INTERVIEW

LONGMAN SERIES IN COLLEGE COMPOSITION AND COMMUNICATION

Advisory Editor: Harvey Wiener
LaGuardia Community College
The City University of New York

INTERVIEW

Marvin Gottlieb

Herbert H. Lehman College of
The City University of New York

Longman
New York & London

Executive Editor: Gordon T. R. Anderson
Production Editor: Ronni Strell
Text Design: Nina Tallarico
Cover Design: Steven August Krastin
Text Art: J & R Services, Inc.
Production Supervisor: Eduardo Castillo
Compositor: Crane Typesetting Service, Inc.
Printer and Binder: The Alpine Press, Inc.

Interview

Longman Inc.
95 Church Street
White Plains, N.Y. 10601

Associated companies:
Longman Group Ltd., London
Longman Cheshire Pty., Melbourne
Longman Paul Pty., Auckland
Copp Clark Pitman, Toronto
Pitman Publishing Inc., Boston

Library of Congress Cataloging in Publication Data
Gottlieb, Marvin R.
Interview.
(Longman series in college composition and communication)
1. Interpersonal communication. 2. Interviews—Psychological aspects. 3. Interviewing—Psychological aspects. I. Title. II. Series.
BF637.C45G66 1985 158'.3 86-92
ISBN 0-582-28389-2

86 87 88 89 9 8 7 6 5 4 3 2 1

Contents

Preface

Anyone who looks into the question of interview, or "the Interview," as it is usually termed, is immediately struck by the importance of this interpersonal phenomenon to virtually every productive aspect of our lives.

Since nearly everyone is employed at one time or another, interview stands out as a central feature in determining the course a life may take. In addition to job interviews, we are interviewed by doctors, lawyers, police officials, poll takers, market researchers, teachers, preachers, and many other people. We also find ourselves on the other side of the coin as well, conducting interviews that have important outcomes for us. In short, life without interview is unthinkable.

Why then has the subject not brought forth a library of information to show us how to do it? Probably because the focus of interview has always been wrong. References to interview reach back into classical times, and the focus is usually on the individual's performance rather than on the dynamics of the interaction itself.

With the rise of interest in the study of interpersonal communication in the late 1960s and early 1970s, we began to see experimentation with interview methodology. Theories were stated, models were constructed, terminology was established. From the mid-1970s on, materials on interview were developed basically as a response to Equal Employment Opportunity Commission (EEOC) and Affirmative Action regulations. The focus was on performance appraisal and how to interview minority people or women for jobs without indicating that you have noticed either their color or their sex. In short, interview study became a defensive enterprise. The materials produced during the last several years have been primarily geared for the employer or personnel professional trying to avoid legal problems.

Hence, we find the reason for this book. It is a text that takes a comprehensive look at interview from the perspective of all the participants and that carves out a place for interview as a field of inquiry, develops an appropriate lexicon, and presents a how-to approach to interview training.

The book is divided into two major parts. Part I, "Gaining Perspective," concentrates on building the framework for understanding and functioning in the interview situation. It consists of three chapters that provide the student with the basic knowledge of the skills and attitudes needed to conduct interviews effectively. Part II, "The Interview Spectrum," consists of seven chapters. Each chapter considers a different type of interview. The chapters have been arranged in order of strategic complexity, with the basic research interview first and the counseling interview last. Each chapter is a self-contained unit, although periodically, references are made to examples or principles set forth in other chapters. The student can read the chapters in any order or selectively without confusion. The chapters are further subdivided into two main sections—one from the perspective of the interviewer, the other from the perspective of the interviewee.

The methodology of this text is built on the concept that interview is a pragmatic enterprise. As a discipline, it is a subcategory within the broader field of interpersonal communication. Because it is a pragmatic enterprise, the study of interview depends greatly on developing awareness. This awareness must be attained in three areas: self-awareness, situation awareness, and strategic awareness. This text addresses these three areas in a developmental way.

The student is first introduced to interview as a phenomenon that has structure and processes that will yield to analysis and definition. The student begins to see that interview is one entity, that it has remarkable consistency across a wide spectrum of applications, and that different types of interview vary only slightly in process.

Interview is then presented as a game, a game between adversaries who are sometimes friendly, sometimes not. An analogy is drawn between interview and chess. This, along with some basic communication theory, helps build a vocabulary to transmit information effectively about the interview process.

The next step places emphasis on the student as an interview participant. The concept of empathy is introduced. The whole matter of perception, values, attitudes, beliefs, biases, and prejudices as they impact on the interview situation is explored. This emphasis on self-awareness also covers active listening and nonverbal awareness. Once the student has gained this perception of interview as a totality of self, situation, and strategy, the text considers the various interview categories from the point of view of the competencies required to perform effectively in each.

This book presents interview as something that can be understood, practiced, and mastered with effort and determination. It develops an awareness of the interview situation, allows the student to see himself or herself as a part of the experience, gives concrete situations to perform, and develops the student as a participant in, rather than a potential victim of, the interview experience.

I would like to thank the many people who supplied inspiration and guidance during the development of this book. In particular, I am grateful to Dean Martin Stevens for steering me in the right direction at the beginning of the project and to my friend and colleague Robert Longo, a true personnel professional, for providing me with both sound advice and opportunities to develop examples for this text.

Marvin Gottlieb

part I

GAINING PERSPECTIVE

Part I lays the groundwork for your understanding of interview as a communication event. Some models of interview are developed that demonstrate the process and provide some of the fundamental vocabulary. Basic skills are covered, which are essential regardless of the type of interview. Part I also establishes the inductive format, which acquaints the reader with the process of working from example.

1

Understanding Interview

Key Concepts

- The mutual need for information
- Factors that control and shape information
- The vocabulary of communication
- Repetition and mirroring

It is one of those very special, very beautiful fall days in New York. Just enough warmth to temper the crispness of the air, but not enough to make you feel uncomfortable in your wool clothes. Just enough wind to blow the Manhattan sky clear and let the buildings stand out in high relief.

I walk into the lobby of the Algonquin Hotel and quickly scan the people sitting or standing in various places in the room. I have an appointment with a young woman. She is interested in being employed on a project with which I am becoming involved. Whether she gets the job or not is partially dependent on me, but today I am introducing her to another person with whom the final decision really rests.

She and I have met socially on occasion, and I know her work. On that basis I have recommended her for the position. It is now 2:30, the appointed time of our meeting. I am eager to give her some background information on the project and Mr. Smith, the person we will meet at 3:00. She's not there. I sit down on one of the couches. The waiter comes over and I order a drink.

She arrives five minutes late and goes to the newsstand and starts looking at the selection of magazines. I call to her. She doesn't hear me. I get up and go over to her. She is surprised to see me. We both go back to the couch and sit down. The waiter arrives with my drink and we order for her. I feel now a little rushed for time, so I dispense with the social talk quickly and begin discussing the matter at hand.

Mr. Smith arrives at 3:00, sees that we have drinks, and apologizes for being late. We assure him that he is on time. Introductions are made. Mr. Smith orders a drink.

The next 20 minutes are spent listening to Mr. Smith explain his background, other involvements, and finally the current project. Then he says, "Well, I have kind of dominated the floor here. Ms. Day, why don't you tell us where you see yourself in this picture?"

Ms. Day jokingly fluffs her hair and says, "Oh, wow, I guess it's interview time."

There are several popular misconceptions about interviews that can be examined using this little scenario. First, let us give Ms. Day the benefit of the doubt. She probably did not really believe the "interview" was beginning at the point she used the term. But her response is instructive. Many people believe that the boundaries of the interview phenomenon are finite, that an interview begins on a certain signal and ends on a signal. This is only partially true.

CONCEPT OF INTERVIEW

If you want to be a skilled interview participant, you must expand the concept of interview to include other elements. From a practical standpoint, think of the beginning of the interview as the moment interview becomes a necessary means to an end. Interview begins as soon as you see a job listing in the paper that appeals to you. Interview begins as soon as you decide to include testimony in your report, your article, or your case. Interview begins as soon as you decide to sell a product or service. Interview begins as soon as you identify the need to counsel or be counseled, to appraise or be appraised, to discipline or be disciplined. In short, interview begins when it becomes necessary to prepare for the interpersonal encounter we commonly call *interview*.

This preparation should take several forms:

1. It can be thought or "internal" role play.
2. It can be background research of subjects, people, companies, or all of these.
3. It can be consideration of location, timing, dress, and appropriate personality effect.

There are only two outcomes. Either you are prepared for the interview or you are not. There is no such thing as overpreparation for an interview. If you have prepared well, then you will perform well and your chances of achieving your end are greatly enhanced. If you are unprepared or less than adequately prepared, you will most likely not achieve your end.

Let us focus on this interpersonal encounter, interview. How do we describe it? What communication principles are in operation? What characteristics are consistent and present in every interview regardless of type?

According to the Oxford English Dictionary, the term *interview* comes from the French *s'entrevoir*, meaning "to see each other." Circumstances and the natural tendency for meanings to change over time have had the effect of making the word *interview* more specialized than its original meaning. One immediately thinks of the journalistic interview or the cross-examination, both of which have the sparkle of an adversary encounter. The medical and psychiatric interviews, which are used for diagnosis and treatment, also come to mind. Perhaps because of these connotations, interview takes on an aspect of "one-sidedness," a situation within which one individual is called on to disclose more than another individual.

While this is true of many interview circumstances, like the journalistic and psychiatric constructs, it is not conceptually true of interview as a process.

BASIC CHARACTERISTICS

Like most other communication events, the lines that delineate the interview situation are not firmly drawn. The basic characteristics of interview most closely resemble conversation. In fact, it is useful to begin with the idea that interview differs from conversation in degree and not in kind.

What are the basic characteristics of conversation?

1. There are two or more people.
2. There is a motive for speech.
3. There is a low level of structure.
4. There is a low level of purpose.
5. There is satisfaction of a basic social need experienced by all people.

What are the basic characteristics of interview?

1. There are two or more people.
2. There is motive for speech.
3. There is a high level of structure.
4. There is a high level of purpose.
5. There should be satisfaction of a basic social need experienced by all people.

Thus, the difference between the interview and the conversation is the degree to which the interaction is either purposeful or structured or both. Conversations often have moments or segments of interview while much of what occurs during interviews can be as accurately described as conversation.

Interview is a structured, purposeful conversation between two or more individuals.

In many interview situations, there are more than two people present, and each person may have a separate and distinct purpose. Recall our little scene at the beginning of this chapter. Clearly, Ms. Day is not only being interviewed by Mr. Smith but by me as well. In fact, I should add that she seems perilously unaware of it! It is important for anyone who, for one reason or another, becomes involved in an interview situation to understand that often more than one person will be encountered who will have a direct or indirect influence on the outcome. In many instances, as with Ms. Day, that person may actually be present while the interview is taking place.

While hardly commonplace, there is another situation where more than one person is present at an interview. This is a current practice, particularly in government, of interviewing several candidates for a position simultaneously. It is still uncertain if this method will become popular, but you can imagine how the situation changes during an employment interview if your competition is present.

To some degree everyone in the interview situation is seeking information.

Let us consider Ms. Day's interview again. Certainly, Mr. Smith is concerned about getting information about Ms. Day. But Ms. Day is also, or should be, interested in getting information about the position and about Mr. Smith, her prospective employer. Since I am involved with the project, Mr. Smith is interested in furthering his understanding of me, as I am of him. I am also interested in filling out my information about Ms. Day in order to confirm my recommendation of her as a candidate.

SELF-DISCLOSURE

If we must differentiate between the "interviewer" and the "interviewee" in this or any other situation, the answer is not determined by who is giving and who is receiving information but rather by who is under the greatest pressure for self-disclosure.

This pressure for self-disclosure may be demanded because of the circumstances, as in the case of the employment interview. Obviously, Ms. Day must tell us about herself if she wants the job. Mr. Smith also feels pressure for self-disclosure, perhaps because the job requires that he work closely with Ms. Day; therefore, he wants her to be sure she understands what the job will entail. But Mr. Smith has an option; Ms. Day does not. This option delineates who is interviewing whom.

If a doctor is asking you to describe the symptoms of your illness or if a poll taker is probing your political views, you are under pressure for self-disclosure. However, if that same doctor has checked you into the hospital and has examined you for the last three days without telling you anything, chances are you will apply some pressure for self-disclosure on the doctor's part.

In that circumstance you become the interviewer and the doctor becomes the interviewee. You are asking the questions; the doctor is under pressure to disclose the answers.

To summarize this point, let us repeat an important principle: To some degree everyone in an interview situation is seeking information. Even when you are clearly the interviewee, as in an employment interview, it is useful to keep in mind that you should have questions that demand answers. Your chances of success are increased if you perceive the interview as an opportunity for you to gather information to help you make a choice.

Always try to see yourself as an active participant in the interview rather than as the potential victim of it.

Interview really does mean *inter-view—s'entrevoir*—"to see each other." Individuals participating successfully in the interview phenomenon will balance the need for information with the pressure for disclosure and will be a part of, rather than just an object of, the experience.

INTERVIEW AS A COMMUNICATION EVENT

As with all events involving people and the necessity for understanding, interview study begins with basic principles of communication. Let us review some of these basic principles and see how they operate from the interview perspective.

The most basic principle is accuracy. Without accuracy interview is a failure, a waste of time. In practical terms the right person may not get the job, the journalist may be sued for libel, the patient may die.

There are many factors that interfere with accuracy. All participants in the interview must strive for accurate communication. The model of communication in Figure 1 shows the exchange of information and points out where trouble can occur. It also provides us with some of the vocabulary of communication.

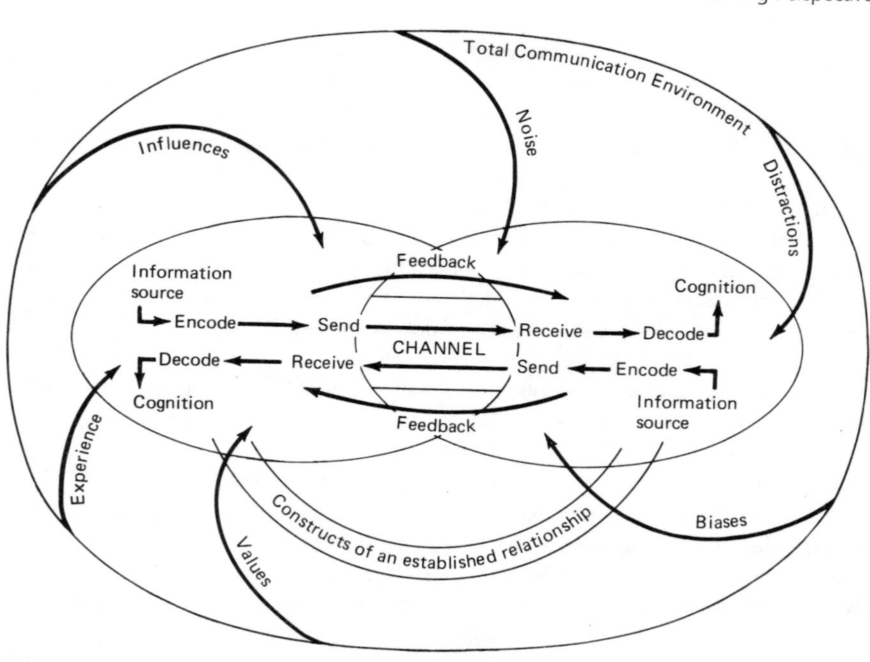

Figure 1

The model also demonstrates the three basic concepts of communication: linear, interactional, and transactional. The *linear* approach is useful as a simple demonstration of the process, and it helps us develop a vocabulary for describing occurrences within the interview situation. The *interactional* aspect of the model shows the effect of feedback as it is observed in the overlapping perceptual field and influences the development of messages internally. The *transactional* characteristics of the model lie in the constructs of an established relationship that influence the formation and interpretation of messages. The model also incorporates the potential influences of outside stimuli that may be present at, although peripheral to, the interview.

The type of interview and the relationship between the participants will determine which aspects of the model are most appropriate. In a research interview, such as taking a poll, the transactional elements are irrelevant and the linear elements are very important. During a cross-examination, the interactional elements become very significant. Transactional elements are important when the interview takes place between people with a relationship, that is, when they have interacted in a variety of communication settings for a period of time. Interviews such as performance appraisals or counseling sessions can benefit from the transactional view. This cycle of information exchange provides us with some necessary vocabulary.

The Communication Cycle

The *information source* is the thought, feeling, idea, impression, sensation, or other brain activity resulting from external and internal stimuli that requires the response, clarification, denial, confirmation, or acceptance of another human being.

Before this can be accomplished, however, this thought, feeling, and so on must be put into transmittable form; it must be *encoded*. The most common codes are language, signs, signals, paralinguistic utterances, and the whole range of nonverbal manifestations. For now, let us attend primarily to language as basic to all interview situations. You will select words that are consistent with your vocabulary and experience. However, language is an imperfect tool. Your vocabulary and experience may not be the same as the person with whom you are communicating.

Once your message has been encoded, it must be sent or *transmitted* to the other person. Your transmission apparatus is no more perfect than your ability to encode, and errors such as mispronunciations may interfere with the accuracy of your transmission.

Another feature to be considered is that the signal that you have transmitted must travel across open space called the *channel*. There is always *noise* in the channel. Noise is any stimulus other than your message that competes either actively or subliminally for your listener's attention. In addition to *external noise*, you are also competing with *internal noise*. As much as you might like to think that your message is the only thing that matters to the recipient, he or she probably has other things to think about. Also, the recipient brings a complex structure of attitudes, values, beliefs, biases, and prejudices to the interview situation.

The same difficulties that may arise in transmission are present when the message is received; a word may not be heard correctly or may be missed altogether. Real difficulty enters when the message is *decoded* since meanings are not consistent from one person to another even in the same language.

Communication depends on our ability to share common patterns of symbolism. As Gerhard Hanneman puts it, the effective transmission of information is dependent on several variables:

> The critical point here is that information is a potential. Its significance is "in the eye of the beholder." Information is *not* conveyed *in* the message; neither is the meaning. We *derive* information from the messages that we communicate by virtue of the meanings and experiences that we bring to the communication transaction. This is known as "frame of reference," and thus we say that meanings are in people.
>
> The concept that meanings are in people, however, implies that unless someone was raised in an environment similar to yours, the probability of perfect communication can never be high. Two people must share at least some of the same experiences for any type of meaningful communication to occur.[1]

With so many pitfalls along the way, accuracy must be considered at a premium in the interview situation. Making your message arrive at its *destination* (the conscious mind of the recipient) more or less in the manner it was intended is a primary objective of interview.

Repetition and Mirroring

We have already seen that there are a number of problems to solve before we can be certain that our messages have reached their destination with any degree of accuracy. However, we are not without means to address these problems.

A most important factor is the *feedback* we receive from the recipient in the form of verbal and nonverbal response. If we are adept at reading this feedback, we can generally tell whether or not our message has been received with some degree of accuracy. Certainly, the effective interview participant will be a good listener. Without good listening skills, any other factors brought to the interview situation will be ineffective.

Accuracy can be brought to the transmission part of the interview encounter through repetition and mirroring. These are the two most important concepts in understanding the interview and in developing strategy and technique. Mastery of these two skills will help ensure that effective communication is taking place. When developed as a strategy, they provide a powerful tool for use in interview.

Repetition is the restatement, in the same or other words, of the question, answer, or series of questions previously asked.

The concepts of repetition and mirroring have many similarities and some subtle but significant differences. Repetition is employed when:

1. Feedback indicates that your question has not been understood.
2. Feedback indicates that your response has not been understood.
3. The answer to your question is unsatisfactory.
4. You are pressing for an answer from a reluctant respondent (as in investigative interviewing or cross-examination).

Consider the following interview segment between Ms. Day and Mr. Smith:

MR. SMITH: Ms. Day, are you aware that this is an ongoing project even though we have placed great emphasis on the first year?

MS. DAY: Well, all we have talked about is the first year.

MR. SMITH: That's why I want you to understand that this is an ongoing project. Are you prepared to make a commitment that goes beyond one year?

MS. DAY: Of course, I can make a better judgment about that after I get into it.

MR. SMITH: Assuming that all goes well, can you foresee staying with the project beyond the first year?

MS. DAY: There are always things that can't be anticipated, but I can't foresee anything that would interfere with my continuing beyond one year. I do have some concern about the level of travel.

MR. SMITH: Well, you won't always be flying first class, but the travel budget is quite substantial.

MS. DAY: No, I mean the level of travel.

MR. SMITH: Where you will be going?

MS. DAY: No, how much of it I may have to do.

MR. SMITH: Oh, I see. That's hard to determine at this stage.

MS. DAY: You must have some idea.

MR. SMITH: I haven't really thought it through, but your point is well taken. You will probably have to visit four or five major cities during the year—some maybe twice. My best guess would be that you will be out of town a few days each month.

MS. DAY: That's not too bad. I was afraid I would be on the go all the time.

MR. SMITH: Okay, check me on this: You are willing to commit beyond the first year, and traveling a couple of days each month would be acceptable.

MS. DAY: Yes.

Mirroring is an instant replay of a communication segment to allow for confirmation, denial, adjustments, or other operations to ensure understanding.

Many unsophisticated interview participants are afraid to use repetition because they do not want to appear either "stupid" or offensive. They feel that they will be responded to negatively if they indicate that they did not understand something or that their question was not answered adequately. Actually, a repeated/restated question or response can build considerable good will in a situation where the other participant(s) is (are) stuck for a response or a follow-up question.

Besides being important for clarification, the use of repetition builds an element of assertiveness into your interview style. Assertiveness is generally viewed as a positive characteristic in most interview situations.

Mirroring is employed when:

1. You want to be certain that you received the message correctly.
2. You want the other participant(s) to know that you received the message correctly.
3. You wish to confront the other participant(s) with their own words.

4. You are probing for additional information.
5. You are summarizing an interview segment.

The final point, summarizing an interview segment, requires some explanation and expansion. Because of the unpredictable nature of interview dynamics, it is difficult to build an analytical model that retains its validity in any but the most highly controlled interview situations. However, the interview process does yield to analysis as long as we accept an element of flexibility as a basic characteristic of interview interaction.

Interview strategists have tried for some time to describe interview based on the sequencing of questions. However, this text sees interview as a segmented process of communication.

Each segment in the interview continuum can be identified as a separate and distinct attempt to gain information.

The individual segments will vary in length one from the other in the natural ebb and flow of the interview process. When interview is effectively happening, however, there will occur at these varying intervals the moment when the information received must be digested, when a new approach must be initiated, when someone needs confirmation, denial, or modification of some content. Such moments almost invariably produce mirroring behaviors.

The mirror provides a natural stop or resting place for the participants to check for accuracy of their own perceptions or to regroup their thoughts in order to come at the problem in a different way. When mirroring is applied deliberately, it gives a large measure of control to the participant applying it as a technique.

The basic interview model is very simple in theory. It presents the interview as a series of varying sized links in a chain. Each link contains a sequence of questions. At the juncture of each link with another is either a mirror statement or a mirror question.

Recall the previous example used for repetition. Mr. Smith says, "Okay, check me on this," and then proceeds to play back his understanding of the information contained in the segment for Ms. Day's confirmation, denial, or modification. Let us take a look at the next segment:

MR. SMITH: Well, what other areas do we need to cover?
MS. DAY: To tell you the truth, I'm not at all certain of what my specific role would be.
MR. SMITH: You would essentially be in charge.
MS. DAY: I would be in charge?
MR. SMITH: You would be in charge in the sense that you would be in com-

plete control of your end. I won't be hanging over you telling you what to do. In fact, you are being considered for this position precisely because you have more experience doing this type of work than I do.

MS. DAY: Does that include financial control?

MR. SMITH: By financial control do you mean will you have your own budget?

MS. DAY: I hadn't thought of it in terms of a budget, but, yes, that's essentially what I mean.

MR. SMITH: Ms. Day, to be perfectly honest, I am going to be so busy with my end of this deal that I don't even want to think about administering your side. You would be allocated a budget to use as you see fit. In fact, one of the first things you would have to do is make budget recommendations. This budget, of course, must be based on sound projections, and periodically you will have to justify your expenditures.

MS. DAY: What you're saying, then, is that my role is both administrative and functional.

MR. SMITH: Are you suggesting that administrators aren't functional?

MS. DAY: *(Laughs)* Come on, give me a break! I mean doing the job and overseeing it at the same time.

MR. SMITH: *(Laughs)* You've got it. Sort of like a dog chasing its own tail—hopefully with better results.

This example is rich with mirroring. Ms. Day and Mr. Smith are using it in a variety of ways. Ms. Day probes with a mirror, "I would be in charge?" Mr. Smith clarifies with a mirror, "By financial control do you mean will you have your own budget?" Ms. Day summarizes the information segment with a mirror, "What you're saying, then, is that my role is both administrative and functional." Mr. Smith asserts his authority by using a mirror to put Ms. Day on the defensive, "Are you suggesting that administrators aren't functional?" This is a natural tendency where the interviewee has controlled a segment and forced self-disclosure. Ms. Day has clearly controlled this segment. She has gotten the information she wanted and discovered another important fact in the process, ". . . you are being considered for this position precisely because you have more experience doing this type of work than I do." Having been this revealing (perhaps with some regret), Mr. Smith feels the need to reassert himself as the boss.

Mirroring and repetition are the basic building materials of the interview chain. They are observable phenomena that occur naturally during the process of interview. They can be analyzed and harnessed for use as effective tools to enhance accuracy, sharpen technique, and develop efficiency and control in the interview situation.

SUMMARY

This chapter has provided you with an overview of some of the more important elements at work during interview. The objective has been to provide you with a framework of understanding on which you can build the more specific information provided in subsequent chapters.

We have discovered that interview is a structured, purposeful conversation and that everyone involved in the interview situation is seeking information. We have learned to differentiate between interviewer and interviewee based on which person is under the greatest pressure for self-disclosure. The chapter provides this advice to all who would involve themselves in interview:

Be an active participant rather than a victim.
Focus on the need for accuracy as a primary objective.
Assert your control over the flow of information through the use of repetition and mirroring.
Be as prepared as possible.
Have fun! Yes, even if you are the interviewee.

Questions for Study and Discussion

1. What were some of the things that Ms. Day did wrong prior to the actual beginning of the dialog portion of the interview?
2. What is meant by the statement that interview begins at the moment it becomes a necessary means to an end?
3. What characteristics do interview and conversation have in common?
4. What is the role of self-disclosure in the interview situation?
5. What is the difference between external and internal noise? How does noise affect the interview situation?
6. What is the difference between repetition and mirroring?

Suggested Activities

1. Describe an experience from your own life when you felt like a victim during an interview.
2. Have someone ask you a question. Turn it into a mirror. Next, try it with a series of questions.
3. Have someone ask you a question. Give a wrong or unresponsive answer. Continue until you receive a mirror.

Note

1. Gerhard J. Hanneman, "The Study of Human Communication," in Gerhard J. Hanneman and William J. McEwen, eds., *Communication and Behavior* (Reading, Mass.: Addison-Wesley, 1975), 29.

2

The Interview Structure

Key Concepts

- The basic chain model
- The three parts of the interview game
- Probing
- The types of questions
- Technique and strategy

In the last chapter, we introduced the concept of interview consisting of a series of definable segments that fit together as links of a chain. These links vary in size because interview segments vary in length. Each segment ends with a mirror question or mirror statement that also serves quite often as the beginning of the next interview segment.

While the interview is one continuous chain from beginning to end, it can be subdivided into three main parts. In fact, all communication events can be divided into beginning, middle, and end. Speeches, conversations, and stage presentations all yield to the three-part division. In order for the divisions to be meaningful and useful to a student of interview, we must develop a more active analogy.

Perhaps some of you are chess players. If you are, you will take quite easily to the example that will be developed here. If you are not a chess player, you probably use some terminology that finds its origin in the game of chess. "Open and aboveboard," "He's only a pawn," "rank and file" are phrases regularly used in chess. In order to gain an understanding of this important aspect of interview structure, you will not be expected to learn chess, but rather three phrases of chess terminology.

The interview chain has three main divisions that we will call *the opening game*, *the middle game* and *the end game*. These terms are borrowed from chess because the game is a good metaphor for interview. Although the object of most interview situations is not containment or defeat, as in chess, interview is an encounter between two individuals who have objectives and who will apply strategy and hope to gain from the experience.

THE OPENING GAME

During the opening game of a chess match, the players focus their attention on the control of the center of the board. Each player attempts to discover the other's strategy and to place pieces in effective locations for future development. There may be some exchanges during which pawns on both sides are captured, but rarely is an important piece lost at this stage. The opening game establishes the format of the board. The alignment of the pieces during this phase will have enormous influence on how the remainder of the game is played.

The opening-game phase of the interview has many of the same characteristics. As in chess, this is an extremely important part of the interview because the format for the entire encounter will be established here. The student of interview needs to focus on three main elements in the opening game: establishing rapport, maneuvering for control or establishing position, and orientation to the matter at hand.

Establishing Rapport

It is a basic principle of this text that interview requires the active participation of all parties involved. Regardless of your position in the interview situation, building rapport is an important task. There are exceptions, of course. For example, a poll taker would be much more concerned with building good rapport with the subject than the subject would with the poll taker.

However, in an employment interview, the applicant can create a favorable impression by demonstrating rapport-building skills. Certainly, the potential employer in the same situation will be more likely to elicit the necessary responses for a judgment if good rapport has been developed with the applicant.

The rapport-building process consists of three steps: the greeting ritual, an expression of interest and concern for the other party, and self-disclosure. The greeting ritual becomes more formalized and predictable when the individuals involved know each other very well. Between strangers, the ritual is less predictable in form and sequence, but it is always present to initiate interaction in the interview situation.[1] Generally, the greeting ritual begins with a smile, followed by a handshake, followed by the finding of appropriate positions, followed by a pause. During this ritual, both participants should be busy drawing conscious inferences about one another. Make a note of your first impressions so that you can later probe either to dispel doubts or to confirm suspicions. Pay attention to what you see and hear. How does the person stand? What is the posture like? How is the person dressed? What does the sound of the voice tell you?

The expression of interest and concern may be a distinctly separate element or integrated with the greeting ritual. It can range from nonrelated personal comment to the specific purpose for the interview. The purpose is to indicate that you are interested in the participant as a person as well as an applicant, a research subject, a news story, an employee, or a patient. When interest and concern have been exchanged, the participants will become more at ease and be motivated to exchange information. Expressions of interest and concern tend to build trust. Trust is the most important component for stimulating the free flow of truthful self-disclosure.

Appropriate self-disclosure is best understood as any revelation about the self that is not readily apparent through observation or prior knowledge. It is not confined to intimate revelations or confessions of socially deviant behavior. Used with care and discretion, self-disclosure can be an effective tool for achieving a desired interview goal as well as a desired goal itself. There has been much examination of how persons respond when they are disclosed to by others. Jourard has shown that responses to disclosures will be primarily positive or affirmative.[2] This happens because when we reveal information about ourselves, information that can only be learned from us, we appear trustworthy. Studies also show that high self-disclosure is an indicator of mental health.[3]

Another factor that is very important for the success of the interview is the reduction of uncertain feelings about the other participant that is brought about by self-disclosure.[4] Studies have also indicated that when one person in a communication dyad escalates the level of disclosure intimacy, the other will follow suit. This will occur even in situations when the discloser is initially disliked.[5] In the following sequence, John Jones, college recruiter, uses the three rapport-building steps in the opening game with potential student Joe Greer:

JOHN: (*Moving forward, smiling, extending hand*) Hello, Joe, it's good to meet you.

JOE: (*Also moving forward, extending his hand to take John's*) Same here, Mr. Jones.

JOHN: "Mr. Jones" is what they call my father, Joe. Why don't you just call me "John"? I hope you didn't have any trouble finding me.

JOE: Well, I got a little turned around, but I finally asked someone who pointed me in the right direction.

JOHN: This is quite a large campus, Joe, as I'm sure you've noticed. It takes a little getting used to. The first time I saw a college campus, all I kept saying to myself was, "No way, I'll be lost here for sure."

JOE: I've been here once before, a few years ago with my mom and dad for a football game. But somehow, coming here alone, you know, it's different . . . scary, sort of.

JOHN: It's not the size of the place, it's the "alone" part that gets you down at first. Can I offer you some coffee or a soda?

John moved quickly through the greeting ritual and immediately began to establish an informal pattern. While Joe is still understandably reluctant to call John by his first name, the offer has been made. Perhaps when Joe relaxes more and develops more trust in John, he will be able to reciprocate on a first-name basis. For the time being, he is content not to use any name, thus avoiding the dissonance created by the prospect of calling an unknown older man by his first name. Sensing Joe's disorientation and learning that he has had some difficulty finding his way, John discloses a feeling that he had when he first entered a large college campus. This disclosure unlocks a valuable disclosure from Joe. He describes what he is feeling and gives John the opportunity to probe his sensitivity.

John Brady describes how Truman Capote used self-disclosure to gather extremely sensitive material from Marlon Brando:

> Truman Capote was sent to the movie set of *Sayonara* in Kyoto, Japan to profile the actor for the *New Yorker*. Brando was remarkably candid, even telling Capote about his mother's alcoholism . . . "I didn't care any more. She was there. In a room. Holding on to me. And I let her fall. Because I couldn't take it any more—watch her breaking apart, like a piece of porcelain. I stepped right over her. I walked right out. I was indifferent. Since then, I've been indifferent." Brando was understandably disturbed when he saw the piece, and his friends were astonished that he had let it happen. "Well, the little bastard spent half the night telling me all his problems," explained the actor. "I figured the least I could do was tell him a few of mine."[6]

We can see how the rapport-building phase sets the pattern for the early stage of the interview. The skillful application of the greeting ritual, expression of interest and concern, and the use of self-disclosure puts both participants at ease, starts the flow of information, and begins to build mutual trust. With the groundwork thus laid, the participants can now move to the control/position phase.

Establishing Position or Control

In most interview situations, the participants know what their relative positions are. In the employment interview, it should come as no surprise to the applicant that he or she is under the greater pressure for self-disclosure. However, even in employment interviews, this is not always the case. In today's high-powered employment market, top executive talent is at a premium. Search firms and even prospective employers often find themselves in the position of having to convince a potential employee that they and their company are worthy of the executive's consideration.

In most instances in the opening game, the establishment of position or control is accomplished at the same time as the third phase, orientation to the matter at hand. But consider the following possible sequence between John and Joe:

JOE: I know this college has a good reputation in my field, but I'm not convinced that the program has the kind of flexibility I'm looking for.

JOHN: I can understand your concern, Joe, but let's hold off on that for a bit. The program you are applying for is highly selective. We will probably only take in 25 students for that program this year. I think our time would be better served if we first assess your qualifications for this program; then, assuming that your candidacy is viable, we can cover your concerns about flexibility and other aspects of the program.

In this sequence John makes it clear that he is going to control the interview. He indicates a willingness to respond to Joe's concern, but not until his demands for information have been satisfied. Unless Joe is going to be outright belligerent at this point, he has no choice but to go along with the pattern that has been laid out by John. In fact, there is nothing to be gained by continuing to challenge John's control of the exchange. By accepting the ground rules, Joe can concentrate his efforts on ensuring that the "assessment of his qualifications" is favorable so that he can have his turn at control later in the game. As mentioned earlier, position or control is often established simultaneously with the third phase of the opening game, orientation.

Orientation

Orientation, like the other parts of the opening game, can consist of several parts. In most interview situations, it will not be necessary to explain why the interview is taking place. It is the nature of interview to be purposeful, and for interview to be successful all participants must know and understand the purpose. As always, there are exceptions. The poll taker must make his or her purpose known to the person being polled, who is without purpose—at least initially. The investigator or the lawyer engaged in cross-examination may seek to obscure the purpose of the interview but must still orient the other party as to the framework, expectations, or procedures to be followed as, for example, when a person is "read his or her rights" after being arrested. Even outside the investigative setting, it is ethical and desirable to explain to the disclosing participant how the information will be used.

In the preceding sequence between John and Joe, John was orienting Joe to the matter at hand while establishing control. He stated that an assessment of Joe's qualifications would be made, thus informing Joe how information provided by him would be used. John continues the orientation process in the next sequence:

JOHN: During the next half hour, Joe, I'd like to explore with you your general background, your experiences as a student—particularly those experiences that you feel have strongly influenced you. We'll look into how your interest in science developed, and how you came to learn about our program. Okay?

John uses a summary, which is a very effective means for orientation. He sets a time frame and clearly states his interview expectations.

In most interview situations, the summary will be a good choice for orientation. However, there are times when it may not be the best possible choice. In our scenario Joe has a great deal of incentive to cooperate in the interview. This is not always the case. If you are taking a survey, the people whom you approach may not readily submit to your questioning unless they see that there is some potential benefit to them.

If you are interacting with a politician, spokesperson, or other individual with a known position on an issue, you can orient the person by making a direct reference to the issue and his or her position concerning the issue. In this case it is always a good idea to be somewhat flattering. The following is an example:

"Ms. Carver, as an important figure in the 'right to life' movement, your views are well known. My readers would be interested to know what your feelings are about the legislation currently being considered in the Congress."

In general terms, orientation establishes the parameters of the interview. It clarifies for all of the participants what the subject matter is going to be, what the time frame is going to be, and it helps establish the relative positions of each person involved. Again, as with all parts of the interview, orientation is a two-way street. Even when you are called on to be the major discloser, as in the last example, you can contribute to the orientation phase.

"Surely, you understand my feelings about the bill, Mr. Jenkins. I would like to convey to your readers some of the reasons why I feel the way I do."

The respondent modifies the thrust of the interview by adjusting the orientation to fit her needs.

In summary, the opening game requires the participants to establish rapport by means of greeting rituals, self-disclosure, and other friendly gestures, such as expressing concern, so that the channels of communication can begin to open. When good rapport is established, the participants begin to build trust in each other's integrity. Next, there may be a need to maneuver for control or to establish the relative positions of the participants. This is often established beforehand, as in the common employment interview, or during the orientation process. Orientation sets the parameters of the interview—the subject matter, the purpose, and the time frames. Having reached this stage, interview moves into the middle game.

THE MIDDLE GAME

In chess the middle game begins when there is a major exchange of pieces. During the middle game, both players develop their strategy and probe each other's defenses. While there are interview situations where this is exactly what occurs, as in the investigative interview, the middle game during interview is generally more benign. The key word here, *probe*, is also the key concept. Remember, the object of the interview is to gain information, and probing is the key that opens the informative doors.

To be effective in the interview situation and to gain your desired ends, you need to develop both technique and strategy. *Technique* refers to your understanding and ability to frame the different types of questions effectively. *Strategy* refers to your ability to organize the various types of questions into the most effective patterns. Most of the questioning will be contained in the middle game of the interview, so let us look at the various types of questions and how they can be used to get the information you want.

Open Questions

Question type is determined by questions intent. If you are asking for a broad spectrum of response, the question type is called *open*. Open questions only specify the topic and therefore give the respondent complete freedom to respond in any appropriate way. The following are examples of open questions:

How are you doing?
What are your feelings about going to college?
Tell me what you know about our company.
Tell me about your company.
What do you think about the current economic condition?

Open questions generally elicit longer responses than other types of questions. The more words a respondent uses, the more opportunity there is to gain information. Participants usually feel more relaxed responding to open questions because they appear to be nonthreatening when asked with a neutral intonation. For this reason, they are effective to use at the beginning of a questioning sequence.

Not all people respond to open questions in a comfortable way. If a participant has some conflict or emotional involvement with a particular subject area or is generally suspicious of you or the purpose of your question, the response will not be extensive. You can determine immediately if the person is hostile or suspicious by the response you do get. This will usually take the form of a question that forces you to be more specific, as shown in the following exchanges:

LARRY: How are you doing?
MARY: What have you heard?

HARRY: Tell me about your company.
TERRY: What do you want to know?

Consider the question that John asks after the orientation sequence:

JOHN: During the next half hour, Joe, I'd like to explore with you your general background, your experiences as a student—particularly those experiences that you feel have strongly influenced you. We'll look into how your interest in science developed, and how you came to learn about our program. Okay?
JOE: It sounds okay to me.
JOHN: Good. Some people say there are advantages to growing up in a small town like you did. What do you think about that?

You can be more specific and still keep your questions open. Use the same approach—asking for feelings, experience, impressions, or knowledge—while giving more information about your expectations for the answer. The following list provides some examples:

How are you doing in law school?
What are some of the problems you are having in college?
Tell me what you know about our company's marketing program.
Tell me about your company's plans for the future and how I might fit in.

The disadvantage inherent in open questions is that you are going to get a lot of information you either do not want or do not need. This can become a time-consuming and frustrating affair that taxes your ability to maintain a high-attention level.

Many beginning interview players have difficulty framing open questions. They are certainly less natural to us than the closed variety. This is a result of the language-development process that begins at birth. Parents are most likely to phrase questions to children in a nonopen way:

Are you hungry?
Did you brush your teeth?
Do you want to go to the movies?

This occurs because these are the types of questions parents were asked by their parents, and it is easy to fall into the same pattern. They are generally *bipolar*, requiring either a yes or no answer. It also occurs because children, by and large, are a secretive lot. The early years are spent carefully guarding an internal privacy since most external privacy is denied to children. Therefore, they do not readily respond to open questions, as is evident in the following exchange:

"Where did you go?"
"Out."
"What did you do?"
"Nothing."

In the interview situation, you must make a conscious effort to phrase your questions in an open mode, particularly at the beginning of an interview segment. It is very useful and highly recommended that you have a prepared list of open questions—many of which are applicable to a number of different interview situations—that you can use at any point to move the interview forward and avoid being "stuck for a question."

The *laundry-list question* is one time-tested and effective means of partially closing in on an open question without severely limiting the potential response. This type of open question provides a framework of acceptable responses from which the respondent may pick and choose. Richard Fear, an early proponent of this method, demonstrates how the laundry-list question is used in an employment interview:

> Applicants almost invariably find some areas more difficult to discuss than others. Confronted with a question that requires considerable analysis, they frequently "block" and find it somewhat difficult to come up with an immediate response. In such a situation, the interviewer comes to the applicant's assistance with a laundry-list type of question. As the name implies, this type of question suggests a variety of possible responses and permits the subject to take his choice. If the subject blocks on the question, "What are some of the things that a job has to have in order to give you satisfaction?" the interviewer may stimulate his thinking by such a laundry-list comment as, "You know some people are more interested in security; some are frankly more interested in money; some want to manage; some want an opportunity to create; some like a job that takes them out-of-doors a good bit of the time—what's important to you?" Given a variety of

possible responses, the applicant is normally able to marshal his thinking and supply a considerable amount of information.[7]

Closed Questions

Each time you become more specific about your expectations for the answer, you focus on or point to the specific area of your interest. This involves the use of *closed* questions. There is a large middle ground of questions that is both open and closed because of their wording or the intonation used in asking or the nonverbal behavior that accompanies the question. While you may be after specific information, open-closed questions in this middle ground demand a more comprehensive response:

What person influenced you most in your life?
What do you do for relaxation?
What was your greatest opportunity?
What do you believe about people—can they be changed for better or for worse?

However, at the opposite end of the spectrum from the open question, we can identify questions that are distinctly closed in form and intent. When you use a closed question, you intentionally limit the range of responses available to the respondent. Here are some examples:

What is your name?
Have you seen Joe?
Do you want this job?
What is your favorite sport?
Which side are you going to support on this issue?

In the following exchange, John uses closed questions to probe Joe's academic style:

JOHN: What's your grade point average, Joe?
JOE: 3.85.
JOHN: That's pretty good. Does studying come easy to you?
JOE: Some subjects are easier than others.
JOHN: What is your worst subject?
JOE: History.
JOHN: Too much reading?
JOE: Yes.

As you can see, closed questions are usually answered with a yes or a no or with only a few words. There is no doubt that closed questioning is more efficient than open questioning. By limiting the range of choices, the participants can gain a large amount of information in a relatively short time. The answers are easier to systematize, code, and analyze, thereby facilitating research. As long as the questions ask about nonpersonal things, they are generally perceived as easier to answer than open questions. Where intimate self-disclosure is required, they are generally perceived as more threatening than open questions.

Probing Questions

In one sense of the word, all questions "probe." The question is the tool with which we, like archaeologists on the search for hidden treasures, remove layers of material in order to arrive at the information we seek. However, in order to identify this third category of questioning technique, think of probing as a follow-up to an original question. *Probing grows out of a felt need for more information*; a feeling on the part of anyone involved in interview that the answer received from the initial question did not provide the full or correct response needed. In the following sequence from Arthur Miller's *A View from the Bridge*, Beatrice probes a reluctant Catherine to discover where her feelings really lie:

BEATRICE: Listen, Catherine. (*Catherine halts, turns to her sheepishly.*) What are you going to do with yourself?

CATHERINE: I don't know.

BEATRICE: Don't tell me you don't know; you're not a baby any more, what are you going to do with yourself?

CATHERINE: He won't listen to me.

BEATRICE: I don't understand this. He's not your father, Catherine. I don't understand what's going on here.

CATHERINE: (*as one who is trying to rationalize a buried impulse*) What am I going to do, just kick him in the face with it?

BEATRICE: Look, honey, you wanna get married, or don't you wanna get married? What are you worried about, Katie?

CATHERINE: (*quietly trembling*) I don't know, Bea. It just seems wrong if he's against it so much.

Although not a trained interviewer, Beatrice, in the preceding sequence, demonstrates excellent investigative strategy. She begins the segment (chain link) with an open question, "What are you going to do with yourself?" Receiving an unsatisfactory answer, she probes by restating the question more emphatically. Catherine responds with a part of the answer, "He won't listen to me." Having partially broken through, Beatrice uses an open probe to force Catherine to broaden her response, "I don't understand this. He's not your father, Catherine. I don't understand what's going on here." Catherine reveals the source of her conflict, "What am I going to do, just kick him in the face with it?" Beatrice, having successfully arrived at the information she sought, closes the segment with a mirror, "Look, honey, you wanna get married, or don't you wanna get married?" and shifts to an open question to begin a new segment, "What are you worried about, Katie?"

Good probes must suit the occasion. There are three basic varieties: assertive, neutral, and silent.

Assertive Probes. Beatrice's emphatic restatement of the same question assertively communicated to Catherine that she was not satisfied with the answer. An assertive probe demands a fuller response:

What do you mean by . . . ?
Could you go into that more?
What happened then?
Do you expect me to believe that?
How did that happen?

Neutral Probes. In most interview settings, you will use more neutral probes than assertive ones. Neutral probes lead or push the respondent toward a fuller response. You are again communicating that you are dissatisfied with the answer as it stands:

I see.
Really?
Uh huh.
Hmmm.
And?

Silent Probes. One characteristic that distinguishes the novice from the skillful interviewer is the fear of silence. Many people feel the need to fill every moment with noise, appropriate or otherwise. Silence correctly understood and effectively used is one of the best probing techniques available to you. If you are sensitive to this universal need to fill silence with verbiage, you can pressure a respondent for more information by simply leaving silent space that he or she may be compelled to fill. The use of silence is enhanced by appropriately applying a wide range of nonverbal behavior. A smile, a frown, a nod of the head, a raised eyebrow, and the like communicate an expectation and will usually elicit a response from most participants.

In summary, probes are questions that are either open or closed. They can be assertive and direct or neutral and indirect. They can even be silent. What distinguishes probes from open and closed questions generally is that they are used to dig deeper into a subject area rather than to open a new area. Of course, the nature of communication being what it is, you may in fact open new areas to explore when you do not expect it. But when an interview participant employs a probe, it is usually as a follow-up to an open question that initiates a segment.

Leading Questions

A leading question is formulated in such a way that it is obvious what answer the questioner is looking for. Most leading questions are unintentional. They reflect the particular bias of the questioner that has gotten mixed in with the information-gathering process. Depending on the respondent's point of view, the leading question is either easy to answer or creates cognitive dissonance, that is, it is mismatched with the respondent's attitudes, values, beliefs, or perceptions of the subject being discussed.[8] As Festinger says:

> Just as hunger is motivating, cognitive dissonance will give rise to activity oriented toward reducing or eliminating the dissonance. . . . In other words, if two cognitions are dissonant with each other there will be some tendency for the person to attempt to change one of them so that they fit together, thus reducing or eliminating the dissonance.[9]

The following leading questions all contain the answer sought:

You are going to college, aren't you?
Isn't Sally's dress disgusting?
Wasn't that a ridiculously hard test?
So you're a Virgo, that means you're supercritical, right?
Don't you think that an unborn child has the same right to life as any other human being?

Leading questions present the respondent with a choice. The easy choice is to provide the answer that the questioner is looking for. In many instances the respondent already shares the bias represented in the question, so the leading aspect passes virtually unnoticed. When biases are shared, leading questions can function as rapport-building aspects of the interview, as the participants discover they hold many of the same opinions, attitudes, and beliefs. The hard choice occurs when the bias represented in the leading question is not shared by the respondent. Even here, the respondent may simply provide the answer sought for in order to avoid confrontation. The degree to which confrontation becomes a possibility is directly related to the respondent's perceived importance of the question. If providing the expected answer puts the respondent in direct conflict with his or her system of values and beliefs, it will be resisted. If the question concerns a peripheral issue that is less important to the respondent than the overall outcome of the interview, the answer will most likely be provided. In addition, the relative positions of the individuals—power, authority, prestige, age, or other sociolgical factors—will increase or decrease the felt need to provide the expected response.

Studies conducted at Yale University that sought to examine the resolution of cognitive dissonance concluded the following:

1. The preferred solution to a temporary dilemma is the one involving the least effortful path, and
2. In resolving cognitive discrepancies, subjects seek not only the attainment of balance and consistency, but also the solution that maximizes potential gain and minimizes potential loss.[10]

Loaded Questions

Loaded questions are leading questions that directly provoke an emotional response. This can be caused by the selection of emotionally charged language, such as, "You're lying to me, aren't you?" or stronger, "Don't you think that remark shows just what kind of creep you are?" An emotional response can also be provoked by questions that set obvious traps and leave little or no escape, such as, "Are you still beating your wife?" or stronger, "What kind of a creep are you?" There is no way the respondent can answer these questions directly without accepting the basic assertion contained in each question. In other words, the questions assume that he is beating his wife and that he is a creep. The only issue at question is whether or not he is *still* doing it and what *kind* of creep he is.

Leading questions, including those of the loaded variety, can be very effectively used in interview. Leading the customer in the direction you want to go is a key strategy of the persuasive or sales interview. There are other situations, as in employment interviews, where you want to test the resolve of a candidate on a particular issue. Reporters frequently use leading and loaded questions to provoke a fuller or more newsworthy response from a reluctant subject. Lawyers employ them as a regular part of the cross-examination process.

In the following excerpt from the trial record of *Rhinelander* v. *Rhinelander*, Lee Parsons Davis, former Westchester County District Attorney, cross-examines Leonard Rhinelander. Mr. Rhinelander brought an annulment action against his wife Alice, claiming that she had represented that she was of pure white extraction when in fact her father was black. Mr. Rhinelander's lawyer had sought to convey that Mr. Rhinelander was an innocent, weak-minded society youth who had been trapped by an older and unscrupulous black woman. To enhance this impression, he pointed out Mr. Rhinelander's tendency to stutter when excited. At the outset, the jury was clearly sympathetic to Mr. Rhinelander and his family. Mr. Davis skillfully uses a series of leading questions to overcome the prevailing impression of Mr. Rhinelander's condition:

Q. Mr. Rhinelander, because of your affliction of speech, I want to be just as gentle as I possibly can with you. Do you understand that?

A. I do.

Q. And will you keep carefully in mind that if I ask you any question that you don't understand, you are at liberty to tell me so?
A. Yes.
Q. I will try to make my questions clear to you. Your mind is all right, isn't it?
A. I believe it is.
Q. Your trouble is that you stammer? Is that right?
A. It is.
Q. (*Sympathetically*) You don't want Judge Mills and this jury to gather the impression that you are an imbecile?
A. No.
Q. You don't want this jury to have any impression that you are mentally unsound?
A. No.
Q. Your only difficulty is that you have this unfortunate impediment of speech?
A. Yes.
Q. In 1921 was your mind all right? [The year he met his wife]
A. Yes.
Q. (*Slightly more emphatic*) You knew what you were doing every minute of that year, didn't you?
A. Yes.
Q. (*Still more emphatically*) You don't want this jury to get any impression from anything that Judge Mills said that you didn't know what you were doing in 1921, do you?
A. No.
Q. Your only trouble back in 1921 was the fact that you stuttered? Is that right?
A. It is, yes.[11]

By confining Mr. Rhinelander's answers to yes, no, or short phrases, Mr. Davis enhances the impression that Mr. Rhinelander is mentally competent. At the same time, he leads him to assert to the jury that he does not want the jury to picture him as mentally unsound and that he did know what he was doing at the time he met Mrs. Rhinelander. About midway in the segment, Mr. Davis uses a loaded question to draw a more emphatic response, "You don't want Judge Mills and this jury to gather the impression that you are an *imbecile*?" Again, the segment ends with a short mirror that summarized the central question, "Your only trouble back in 1921 was the fact that you stuttered? Is that right?"

To summarize, leading and loaded questions can be effective techniques for interview. They clearly indicate the response that the questioner is expecting. Often, leading questions are asked unintentionally. You need to guard against framing leading questions when you do not mean to because of a particular bias you may have about the subject or the circumstances of the interview. By nature, leading and loaded questions are very assertive. They demand control of any interview segment in which they are used. Your understanding of the other participant should tell you if you will achieve your end or trigger a confrontation.

Mirror Questions

The technique of mirroring has already been covered in some detail in Chapter 1. Remember, mirroring is an instant replay of a communication segment to allow for confirmation, denial, adjustments, or other operations that will ensure understanding. We have also already seen how interview segments are ended with a mirror of the important information components contained within the segment. Mirror questions, however, can and do appear at other points during interview segments:

MARY: I want to eat at Joe's.
SUE: You want to eat there?

JACK: I've told you a thousand times not to do that.
JILL: A thousand times?

When mirrors are used within the segment, they may be thought of as *reflective probes*. As with leading questions, the reflective probe is a control device. It demands a clarification or modification from someone while conveying either a negative or skeptical attitude.

Mirroring is the most underused technique available to the interviewer. Participants who are not comfortable with structured interpersonal situations like interview are reluctant to use mirrors. They fear that by using mirrors they will communicate a lack of understanding that may be mistaken for inattentiveness or ignorance. In fact, just the opposite is true. Mirroring affirms that you have been listening attentively as well as your interest in the subject being discussed. Like the technique of open questions, mirroring is a technique that must be learned—we do not come by it naturally.

Here is the overview of questioning technique. As a practiced middle-game player, you will understand the different types of questions and the responses that can be expected from each. The main types of questions include the following:

1. *Open Questions*. The primary characteristic of these questions is the wide possibility for response. They are generally used at the beginning of an interview segment to draw out information worth probing further.
2. *Closed Questions*. These questions intentionally limit the range of responses available to the respondent. In their bipolar or yes-no form, they require only one of two possible answers. While not appropriate

for situations where a freer response would be more informative, closed questions are efficient at gathering a great deal of information in a short period of time that is easily systematized, coded, and analyzed.
3. *Probing Questions*. These questions grow out of a felt need for more information. Probes can be assertive and thereby demand a fuller response. They are usually neutral, which nudges a respondent toward a fuller response. They can even be silent, leaving space in the interaction that the respondent may feel compelled to fill.

Knowing how to use the different types of questions effectively and appropriately constitutes your technique. Developing and delivering an effective question sequence constitutes your strategy.

Strategy

A skilled boxer goes into the ring with his arsenal of punches. He has practiced his left and right jabs, his body punches, his uppercut, and his roundhouse right. Punches, like questions, are usually ineffective when applied at random. Let us return to the metaphor of chess. A player can have an in-depth understanding of how each piece moves on the board, but he or she can quickly discover that in order to play effectively the pieces must be deployed in skillful combinations. What follows is an overview of basic strategies, including *funnel*, *tunnel*, and *quintamensional* sequences. We will also examine the basic chain-link strategic model.

Before we dig too deeply into the question of strategy, we need to understand the forces that govern strategic choice. The most commanding element that influences strategy is *purpose*. What is the purpose of the interview? What do you or the other participants hope to gain from this encounter? Certain points should be obvious. If, on the one hand, your purpose is to gather information for a survey, and on the other hand, to conduct a psychiatric assessment, the structure of your approach to each situation will differ. So, strategy is determined by the following hierarchy:

Purpose: What information do you need to give or acquire?
Structure: What degree of control needs to be asserted in order to ensure that the purpose is accomplished?
Strategy: What is the most effective question sequence to use within the structure?

Interviews are generally one of two types: *high structure* (sometimes called *directive*) or *low structure* (sometimes called *nondirective*). While most interviews will exhibit both high- and low-structure segments, the dominant feature determines the type. How an interview is structured will be determined by the purpose. Each type of structure has advantages and disadvantages.

High-Structure Interview. High-structure interviews are efficient. They generally take less time and get to the necessary information quickly. They minimize the possibility of getting off the track, maintain a relative neutrality between the participants, and yield data that are easily organized, quantified, and subjected to analysis. High-structured interviews are used for research (questionnaires), induction procedures, and some investigative situations.

Nevertheless, high structure limits the potential response patterns to a narrow range. Participants are not given the opportunity to probe for deeper or more significant responses, and mirroring is confined to summaries at the end of long sequences or at the very end of the interview. The application of technique is also limited since the pattern of questioning is established beforehand.

Low-Structure Interview. The low-structure interview places fewer constraints on the direction of the interview. Respondents are free to probe and follow a variety of paths as they develop naturally out of the interaction. The low-structure interview invariably takes more time and as such is less efficient than the high-structure form. However, the results of a low-structure interview usually show more depth across a broader range of responses, a fuller and more productive relationship between the participants, and a sense shared by all parties that the interview has been a valuable experience. Low-structure interviews are used for several interview settings. In their most extreme form, they are effective for counseling and problem solving.

On the negative side, low-structure interviews often allow or even encourage participants to digress. The information acquired is generally disclosed in a way that does not lend itself to quantification and analysis. For a low-structure interview to be successful, the participants must have interview skill. They must mirror frequently for confirmation and clarification, and they must listen very effectively. The low-structure setting allows for a variety of strategies that can either be planned in advance, developed as the interview progresses, or both.

Funnel Strategy. The funnel strategy employs a questioning sequence that moves from the general to the specific. The question that begins the sequence is very open and demands a general response. Each subsequent question becomes more closed and restrictive to the available responses, as seen in this exchange:

MARY: What do you think of the space program?
BOB: I think it's a generally good program. It seems to me that there have been some good things that have come out of it.
MARY: What "good things" do you mean?
BOB: Well, you know, there has been a great advance made in commu-

nication through the use of satellites, there has been a lot of medical research, the program carries a great deal of prestige for the country.

MARY: Do you have any idea how much the space program has cost?

BOB: Not exactly, but I know it has been billions and billions of dollars.

MARY: Of the "good things" you list—communications, medicine, and prestige—which one do you consider the most important?

BOB: I guess if I had to pick one, it would be medicine.

MARY: Do you think if all those billions and billions of dollars were applied to medical research directly we would have made the same advances?

BOB: Probably more.

MARY: What do you think then, Bob, has the program been worth the money it has cost?

The funnel sequence is effective in several interview settings. It can be used as a strategy for investigation. It can be used in a sales interview to lead a prospective customer to the "right" conclusion. It can be used by a journalist to elicit more facts, names, or circumstances concerning a particular event. The funnel strategy is a good one for beginning interviewers to practice. It requires the formation of an open question at the outset of a questioning segment, and sensitizes the questioner to the need for follow-up probes.

Quintamensional Design Strategy. First described by George Gallup in 1947, the quintamensional design is built, as the name suggests, on five questions that probe for the intensity of an attitude or opinion.[12]

1. Awareness: What do you think of the space program?
2. Uninfluenced attitudes: Can you tell me what has come out of the space program?
3. Specific attitude: Do you approve of the money spent on the space program?
4. Reason why: For what reason?
5. Intensity of attitude: On a scale of one to ten, how strongly do you feel about this issue?

The quintamensional design differs from the funnel sequence in that it has limited objectives. Otherwise, it is quite similar. The fifth question is the determinant since the objective of the quintamensional design is to produce quantifiable data.

Tunnel Strategy. The tunnel strategy uses a series of questions that require quantifiable answers to each question in the series. The questions always involve a "forced choice," which means that the respondent is given a finite number of possible responses and must select the one that is most satisfactory.

1. Do you approve or disapprove of the space program?
2. Do you feel that what has come out of the space program has been worth the money or not worth the money?
3. If the money were spent in another way, would you prefer that it were spent on medical research, rebuilding urban areas, or welfare?
4. In the future, should the space program be expanded, maintained at the same level, or severely curtailed?

Besides being useful for getting a quick index of someone's attitude toward a particular subject, the tunnel sequence is useful in psychological profiling. A long series of forced-choice questions containing several reworded questions on the same issue will indicate a consistency of response. This is also effective for investigative interviewing since it makes sustaining a lie very difficult.

The Chain-Link Strategic Model. Each interview situation is unique in itself. Even in high-structure interviews, the answers are not always predictable or expected, as in the proverbial answer, "Occasionally," to the question, "Sex?" However, one advantage of the high-structure interview, as has already been pointed out, is that the questions are prepared in advance. This relieves the interviewer from the potential of "getting stuck" for a question. But high-structure interviews account for only a small percentage of interview situations. Most interviews contain both elements of high and low structure but with emphasis on the latter. In the low-structure interview or interview segments, it is quite easy to suddenly find yourself at a loss for an appropriate question. The chain-link strategic model, once internalized, will provide a framework from which either participant can move the interview forward productively without embarrassing lapses.

The model in Figure 2 always begins with an open question. Open questions, as we have already seen, generally elicit a fuller response. Not only does this give the participants time to think, but it also provides more material for further questions. In the ideal situation, a response to an open question will provide some point of interest that the questioner will desire to know more about. This calls for a probe. The model shows two probes in succession because a single probe often does not get at all of the specific information being sought. A closed question that requires a yes or no response or provides a forced choice is many times a good follow-up to a series of probes. It asks the respondent to be very specific about the information just provided. The segment ends with a mirror that plays back the information as the questioner has understood it. This allows the respondent the opportunity to clarify, confirm, or modify the information. Following the mirror, a new segment is begun with an open question.

It is neither possible nor desirable for interview segments to follow this model consistently and accurately. Rather, it should be employed as a loose

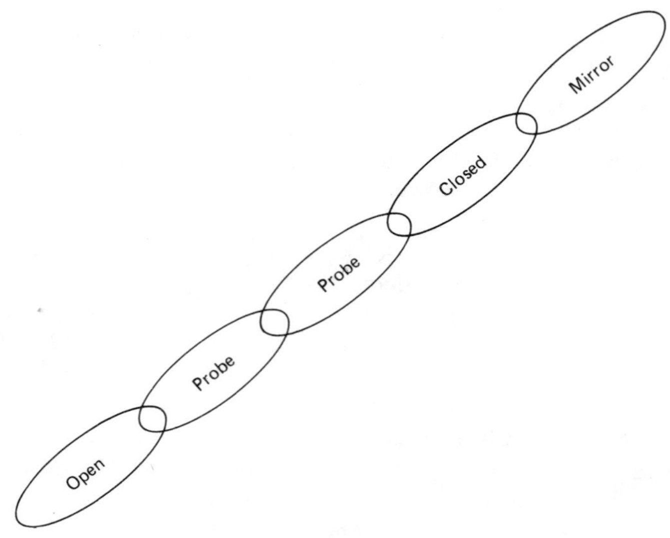

Figure 2

framework that plays in the background of the interaction. Understanding the basic chain-link model will allow the skilled interview player to differentiate between various types of interview through comparisons of their strategic models. The following segment from *Pygmalion* by George Bernard Shaw demonstrates the basic chain-link model:

LIZA: What did you do it for if you didn't care for me? [Open question]
HIGGINS: Why, because it was my job.
LIZA: You never thought of the trouble it would make for me. [Probe]
HIGGINS: Would the world ever have been made if its maker had been afraid of making trouble? Making life means making trouble. There's only one way of escaping trouble; and that's killing things. Cowards, you notice, are always shrieking to have troublesome people killed.
LIZA: I'm no preacher: I don't notice things like that. I notice that you don't notice me. [Probe]
HIGGINS: (*jumping up and walking around intolerantly*) Eliza: you're an idiot. I waste the treasures of my Miltonic mind by spreading them before you. Once for all, understand that I go my own way and do my own work without caring twopence for what happens to either of us. I am not intimidated, like your father and your stepmother. So you can come back or go to the devil: which you please.
LIZA: What am I to come back for? [Closed question]

HIGGINS: *(bouncing up on his knees on the ottoman and leaning over it to her)* For the fun of it. That's why I took you on.

LIZA: And you may throw me out tomorrow if I don't do everything you want me to? [Mirror]

The choice of a segment from a play to demonstrate the basic chain-link model brings to light a very important concept. The chain-link model is a basic model for producing dialog, which is exactly the objective of interview.

So, we have seen how strategy is the effective arrangement of questions of various types in a sequence. The choice of strategy derives from the structure of the interview situation. High-structure interviews are efficient but limit the potential for response. Low-structure interviews take more time but provide for a greater range of response. We have examined some standard strategic approaches including funnel, tunnel, and quintamensional design sequences. The chain-link model was introduced as a basic form to follow as a framework to produce dialog in the interview situation.

As was pointed out at the beginning of this segment on the middle game, the focus during this part of interview is on the development of technique and strategy. The objective of interview is to gain information, and most of it is gained during the middle-game phase. Once the objectives of the middle game have been achieved or it is evident that no further purpose can be served by continuing strategic application, interview moves to the final phase, the end game.

THE END GAME

The primary objective of the final phase of interview is the termination of the interaction, at least temporarily. The key concepts for successfully terminating interview are *summarizing* and *projecting outcomes*. In the same manner that we can identify a greeting ritual, we can also identify a closing ritual. The closing ritual is generally initiated by some combination of body language in concert with a summary statement:

GEORGE: *(putting his hands on the arms of the chair and rocking first forward as if to rise and then leaning far back in the chair)* Well, this has been a most illuminating discussion, Sam. I'm glad we had the opportunity to meet at last.

SAM: So am I, George, and I want to thank you for taking the time to see me on such short notice. *(He places his hands on the arms of the chair, rocks forward and holds the position as if about to rise.)*

A summary statement is not the only verbal means of signaling a closing. Often, one participant will claim sufficiency, such as, "Well, that covers all of the issues on my side. How about you?" Another approach is to ask if there are any questions, "If you have any questions, I'll be glad to answer them," or, "What else do you need to know?"

Regardless of the approach, the end-game portion of the interview, although proportionally short, is an important stage of the process. Even if you are convinced that there will be no need for future interviews, common courtesy dictates that you maintain some level of rapport until the end, that is, of course, if you are not engaged in a difficult interrogation or cross-examination of a hostile witness in a courtroom. The closing moments of interview allow the respondents to make any statements or ask any questions that may have been neglected during the middle game. They can clarify, confirm, or delete an impression made earlier by emphasizing or recanting one or several of the earlier responses.

As part of the end-game process, the participants should be left with a clear understanding of what the outcome of the interview will be. Will there be additional interviews? Will the results appear in print? Will one of the participants be notified about a hiring decision? A good habit to develop is to include a summary or "recap" in the closing phase of every interview. This not only clarifies your understanding of the main points that have been discussed, but it also gives the other participant the opportunity to see how you have perceived the interview. This provides a "reality check" of whether or not both participants are seeing things the same way.

As always, the closing will be greatly influenced by the amount of structure and the type of interview conducted. While a research interview and a journalistic interview may end in much the same way, both would differ from the ending of a counseling or a sales interview.

The end game should summarize and provide an understanding of future actions or outcomes. Where appropriate, endings should be courteous and maintain rapport. The best endings leave each of the participants with the feeling that they have gotten as much as they could out of the encounter and that the closing came at the appropriate time.

SUMMARY

This chapter has shown how the interview is divided into parts that can be dealt with separately to enhance your skill. You should now know the different types of questions and how to frame them. Your ability to frame different types of questions at will is your technique. You have also learned how to align these questions in some of the basic interview sequences. This facility with alignment is your strategy.

Questions for Study and Discussion

1. What are the three main elements of the opening-game phase of interview?
2. What is meant by "appropriate self-disclosure"?
3. Explain the difference between technique and strategy.
4. What is a "laundry-list question" and how is it used?
5. Why is the closed question considered efficient?
6. What distinguishes probing questions from either open or closed questions?
7. What element in the interview situation determines your strategy?
8. What are the basic differences between high- and low-structure interview?
9. What are the two key factors in the end-game phase of interview?

Suggested Activities

1. Make a list of closed questions requiring a yes or no answer. Now convert them all to open questions.
2. Select a partner and interview him or her about hobbies, career goals or other interests. Try to frame your questions to fit one of the following: (a) the chain-link sequence, (b) the funnel sequence, or (c) the tunnel sequence.

Notes

1. Paul D. Krivinos and Mark L. Knapp, "Initiating Communication: What Do You Say When You Say Hello?" *Central States Speech Journal* 26 (1975): 115–125.
2. Sidney M. Jourard, *The Transparent Self* (New York: Van Nostrand Reinhold, 1964): 74.
3. Sidney M. Jourard, "Healthy Personality and Self-Disclosure," *Mental Hygiene* 43 (1969): 499–507.
4. Charles R. Berger and Richard J. Calabrese, "Some Explorations in Initial Interaction and Beyond: Toward a Developmental Theory of Interpersonal Communication," *Human Communication Research* 1 (1975): 99–112.
5. James J. Bradac, Lawrence A. Hosman, and Charles H. Tardy, "Reciprocal Disclosures and Language Intensity: Attributional Consequences," *Communication Monographs* 1 (1978): 2.
6. John Brady, *The Craft of Interviewing* (New York: Random House, Vintage Books, 1977), 54.
7. Richard A. Fear, *The Evaluation Interview: Predicting Job Performance in Business and Industry* (New York: McGraw-Hill, 1958), 92–93.

8. Leon Festinger, "The Motivating Effect of Cognitive Dissonance," in Gardner Lindzey, ed., *Assessment of Human Motives* (New York: Holt, Rinehart and Winston, 1958).
9. Ibid., 69–70.
10. Carl L. Hovland and Milton J. Rosenberg, eds., *Attitude Organization and Change*, vol. 3 (New Haven: Yale University Press, 1960), 204–209.
11. Francis L. Wellman, *The Art of Cross Examination* (Garden City, N.Y.: Garden City Books, 1936), 256–257.
12. George Gallup, "The Quintamensional Plan of Question Design," *Public Opinion Quarterly* 11 (Fall 1947): 385.

3

Developing Basic Skills

Key Concepts

- Perception
- Empathy
- Objectivity
- Attitudes, values, beliefs
- Listening
- Nonverbal communication

(This is incredible. How do I get roped into these things? They actually expect me to interview her for an administrative position? Oh, nuts! Why don't they put the coffeepot back on the hot burner instead of the cold one? I can't stand cold coffee. Now it'll take half an hour to warm up. I'd go downstairs for a cup, but she'll be here in a minute. No coffee. That really ices it. Why is Nancy so positive about her? Probably figures she can lay off some of her work on the new person. I didn't know she was Jim Barton's secretary. I didn't even think she was a secretary. She seems awfully young for the job. I need someone who can think and act fast. Why is Nancy pushing her? She knows the situation here probably better than anyone. She's a friend of hers. Would she let that cloud her judgment? Why did they set this interview up now? It's nearly 4:00. I don't think I'm up for this at all.)

"Mr. Gottlieb?"

"Oh. Yes. Hello, Joan."

"Why are you staring at the coffee machine?" (There I go again with the flip remarks. Nice going, Joan. I don't think he liked being put on the spot like that. But he *was* staring at the coffee maker. Is he weird or what?)

"There's never hot coffee when I want it, but I drink too much coffee anyway. Let's go into my office where we can talk for a while." (She looks tired. I like her approach. She definitely has spunk—"Why are you staring . . . ?"—that must have looked a bit weird.)

"Sit down. Tell me, what do you know about this job?"

"Well, Nancy said you were looking for someone to administer the training program. Truthfully, I'm not sure what that means." (I guess I should have been more definite, but I didn't want to guess.)

"Essentially, that's right. Although we should clarify what 'administration' means. I'm talking about keeping track of the schedule and everyone's whereabouts. In addition, there is a lot of correspondence and general typing that has to be done. Are you a good typist?" (I bet she's only fair.)

"I just took a typing test and scored 96 words per minute." (How do you like that one, buddy?)

"Ninety-six words a minute? Say, you really rip along!" (Ninety-six words a minute? What have I got here? I wonder if she can handle the expenses and billing.)

"Do you have any experience with expense accounts?

"Yes, in my present position I have been involved with auditing expenses." (He is beginning to realize I am not a dumbbell.)

"Let me tell you what I need. I need someone who can work independently. I will not be available much of the time for administrative questions. Besides, I would hope you would know more about that than I in a very short time. I need to know where every member of the training staff is at all times. I need to have exact, up-to-date tallies of all the expenses. Tell me what you have in your background that fits with these needs."

(He's getting serious. He certainly can be direct and clear when he wants to!) "There are several similarities to what I've been doing in the Audit Department. Helping the auditors keep track of all kinds of details has been a daily task. As for working independently, the auditors are on the road most of the time, so I have had to manage everything in the office pretty much on my own."

"What do you mean by manage? What kinds of things do you do?"

"Everything that comes up. I answer the phone, schedule appointments, take care of the filing and correspondence. I occasionally draft letters for Mr. Barton because I know his writing style pretty well."

(That's good. She appears to have initiative. Why does she seem to be depressed?)

"I like what you're telling me, Joan, but what is it about the job that interests you?"

"Well, as you know, the Audit Department is being moved to the regional office in Chicago, and since I can't move, I would like to remain with the company." (That's not a good enough reason.) "Besides, I believe there is potential for growth here. I would be learning new things and meeting new people."

"Do you have any interest in word processing?"

"Yes, I would really like to learn that."

(Let's get to the point.) "Joan, I'm not convinced you want the job."

(He's definitely picked up that I'm in a low mood. How do I deal with this? Well, let's try the truth.) "I'm not in very good spirits. I just got the news of this move yesterday, and my head hasn't adjusted to it yet. I am very interested in the job, I'm just not doing a good job of showing it."

"I can certainly understand your state of mind. Why don't you take a couple of days to think it through. I believe you have the skills I'm looking for, but I want you to be sure it's what you want. Let's talk again on Tuesday. I'll call you at your office in the morning to set up a time."

"That sounds fine to me. I promise to be in a better mood. Oh, and by the way . . ."

"Yes?"

"Why don't we have our coffee delivered to us from the coffee shop downstairs?"

"Great idea! See you Tuesday."

In the scene we just witnessed, all of the key concepts to be discussed in this chapter are present. Certainly, perception is taking place. The perceptions of both individuals are shaped by their attitudes, values, and beliefs as well as their ability to develop objectivity and empathy during the interview. Listening skills and nonverbal communication also play a large role in the outcome of the experience.

PERCEPTION

Perception is the one phenomenon that encompasses most of the important skills needed for success in interview. It is through the act of perception that we gather the information that we seek. When we perceive, we select, organize, and interpret information or other stimuli that are presented to us in a constant stream.[1] During interview, perception is operating primarily on three levels. We have a perception of ourselves operating in the situation, a perception of the other participant(s), and a perception of what is occurring in the form of communication.

Perception is an interpretive process and as such is affected by subjective influences. In order to maintain some sense of order in what appears at times to be a chaos of stimuli, we automatically attempt to impose consistency on our perceptions. These attempts at consistency often form the basis of our attitudes, values, beliefs, and prejudices. In fact, we might say that our very need for consistency breeds bias into our perceptions of the world and the people around us. We also have a need to attach meaning to all of the sensations we perceive.[2]

Gaining an accurate idea of how perception in general and how our own personal perceptions operate is a high-priority item for the student of interview for two reasons: first, because our perceptual apparatus must be highly tuned to what is occurring, and second, because of the need to control, as far as possible, the perception the other participant(s) have of us. Because of the consistency we impose on our perceptions, we have the tendency to hear what we want to hear and see what we want to see. Hastorf, Schneider, and Polefka tell us that human reactions are predictable in three ways:

1. We tend to structure all of the stimuli we receive from the outside world.
2. In addition to structure, we impose consistency. Even though stimuli may differ, we interpret them through the process of perception as being the same. Two individuals who resemble each other will be perceived as being much the same in all respects.
3. We attach meaning to everything we perceive; we "decode" stimuli by filtering them through our language apparatus and our history of experiences, perceptions, and sensations.[3]

This once again leads us back to our earlier point: We tend to see what we want to see and hear what we want to hear. Now, this is not always, if ever, a desirable phenomenon in the interview situation. We are, after all, in search of information—hopefully the right or truthful information—with which we will be making some very important and perhaps costly decisions. Therefore, we must constantly work against our natural tendency to structure and categorize our perceptions according to our patterned formula for consistency. We need to gain objectivity about our perception of ourselves, the other participant(s), and the communication that occurs during interview.

In the opening scenario, prior to my encounter with Joan, I was clearly not receptive to a positive impression. I was tired, frustrated, and burdened with a perception of Joan based on my natural tendency to categorize or stereotype "young people who look like her." However, using the chain-link sequence, my open and probing questions gave Joan a chance to express herself in a way that provided an opportunity for me to be objective about her qualifications. Once I achieved objectivity, I was able to perceive other things, such as her mood and attitude toward me and the position we were discussing.

In addition to perceiving with a greater degree of clarity, we need objectivity to sort out as accurately as possible the variety of stimuli that come at us in the form of verbal and nonverbal codes.

THE SAPIR-WHORF HYPOTHESIS

The importance of language in the interview process is self-evident. However, it falls outside the parameters of this text to engage in an extended discussion of how language develops and functions as a vehicle during interview; yet we need to know some of the things it will and will not accomplish. We have already established that we actively participate in the organization and perception of what we term reality. What we organize and perceive may be controlled largely by our language.

Benjamin Lee Whorf was a fire insurance engineer with a curiosity about the nature of language. Perhaps this curiosity derived from his association with Edward Sapir, who was a linguist and who contributed significantly to the hypothesis that bears both their names.[4] The hypothesis asserts that our perception of reality is determined by our thought processes and that our thought processes are largely determined by the language system we have acquired. The classic example is the word *snow*. Eskimos, it is pointed out, have several words that describe the experience of snow while people from southern climates have the single word *snow*. Accordingly, the person from the south will only see one physical reality regardless of the variety of frozen particles that come from the sky. In contrast, the Eskimo will be able to differentiate among many kinds of snow because he has many different words to describe it. He will in fact see different kinds of snow that appear all the same to the southerner.

Having established the importance of language in interview, we must first try to get a clear picture of how our own language or, even more specifically, our vocabulary shapes our perception of the interview process. Second, we must try, as much as possible within the natural limitations of such an exercise, to get within the perceptual apparatus of the other participant(s) and try to perceive the experience as they do. The language that each of the participant(s) uses not only shapes their perceptions of the experience but also provides clues to their manner of perception. In the end, success will be minimal as far as actually seeing as others do, but the advantage is gained in the attempt. It is this attempt to enter another's perceptual stream that creates the objectivity necessary for successful performance in interview. In order to appreciate fully the importance of this notion, we need to examine how communication occurs during interview.

Language is the most obvious phenomenon during interview. But, as we have already seen, several other phenomena are actively shaping perception during interview. The model in Figure 3 approximates the interview experience and provides an operational vocabulary. Reduced to his or her most basic components, a participant can be represented by two main parts.

The interior functions include the generation of thoughts, feelings, impressions, and other mental activities that form the basis for information-seeking and information-giving behaviors. The interior also functions cognitively to catalog, analyze, and evaluate information being received. The exterior contains the mechanisms, both physical and mental, for processing the information-giving and information-getting activities. On the sending side, thoughts, feelings, and impressions are "encoded" or organized into a medium, such as language or gesture, and conveyed to the "source"—the other participants. On the receiving side, the encoded signals are "decoded" for cataloging, analysis, and evaluation by the cognitive interior.

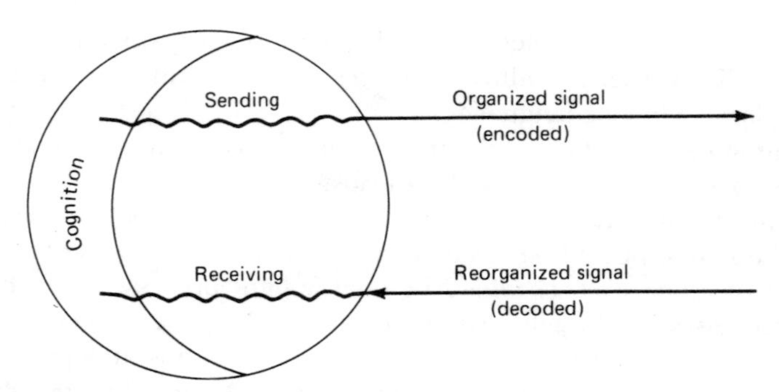

Figure 3

Figure 4 illustrates the process of sending and receiving organized signals. It also diagrams the function of empathy. The broken line curving through the sending/receiving area illustrates the empathic flow of the other participant's attempt to perceive the encounter through this participant's perceptual apparatus. The broken line passing out toward the other participant represents the same attempt on the part of this participant.

The exchange of information is represented by the diagram in Figure 5, which models the entire interview process. The information exchange is illustrated at the center of the model to emphasize the principle of both participants seeking information. The content contained in the information oval is not exhaustive, but it indicates the range of the possible categories of information available and operative during interview. Because of their influence on perception, internal sources like attitudes, values, and beliefs are grouped with outside sources as part of the information spectrum.

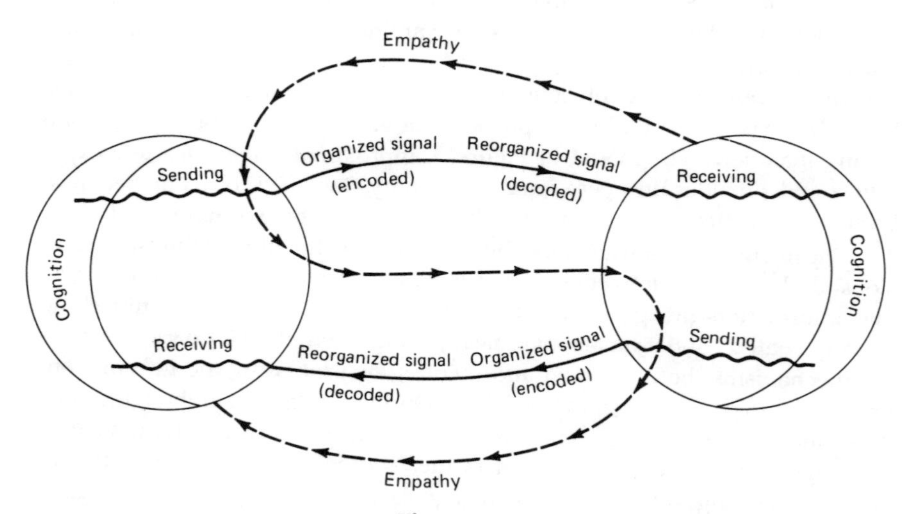

Figure 4

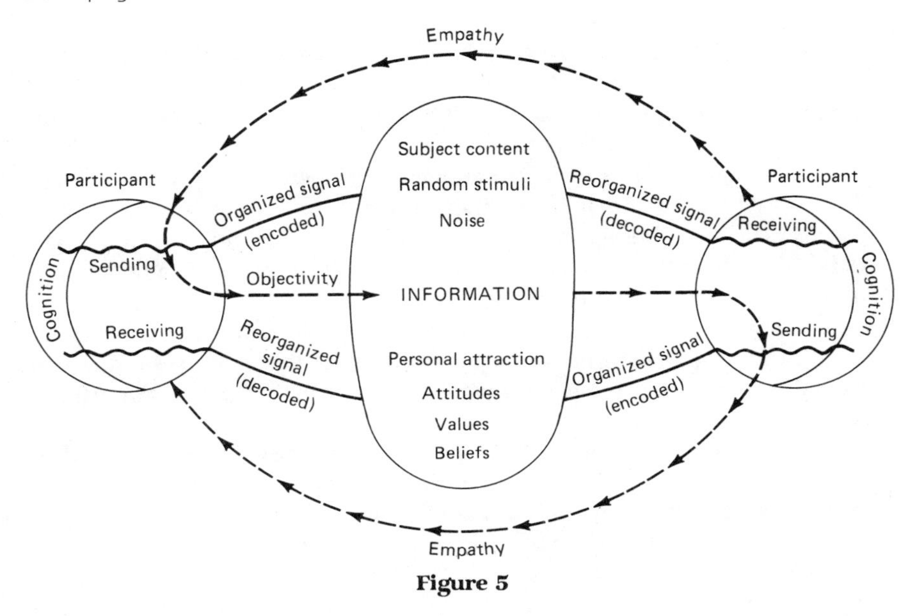

Figure 5

This interview model is useful for several reasons. It clarifies the relationship and responsibilities of the participants. It helps us further break down the subjective phenomenon of interview into observable components. It also points out many of the potential problems that can detract from the information-gathering process. It shows how empathy weaves itself throughout the exchange and becomes a primary interview technique for gaining objectivity, building rapport, and active listening.

RAPPORT-BUILDING TECHNIQUES

Empathy

As has been emphasized throughout this text, the object of interview is the exchange of information. Regardless of our position in the interview situation, we must share something of ourselves in order to get something back. Sometimes this sharing takes the form of a personal disclosure. Sometimes it takes the form of the mirror behaviors discussed in Chapter 1, that is, we share our perception of what the other person is sharing.

In general, sharing involves letting the other person know something about you that would remain unknown if you did not reveal it. The psychologist Sidney Jourard points out that if you do not say what you feel or need, the person with whom you are talking has only two alternatives: to ignore your needs or guess them.[5] The skilled interviewer does not take for granted that the other participant will be skilled as well and is therefore willing to use sharing as an information-getting technique.

The skilled interview participant uses empathy to build and maintain rapport. Sharing your perception of the situation, exploring and discovering common perceptions, testing your objectivity with empathic statements, all serve to put the other participant in a sharing frame of mind. We naturally like to share our feelings with people whom we perceive are in agreement with us or who at least demonstrate a willingness and ability to understand.

Consider my earlier interview with Joan. My perception told me that Joan was hesitant about the job. I decided to share that perception with her, "Joan, I'm not convinced you want this job."

The empathetic statement encourages Joan to share a truth of her own, "I'm not in very good spirits. I just got the news of this move yesterday and my head hasn't adjusted to it yet. I am very interested in the job; I'm just not doing a good job of showing it."

In certain types of interview, empathy is very specifically employed to encourage disclosure of the truth. Investigative reporting often takes this approach. The classic "good cop, bad cop" routine presents a suspect with a choice of dealing with one person who is hostile and threatening or another who appears friendly and sympathetic. The dynamics of the situation enhance the perception of empathy provided by the "good cop," thus creating pressure toward sharing to diminish the threat provided by the "bad cop."

As a general application of technique, empathy is used to gain objectivity, build rapport, and encourage sharing behavior. The following are examples of empathic statements that should be used frequently and appropriately:

"I agree with you."
"If that happened to me, I would feel the same way."
"That must have been (interesting) (exciting) (frightening) (embarrassing) (rewarding) (frustrating)."
"I know what you mean."
"I see."
"I have had that experience."

Listening

The importance of listening is so self-evident it seems superfluous to even make the statement. We have already discussed the function of mirroring to clarify and confirm your understanding of the information you have received in order to close one interview segment and begin another. Clarifying and confirming what you hear is extremely important, but it is not the only component of effective listening. Very often the skilled listener will be called on to interpret aspects of the information spectrum being received. Attitudes, values, beliefs, cultural differences, and other variables cause people to ascribe different meanings to the same or similar words, signs, and symbols. The interview participants, during the course of gathering information, must reach for a genuine understanding of each other.

According to John Stewart and Gary D'Angelo, genuine understanding does not necessarily mean agreement:

> Understanding involves grasping fully what the other person is trying to say—from her or his point of view—and how he or she feels about it. It comes about when you are able to interpret accurately and empathically the cues the other person makes available.[6]

Stewart and D'Angelo go on to say that accurate understanding usually requires "listening" with more than just the ears. You listen with all of your sensory equipment. You hear words being spoken, you listen to the tone of voice, pauses, and sighs. You watch for body movements, facial expressions, eye movements, changes in spatial relationships, and any other observable clues. You have to hear both what is being said and what is not being said. The skilled listener detects feelings in another person without actual words being said.[7]

Stewart and D'Angelo further tell us that it is often unfair to draw inferences about what another person is feeling based primarily on our own perceptions. They speak of the need for "perception checks" that present our understanding and allow the other person to respond to our interpretation. Although labeled differently, perception checking is identical with mirroring. Listening is the fiber that binds the interview segment together. When you actively listen, you absorb every possible scrap of information, both verbal and nonverbal, that your open question, probe, leading question, and so on elicits. You process and interpret this information, and in the course of doing so, you identify discrepancy, ambiguity, and other unclear elements. These elements become the subject of your mirror.

In general, try to keep value judgments out of your mirror responses. If the other participant perceives that you are being judgmental, the result will probably be defensiveness and even hostility. Jack Gibb studied group interaction for eight years and defined defensive behavior as behavior "which occurs when an individual perceives threat or anticipates threat." One major cause of defensiveness is "speech or other behavior which appears evaluative."[8] As there are exceptions to most rules, so there are to this one as well. A well-timed evaluative response can often be very effective for certain types of interview, such as investigation and cross-examination.

Listening is a skill that cannot be taken for granted or given too much attention. There is considerably more nonverbal information during interview than verbal, and usually much more ambiguity than clarity.

Spatial-Territorial Arrangements

Understanding and controlling spatial-territorial arrangements during interview can greatly enhance the outcome. Being unaware or insensitive to spatial-territorial arrangements can create insurmountable problems. Edward T. Hall invented the term *proxemics* to describe "social and personal space and man's perception of it."[9] Hall sees space as an active participant in the communication process. He asserts that "man senses distance as other animals do. His perception of space is dynamic because it is related to action—what can be done in a given space rather than what is seen by passive viewing."[10] He delineates four distance zones: intimate, personal, social, and public. Both the intimate and personal zones are distinguished by the potential for touch. The far phase of personal distance, according to Hall, is four feet.

While as always there are exceptions, the act of touching is out of context with the general interview construct. Most interview takes place within what Hall terms *social distance*:

> The boundary line between the far phase of personal distance and the close phase of social distance marks, in the words of one subject, the "limit of domination." Intimate visual detail in the face is not perceived, and nobody touches or expects to touch another person unless there is some special effort. Voice level is normal for Americans. There is little change between the far and close phases, and conversations can be overheard at a distance of up to twenty feet.[11]

In the close phase of social distance, which is four to seven feet, the head size of each participant is perceived as normal. "At four feet, a one-degree visual angle covers an area of a little more than one eye. At seven feet the area of sharp focus extends to the nose and parts of both eyes; or the whole mouth, one eye, and the nose are sharply seen."[12]

The close phase creates more involvement than the distant phase. Certain types of interview, such as counseling and performance appraisal, will have moments when this degree of closeness is appropriate and desirable. Most interviews will occur in a far phase arrangement, which is seven to twelve feet, as Hall has noted:

> This is the distance to which people move when someone says, "stand away so I can look at you." Business and social discourse conducted at the far end of social distance has a more formal character than if it occurs inside the close phase. Desks in the offices of important people are large enough to hold visitors at the far phase of social distance. Even in an office with standard-size desks, the chair opposite is eight or nine feet away from the man behind the desk. At the far phase of social distance the finest details of the face, such as the capillaries in the eyes, are lost. Otherwise, skin texture, hair, condition of teeth, and condition of clothes are all readily visible. . . . The eyes and the mouth of the other person are seen in the area of sharpest vision. Hence it is not necessary to shift the eyes to take in the whole face. During conversations of any significant length it is more important to maintain visual contact at this distance than it is at closer distance.[13]

Hall's observations are not only helpful in defining proper spatial-territorial arrangements but also in underlining the variety of data available to the skilled observer. During interview we need to be sensitive to individual space needs. These needs vary with the situation and the subject matter; they are also culturally determined. As with all of the other basic interview skills, learning how to control and manipulate spatial-territorial arrangements is an important part of interview training.

SUMMARY

This chapter shifted our focus from interview as a phenomenon to the interview participant as a phenomenon. It outlined the basic skills necessary for the effective interview participation. Perception was discussed as the umbrella under which all the other skills fit. It is through the act of perception that we gather the information that we seek. We looked at some of the limitations of language as demonstrated by the Sapir-Whorf hypothesis, and a model was developed illustrating what occurs during an interview exchange. The importance of empathy for building and maintaining rapport was covered as well as using empathy as a technique to gain objectivity. We also looked at listening and spatial-territorial arrangements as important interview skills.

Questions for Study and Discussion

1. What are the three levels that perception operates on during interview?
2. What is meant by "perception is an interpretive process"?
3. Why can Eskimos see more kinds of snow than we can?
4. Explain how empathy can build rapport and objectivity at the same time.
5. What is meant by "sharing"?
6. What is the difference between hearing and listening?
7. Why do most interviews occur in the far phase of Hall's social distance zone? What are the parameters of the far phase?

Suggested Activities

1. Have several people role play the opening interview, using it as a blueprint, but not necessarily using the exact words or outcome.
2. Try a role play interview and arbitrarily move the chairs closer together at points and farther apart at other points. How does this affect perception? Behavior?

Notes

1. Charles M. Butter, *Neuropsychology: The Study of Brain and Behavior* (Belmont, Calif.: Brooks/Cole, 1968), 39.

2. Albert H. Hastorf, David J. Schneider, and Judith Polefka, *Person Perception* (Reading, Mass.: Addison-Wesley, 1970), 7–10.
3. Ibid., 1–18.
4. Benjamin Lee Whorf, "The Relation of Habitual Thought and Behavior to Language," in John B. Carroll, ed., *Language Thought and Reality* (Cambridge, Mass.: M.I.T. Press, 1956), 134–159.
5. Sidney M. Jourard, *The Transparent Self* (New York: Van Nostrand Reinhold, 1964), 3.
6. John Stewart and Gary D'Angelo, *Together: Communicating Interpersonally* (Reading, Mass.: Addison-Wesley, 1975), 191.
7. Ibid., 192.
8. Jack R. Gibb, "Defensive Communication," *Journal of Communication* 11 (September 1961): 141.
9. Edward T. Hall, *The Hidden Dimension* (Garden City, N.Y.: Doubleday, 1966), 1.
10. Ibid., 108.
11. Ibid., 114.
12. Ibid.
13. Ibid., 115.

part II

THE INTERVIEW SPECTRUM

In Part I we have laid the groundwork for your development as interview practitioners. We have explored the phenomenon of interview, developed some models to make the methodology of interview visible and concrete, and outlined some of the basic skills needed for effective interview participation. Part II attempts to divide the interview spectrum into discrete types based on the primary purpose or need for interview. In pointing out the differences and contrasting the styles, however, we will also see continuous threads of similarity. Certainly, elements of the basic research interview will be present during journalistic interview, medical interview, and even sales interview and cross-examination. The delineation among the types must be viewed as the "overriding purpose" or the primary goals and objectives of the participants.

Each of the following seven chapters considers a different type of interview. Each chapter is subdivided so as to present the point of view of both (or more) interview participants.

4

The Basic Research Interview

Key Concepts

- Defining your purpose
- Maintaining objectivity
- Matching strategy to goals

ME: (*Phone rings.*) Hello.
VOICE: Mr. Gottlieb?
ME: Yes. (*Already skeptical*)
VOICE: Mr. Gottlieb, I'm Roger Fern from the National Society for Life Enhancement, and I wonder if you would mind answering a few questions.
ME: Well, ordinarily I wouldn't, but my turkey vulture has somehow gotten out of the cage and has my kitty cornered in the bathroom. So . . . some other time, Roger. (*Click*)

I readily admit it. I am a terrible subject for spontaneous interviews. I simply do not like to be intruded on in my private space during what I consider private time. The truth is that most people are probably a lot like me in that respect. It is not that I believe providing my opinion is not important or not part of my civic duty. It is just that so many of these calls and knocks on the door through the years have developed into pitches for aluminum siding. Face-to-face and telephone-opinion polling are becoming less prevalent with the development of new methods and technologies.

However, a survey prepared and conducted effectively will yield a higher quality of data—more accurate, more complete. I agree with Stewart and Cash that, "Face-to-face and telephone surveys have a number of advantages over mailed or handed-out questionnaires."[1] Stewart and Cash list some of the advantages:

> For instance, we have no control over who in a family or organization might fill out a questionnaire. Thus, a fifty-year-old female instead of the twenty-five-year-old male we need for our sample may answer the questions. . . . We cannot observe or listen to answers in questionnaires, so we lose the valuable nonverbal clues that survey respondents provide. . . . Questionnaire respondents may not read our instructions or follow the guidelines we provide.[2]

In spite of these advantages, the use of direct mail as a response vehicle has expanded dramatically during the last several years. While this is particularly true for advertising, the same dramatic rise has occurred in the use of questionnaires. There are several reasons for this, the most obvious being that the direct-mail approach can cover populations of extraordinary size in a relatively short period of time for less cost than face-to-face interviews. Even the U.S. Census Bureau used a direct-mail questionnaire the last time around, and they, by definition, sampled the entire population of the country. Another factor is the rise in the sophistication of the respondents. This coupled with more powerful statistical techniques has tended to reduce the error factor. Electronic surveys, such as those conducted by Nielsen, eliminate the human factor entirely and collect data directly.

In spite of all this, there are still times when the face-to-face survey is the best choice to gather your necessary information, and as such, the skilled interviewer should understand its techniques and strategies. According to Stewart and Cash, "The survey is the most meticulously planned and executed of all informational interviews because its purpose is to establish a solid base of fact from which to draw conclusions, make interpretations, and determine future courses of action."[3]

DEFINING YOUR PURPOSE

As with all types of interview, your overriding purpose is the acquisition of information. The amount and type of information sought as well as time and resources will shape the design of your survey. The results of your research interviews will ultimately be tested by how well you have achieved your objectives. Here are some guidelines to follow:

1. Develop a brief statement that tells why you are doing the study.
2. Make a list of the components of information you require.
3. How will you use the information once you obtain it?

4. Using the answers you have provided for the first three guidelines, prepare a list of objectives taking all of these factors into account.
5. What data do you need from respondents in order to achieve each objective?
6. For each objective, draft a question or questions that, when answered, will provide you with the necessary information to satisfy the objective.

The data you collect from a research interview is best understood in the context of your purpose. Harry Alpert, discussing survey use in the field of sociology, supports this notion:

> Operationally speaking, survey results are understandable only in terms of the methods by which they are obtained. To the extent that we wish to organize our research in terms of a systematic, theoretical system, we must make method, including sampling method, the servant, and not the master of our theoretical scientific framework.[4]

SAMPLING

Surveys can be used for a wide variety of basic research problems. In some instances it may be possible to interview everyone concerned with the problem. For example, if you are interested in how your family feels about a certain issue, it is possible to schedule the time to interview each family member. Obviously, a 100-percent sample gives you the greatest accuracy. However, as soon as your interest extends beyond a particular point, you need to concern yourself with sampling techniques. If you were interested in how American families of the middle class feel about a particular issue, you would not be able to get a 100-percent sample.

When you set out to do basic research interviewing, you confront an array of potential human responses: opinions, attitudes, wants, beliefs, prejudices, preferences, intentions, expectations, levels of satisfaction, and morale. In order for your research to be useful, it must contain a large measure of accuracy. Limitations of time and money always place restrictions on the size of any given sample. A good sample is the best feasible compromise between the need for accuracy and the need for economy. What do we do when we sample? Frederick F. Stephan and Philip J. McCarthy, reporting on results of studies done by the former Joint Committee on the Measurement of Opinions, Attitudes, and Consumer Wants, answer this way:

> The basic idea in sampling is simple: (a) we seek information about a whole class of similar objects, (b) we examine some of them, (c) we extend our findings to the entire class. This fundamental aspect of sampling is quite familiar. All our experience with the world is of this partial nature. We learn about people and about physical objects by accumulating experience. We assume that they will

continue to be in the future approximately what they have been in the past. It is in this way, for example, that the common conceptions of national and regional character are formed from a few observations. New Englanders are believed to be cold and reserved. Southerners are easygoing and very hospitable. Scotsmen are thrifty. We can extend the list as we please.

A conception of sampling that applies to all such generalizations from limited experience is too broad to be useful for our present purposes. Something more is needed to make it definite and fully serviceable. It is necessary to restrict further the scope of the notion of sampling. We shall define it in the following way:

Sampling is the use of a *definite procedure* in the selection of a part for the express purpose of obtaining from it descriptions or estimates of certain properties and characteristics of the whole.[5]

Selecting an Appropriate Sample

In order to effectively select a sample, you will need to collect some essential information. Once you have identified the population you wish to survey, you need to ask some questions about that population.

1. How large is the population to be sampled?
2. How is the population situated geographically?
3. What are the characteristics of the population that have a direct bearing on the objectives of the survey? For example, what, if any, of the following factors relate to our projected final outcome?
   a. age groups
   b. race
   c. religion
   d. occupation (laborer, executive, farmer, soldier, student)
   e. economic group
   f. participants in certain activities
   g. members of certain organizations
   h. users of certain products
   i. readers of certain publications
   j. voters
   k. users of particular media (radio, TV, film, stereo, etc.)

Certainly, this list is not exhaustive. However, it provides some insight and direction for examining your population. Decisions that you make to either include or exclude certain subgroups from your population will redefine your population and have important effects on the results of the survey.[6] When the results are examined on completion of the survey, they must be looked at with a clear understanding of what population was sampled in order to have meaning.

Another question to be considered is: What are the prevailing attitudes of your population? One view of sampling proposed by Feller holds that the process of selecting a sample is actually one of drawing a sample from a set or collection of attitude measurements rather than from a population of human biological organisms.[7] Stephan and McCarthy summarize the importance of attitude variables this way:

> Information must be assembled on the attitude variables and other variables that are to be studied because they affect profoundly most of the phases of the entire survey design. They constitute, first of all, the basic criteria of the representativeness of the sample. They determine very largely the kinds of measurement operations that are feasible (e.g., mail questionnaire, personal interview, direct observation, laboratory test, etc.) and therefore influence the choice of methods of getting in touch with the population.[8]

If we assume that personal interviews are necessary in order to obtain information on attitude variables, the sample must be selected so as to avoid excessive travel costs and also, if we are not working alone, the problem of hiring, training, and supervising interviewers.

Sample Size

The size of your sample is determined by many factors. What you are striving for is a sample that is "representative" of the total population. It is possible for a small sample to be representative and a large one not. So, size alone is not a good indicator of accuracy. You must also consider the cost to you in time and other resources. Even if you can decrease the error variance by 10 percent by increasing the size of the sample by 20 percent, you will probably increase your cost by 20 percent as well. The effect of changing the sample size is like the effect of changing other features of a survey. The size of your sample should be chosen to reflect the needs and objectives of the survey procedure. Generally speaking, a larger sample will tend to be more accurate in reflecting the population.

DESIGNING THE BASIC RESEARCH INTERVIEW

If your data is to have any meaning, it is essential that each respondent is put through the same experience. If you are conducting a large survey, it will probably be necessary to hire and train a staff of interviewers. If the interview contains open questions, this process of training becomes more difficult. Even with closed-question interviews, there must be a high degree of standardization in approach, intonation, and questioner response. This is best accomplished through simulation exercises—perhaps with videotape—that focus the interviewer's attention on the details and subtleties of the interaction.

It is beyond our purpose here to delve into the complex problems associated with large survey projects and the training of an interview staff. Rather, we will concern ourselves with your role in the survey interview. Let us begin with the basic assumption that you are conducting research that requires that you involve yourself in several interviews in order to collect the necessary data. You have successfully mastered the techniques and strategies presented in Part I of this book, and the time has come to put some of these concepts to practical use. Let us take a minute to review some of the important aspects of interview.

All interviews divide themselves rather neatly into three parts: the opening game, the middle game, and the end game. Each part has its own rituals and objectives. We also know that the raw material of interview is the question. We know that the question comes in many forms, and our mastery of these forms is our technique. We further know that questions by themselves are ineffectual for gathering the necessary information; they must be placed in some kind of sequence in order to maximize our information-gathering potential. We have learned that this placing of questions in a deliberate sequence is our strategy. We have examined some standard questioning strategies, including tunnel, funnel, quintamensional, and chain-link sequences. The design of your research interview and the strategy you apply are totally interdependent.

Let us consider strategy first. What kind of information do you need? In what form do you wish to acquire this information? Must the information be easily quantifiable for tabulation or computer analysis? Or is the information you seek more subjective? Is the nature of the response to certain questions as important or more important than the answer itself? These and other questions should begin to shape a strategy and consequently, a design for your research interview. For the purposes of discussion, let us look at the questionnaire in the box on page 61.

In the example in the box, the researcher is an employee of a large corporation who has the task of determining what types of changes in sick leave policy and other company benefits would be desirable to the employees of the company. There is a secondary objective also—to determine how the employees' perception of company benefits impacts on morale.

The interview begins with the usual opening-game characteristics: greeting ritual, establishing rapport, etc. This is immediately followed by a statement that orients the respondent to the interview. It is important that each respondent knows what the expectations are. In addition, the respondent is told how the information will be used.

The first 14 questions are closed forced-choice questions that will produce very specific, easily quantifiable data. This data will be cross-tabulated with the help of a computer in order to identify which, if any, sex, age, regional, tenure, or marital status subgroups stand out with regard to any of the survey items.

XYZ Inc.

Reactions to Existing Sick Leave Policy

(Open as follows, being as natural and spontaneous as possible.) Hello, I'm ________. Thank you for your time. I'm going to ask you some questions about our sick leave policy that is currently under review. Your response is very important since changes will be made based on the information we receive. Since these changes will affect you, we want you to have a say in what they will be.

1. Sex (note without asking) ______
2. Age ______
3. Region of the U.S. ______
4. Period of time with XYZ Inc. ______
5. Marital status ______
6. What is your yearly salary range?

   ______ a. below $10,000
   ______ b. $10,000–$20,000
   ______ c. $20,000–$30,000
   ______ d. above $30,000

7. How often have you used sick leave?

   ______ a. frequently
   ______ b. occasionally
   ______ c. rarely
   ______ d. never

8. How well do you feel you understand the current sick leave policy?

   ______ a. completely
   ______ b. somewhat
   ______ c. very little
   ______ d. completely confused

9. If you have taken sick leave, were you satisfied with the way the company handled your situation?

   ______ a. completely satisfied
   ______ b. it was a problem, but it worked out okay
   ______ c. unsatisfied
   ______ d. the matter is still unresolved

10. Do you feel that sick leave policy is applied equally?

    (Check more than one if applicable.)

    ______ a. among regions ______ c. regardless of salary

    ______ b. among departments ______ d. policy is not applied equally

11. As compared to other company benefits, how would you rate the sick leave policy?

    ______ a. one of the best ______ c. average

    ______ b. good ______ d. one of the worst

12. Compared with other companies, how would you rate our sick leave policy?

    ______ a. one of the best ______ c. average

    ______ b. good ______ d. one of the worst

13. Do company benefits affect your morale?

    ______ a. very much ______ c. not at all

    ______ b. somewhat

14. Would you like to have more input regarding decisions about company benefits?

    ______ a. yes ______ b. no

15. What do you believe is the most important company benefit? __________

16. What do you believe is the least important company benefit? __________

17. What should be clarified about current sick leave policy? __________

18. What changes would you like to see in current sick leave policy? ________

19. What other changes would you like to see in company benefits? ________

20. Are there other matters concerning sick leave or other company benefits not covered in this questionnaire that you would like to discuss? ________

(End as in the following.) Thank you for taking the time to answer these questions. Your responses are a valuable resource in the shaping of company policy.

The remaining six questions are all open questions that become increasingly more open as the interview progresses. They provide the respondent with the opportunity to express him- or herself on a wider range of issues. The open questions also provide a reasonable cross-check of the information received via the closed questions. A respondent who claims satisfaction with the policy (#9) may, in response to the open questions, turn out to be highly critical of certain aspects of the policy. As with all open questions, you run the risk of receiving a more voluble response than necessary or having the interview drift toward peripheral issues.

Open questions in a survey have another purpose that is beneficial. They leave respondents with more of a feeling of accomplishment, a feeling that they have contributed substantively to the outcome of the survey. If you are the only person conducting the survey, you can keep reasonable control over the administering of the open questions. This becomes more difficult if several people are involved in the data collection. The key word for open survey segments is *restraint.* The questions must be asked in such a way as to be devoid of expectation. You cannot, through physical action, intonation, or other communication behaviors, present a bias or lead toward an expected or desired response.

In the following example, Roger Fern, a persistent telephone survey person, finally succeeds in capturing my attention:

ME: (*Phone rings.*) Hello.

ROGER: Mr. Gottlieb?

ME: Yes?

ROGER: Roger Fern, again.

ME: Roger . . .

ROGER: Yes, we spoke briefly the other evening, but you had an emergency. Is your kitty okay?

ME: Oh! Hello, Roger.

ROGER: I need only two minutes of your time to answer a few questions being posed by the National Society for Life Enhancement.

ME: Roger, are you selling something?

ROGER: Hopefully, I'm selling a better future for all of us.

ME: Okay, let's have the questions.

ROGER: Thank you, Mr. Gottlieb. Which one of the following issues would you rank as the most important issue for the next ten years:

Control of hazardous waste
Disarmament
Preserving and developing energy resources
Promotion of international understanding

ME: These are all very important issues, Roger. But, if I have to pick one, I guess disarmament is the issue that concerns me the most right now.

ROGER: Are you currently active in any groups or organizations that promote or support this issue?

ME: No.

ROGER: Do you identify yourself with the people you ordinarily associate with activism on this issue?

ME: Actually, no.

ROGER: If you knew of a group that was compatible with your attitudes, values, beliefs, and status and was actively promoting this issue, would you participate?

ME: I might.

ROGER: Would you be more likely to participate actively in person or through financial support?

ME: Most likely through financial support.

ROGER: Would you be interested in learning the results of this survey?

ME: Yes, I would.

ROGER: Fine. Thank you, Mr. Gottlieb. I will send you a package of materials that will detail the results of this survey and will also include some information about the National Society for Life Enhancement.

ME: Okay.

ROGER: Good-bye.

ME: Good-bye.

In this example Roger Fern uses a funnel strategy. He presents a series of closed questions that continually narrow down to a commitment. In retrospect, I can perceive that all of the issues presented for my choice are issues of N.S.L.E. (a fictitious creation for this text, by the way). Roger is interested in finding out which issues have the greatest impact, what levels of activism are operating and, perhaps, how they are distributed geographically. He is also gaining an index of untapped activism based on an expressed lack of source identification. He narrows down to my willingness to be active and, further, to my choice of activity—financial support. He has successfully obtained my advance commitment to financially support N.S.L.E., assuming they present an image I can identify with. We do not need to dwell on why N.S.L.E. conducted such a survey, but Roger has identified me as a primary prospect for financial support, thereby making it worthwhile to send me a package of relatively expensive printed materials.

In both examples presented thus far in this chapter, we have a demonstration of the basic principles of survey interviewing. First, identify your purpose or purposes for conducting the research. The best surveys provide a wide spectrum of data—some peripheral to the main objective—that will ultimately enrich the results, provide tests of reliability, and help in the analysis. You need to select an appropriate or representative sample from the population you are studying. Always think in terms of questions. Continually ask yourself, "What question is going to get the respondent to provide that piece of information?" Finally, shape your questions into a strategy for achieving your objectives.

Analysis

The analysis phase of the research interview is the time when all of the effort comes together. It is during the analysis that the accumulated information turns into meaning. The availability of sophisticated computer analysis techniques greatly enhances your ability to find meaningful results. If you have the skill and access to use a computer, do not pass up the opportunity. If you have the resources, it is even a better idea to involve or employ a computer professional. I have found it extremely valuable to involve such a person early in the research process. How the data will ultimately be analyzed should have a strong influence on how the survey is designed.

A survey is an instrument of measurement and as such should be subject to the same criteria applied to any measuring instrument. All instruments for measurement are judged by their accuracy. This need for accuracy is usually expressed as the "reliability" of the instrument. It is probably impossible to design a survey that is totally accurate. In fact, all measurement scales are only relatively accurate. In order to interpret the findings, however, we must know the degree of accuracy. It is essential, therefore, to determine the reliability of your survey. A detailed examination of statistical methods for measuring reliability would be out of place here and beyond our purpose. There are several tests that can be made to determine if the respondents are responding consistently to the same type of question. The most prominent of these tests is the Pearson product-moment correlation coefficient, which numerically demonstrates the association between two variables.[9]

If you have been careful in setting your objectives and framing your questions, there should not be a significant problem with reliability. If you are conducting a very large study, it may be necessary to run a pilot—a small section of your sample—before beginning the project. This enables you to establish the reliability of your instrument beforehand and enables you to make adjustments to increase the reliability if necessary. A high degree of reliability is helpful when you present your findings since it tends to confirm that sound methods were used in preparing and conducting the study.

The analysis summarizes your findings and allows you to draw conclusions about those findings. If you have used a sample of a large population, you should now be able to generalize your findings across the target population. As with other stages in the survey-interview process, you must work hard to control your biases. Very often we do not get the results we expect, but that does not make the actual results less valuable. In doing any kind of basic research, keep your ego out of it. The value of your study will depend primarily on your objectivity.

Focus Groups

A special form of basic research interview is the focus-group interview. Once only a tool for marketing, focus-group interviews are now being conducted in a variety of settings where in-depth and detailed personal responses to a product, plan, service, or concept are desired. Large insurance brokerage firms are using focus groups to determine which benefits are best suited for a particular company. Companies themselves are using focus groups to determine staff development needs as part of overall strategic planning. Colleges and universities are using focus groups to determine students' needs and evaluate and recommend changes in the curriculum. Of course, advertising agencies continue to use them extensively to test product viability.

Focus-group interviewing is a way of determining the success of a particular approach before expending large amounts of time, effort, and money. It involves assembling cross-section groups and, by means of an open interview strategy, getting their reactions to the product or idea you are presenting. The groups selected must be a representative sample of the whole target population. They would be selected in much the same way as any sample might be for a survey. Each focus group should consist of eight to ten people. A larger group becomes unwieldy; a smaller group does not provide enough interaction. Assemble the group in reasonably comfortable surroundings, perhaps around a table so that it is a circular conversational grouping.

Begin as you would any individual interview; thank them for their participation, tell them how much you value their judgment, and orient them to the purpose of the focus group. Then present your product, idea, concept, or whatever your focus is. When the group is thoroughly familiar with your purpose, you can begin questioning.

As always, you must be particularly careful not to inject your bias into the discussion. Structure your questions so that they elicit reaction. Cynthia S. Smith, in her book *How to Get Big Results from a Small Advertising Budget*, gives us a general overview of how the line of questioning should proceed:

> For instance, if you want to know how they like the look of a product, don't ask a straight like-it-or-not question. The result is useless. Too many people will say Yes because they hate to hurt your feelings, and many will say No because they enjoy being provocative.
>
> Sneak in the back way with a gambit like "Which room would you place this table in?" If it ends up they can't see the piece in any room, then you know you've got a redesigning problem on your hands.
>
> If you want to know what price range the product should fall into, don't ask, "How much would you be willing to pay for this?" Suggest a few prices, and see which range they consider feasible.[10]

Smith goes on to underline the necessity of maintaining control of the levels of participation, such as controlling the more aggressive participants and drawing in the shier ones. She also alerts us to the creative potential of focus groups:

> Keep on the alert for new ideas too. Sometimes a suggestion for a new application for the product crops up. Pick up the lead, and get everyone's opinion on the potential.
>
> Find out what colors they prefer, where they would expect to buy it, for whom in the family they would buy it.
>
> One or two of these sessions, and you will have a pretty fair idea of the dominant marketing theme that should be stressed, what price range the product must fall into, and whether or not it has sufficient potential to bring it in at all.[11]

Recording and tabulating the results obtained from focus-group interviews can be a difficult task primarily because the discussion, if proceeding successfully, is varied and unpredictable. Wherever possible, use a tape recorder. The group will quickly become used to it, and any inhibiting effect is overbalanced by the ability to have total recall of the proceedings. However, whether you are able to record or not, be sure to develop a tabulating system beforehand. Prepare sheets with the general categories you are exploring, such as "color," "price," and "packaging" if the focus is on a product or "medical plan," "dental plan," and "savings plan" if the focus is on company benefits. This will enable you to contain all of the pertinent notes for each category in the same place. Later you can break the information down into finer categories and group the categories for analysis.

In summary, focus-group interviews can be a very effective research tool. In a sense, a focus-group approach is like doing several individual interviews simultaneously, with the added benefit of group interaction.

PARTICIPATING IN THE RESEARCH INTERVIEW

During the course of this chapter, we have discussed several "do's" and "don'ts" about conducting research interviews. It is useful to summarize and expand on these points.

The Opening Game

One unique aspect of the opening game of the research interview is that the subject participant is usually approached without having had time to anticipate the interview. You stop the person on the street or call on the phone. When there is opportunity to select your subjects more specifically, they should be informed and oriented to the purpose of the interview. When this is not possible or desirable, you must make sure that your first impression is a good impression. In *The Craft of Interviewing*, John Brady gives good advice for the opening game of the research interview:

> The first impression that an interviewer makes on his subject is probably his physical appearance: clothing, accessories, and—if the interviewer is female—make-up. 'Clothing should be average,' suggests one researcher who feels that the interviewer's physical appearance should be as neutral as possible. "It should be neither too fashionable nor too plain. The same applies to the accessories of women interviewers." The important thing to remember is not to compete directly with the subject. Women who wear absolutely no make-up or nail polish, however, risk creating an impression "of coldness, even of masculinity. These impressions, whether right or wrong, are to be avoided. The interviewer may feel that he is being asked to mask his personality by suppressing indications of where he belongs in the social matrix. He is being asked to do exactly this, but he should remember that it is part of doing his job well."[12]

While Brady focuses on the face-to-face situation, the same basic principles hold true for the telephone interview. You need to establish the same aura of neutrality. Your opening remarks should be friendly without being ingratiating. Your tone should convey strength without aggressiveness. Some telephone interviewers make the mistake of "putting on" a special voice or accent for their phone interviews. This usually comes across as phony and creates an atmosphere of untrustworthiness.

Remember, your primary purpose in the opening game is to establish rapport and orient your subject to the purpose of the interview. This should be accomplished quickly and efficiently. If you are surveying several subjects, practice your orientation section until you can deliver it virtually the same way to all subjects. If you do not, you will find that your orientation changes somewhat with each subject and eventually may change enough to influence the answers.

The Middle Game

For the basic research interview, you have plotted out your strategy in advance. Except for the most open-ended types of surveys, such as collecting family history or other ethnographic or anthropological data, you will have developed your questions and arranged them in a sequence. Even for the open-ended interviews, you will be guided by the structure you have prepared in advance to organize the information, such as a chronological order or some classification ordering scheme.

It is best to have a form containing your questions and appropriate space for noting the answers. Wherever possible, keep your writing to a minimum. Subjects tend to become nervous and uncooperative if they feel you are being too detailed in your recording of their answers. Also, you lose the flow of the interview if you have to stop after each question to make an extensive note.

State each question clearly and in a conversational manner. It is best to rehearse your questions enough so that you can check the form, determine the question to be asked, raise your eyes from the form, look directly at the subject, and ask the question. Avoid reading the question directly from the form. Reading is annoying to the subject, makes you appear to be less involved or informed than you should be, and is thoroughly unprofessional. Once you have asked the question, remain silent. The next utterance must come from the subject. If the question has been misunderstood, the subject will ask for an explanation. Avoid the natural tendency to elaborate. Instead, restate the question. If the misunderstanding persists, the subject will be more specific about what is confusing. If you must restate or explain, try to be brief and to the point. Each communication segment you employ outside your planned approach will tend to contaminate your data since additional communication, unrehearsed and unplanned, provides an opportunity for questioner bias to enter the process.

Demonstrate your interest and involvement through active listening. The active-listening techniques you use—nodding, smiling, various verbalizations like "I see," "um hmm"—must be consistent throughout the interview. You must guard against being more enthusiastic about answers in one particular direction.

The End Game

The wrap-up for the basic research interview is generally short and to the point. The researcher announces the end, states his or her gratitude, and provides an opportunity for the subject to ask questions or make some final statement:

"Well, Mr. Jones, that covers all of my questions. You have been extremely helpful, and I want to thank you for your input on this project. Do you have any questions or concerns which we have not covered?"

This final gambit can sometimes be very beneficial. The subject may provide information that, while peripheral to the central issues of the study, is extremely useful as background material or helpful in interpreting the data when it has all been collected.

In summary, participation for the researcher in the basic research interview is a highly structured experience. From beginning to end, you must be in total control of your purpose and your presentation. The key words are: control, neutrality, consistency, and preparedness.

If you find yourself as the subject of a research interview, there are some questions to consider and some response patterns to follow. When approached to participate in a survey, you should first find out how the information is going to be used. Who is conducting the survey? For what purpose? Why have you been selected? For a specific reason? At random? When these questions have been answered to your satisfaction, you are in a position to make a judgment about participation.

Many people instinctively decline participation. The feeling is that it will take too much time or that the information you give will not ultimately mean anything anyway or be ill used. In fact, participating in a survey can be viewed as an opportunity to express your views on a variety of subjects. Many times the results of these surveys have significant impact on a diverse group of subjects ranging from national policy issues to the size, shape, and cost of a product.

Certainly, the final decision to participate rests with you. Except in those instances where your company or your government requires you to take part in certain surveys, you have a choice. If you decide to cooperate, here are some guidelines for effective survey participation:

1. Be certain that you have the time to give proper consideration to the questions at hand. In other words, do not start anything that you do not have time to finish.
2. Listen attentively and be sure that you understand the question before you attempt an answer. If you have any doubt, ask the interviewer to repeat or clarify the question.
3. Try to answer the question as directly and honestly as possible. Do not go off on a tangent or rephrase the question to better fit the answer you would prefer to give. Participating in a survey is not an open forum. You need to have some sensitivity to the needs of the researcher, who has specific data to collect and is probably also pressed for time.

SUMMARY

This chapter focused attention on the key issues revolving around the basic research interview. All research, whether interview related or not, grows from some definable purpose. Interview must be seen as the means to an end rather than as an end in itself. We have discussed the importance of selecting an appropriate sample, and some guidelines were provided for sampling. The design of the research interview must match the goals and objectives set down in the purpose. The strategy, the sequencing of questions, are also determined by the preestablished goals of the research. There are other factors to be considered in the design of the survey, including how the results will be analyzed. Steps must be taken to ensure that the instrument you are using is reliable.

Participation in the research interview was examined using our three-part chess game approach for the researcher, and some basic guidelines for the participant as subject. There are many similarities that run throughout the interview spectrum. The research interview is distinguished from other types by the need for a high degree of structure and preplanning.

Questions for Study and Discussion

1. What are the different types of research interviews, and what are the strengths and weaknesses of each?
2. What is meant by Alpert's admonition, "Operationally speaking, survey results are understandable only in terms of the methods by which they are obtained"?
3. Respond to the notion that sampling is actually a process of exclusion.
4. What is a funnel strategy?
5. What characteristics of good interview made Roger Fern successful?
6. What is the purpose of a focus group?
7. Why do you need an aura of neutrality for the research interview? How do you achieve it?

Suggested Activities

1. Select a topical issue that interests you and develop a questionnaire.
   a. Select your sample. Make it feasible within the limitations of your time and resources.
   b. Choose a strategy and then sequence your questions accordingly.
   c. Collect and analyze your data.
2. Develop a product, idea, or concept for presentation to a focus group.
   a. Create a list of questions that you feel will provide the most complete and honest responses.
   b. Facilitate the focus group discussion using your prepared questions and others that evolve naturally from the discussion.
   c. Summarize your findings.

Notes

1. Charles J. Stewart and William B. Cash, Jr., *Interviewing: Principles and Practices*, 3d ed. (Dubuque, Iowa: Brown, 1982), 121.
2. Ibid.
3. Ibid., 103.

4. Harry Alpert, "Some Observations on the Sociology of Sampling," *Social Forces* 31 (1952): 30.
5. Frederick F. Stephan and Philip J. McCarthy, *Sampling Opinions: An Analysis of Survey Procedure* (New York: Wiley, 1958), 22–23.
6. Ibid., 346.
7. William Feller, *An Introduction to Probability Theory and Its Applications*, vol. 1, 2d ed. (New York: Wiley, 1957), 8–12.
8. Stephan and McCarthy, *Sampling Opinions*, 344.
9. Elaboration of these concepts and technical details may be found in A. Anastasi, *Psychological Testing*, 5th ed. (New York: Macmillan, 1982): and L. J. Cronbach, *Essentials of Psychological Testing*, 4th ed. (New York: Harper & Row, 1984).
10. Cynthia S. Smith, *How to Get Big Results from a Small Advertising Budget* (New York: Hawthorn Books, 1973), 15.
11. Ibid., 16.
12. John Brady, *The Craft of Interviewing* (New York: Random House, Vintage Books, 1977), 50–51.

5

The Employment Interview

Key Concepts

- Being prepared
- Need to have versus nice to have
- Anticipating key questions
- Projecting the appropriate image

"Why is it?" he said, his hand raising and lowering, softly stroking the table for emphasis. "I can't understand it. I hired four new people last month and three of them have already gone sour."

"What do you mean 'sour,' George?" I asked, trying to be neutral but concerned.

"One guy can't seem to get along with anyone in his work unit. Another's manager calls yesterday to tell me he is putting him on probation because he lacks the technical skills needed for the job. And this morning I get a resignation letter from a new supervisor who claims that she is not doing the job she understood she had been hired to do." He stirred his coffee abstractedly, as if he were looking for the answer somewhere in the cup just below the surface. "What particularly bothers me is that I hired that supervisor myself. She's absolutely right for the job. I really thought she was going to make some waves in that department."

"What did her manager say?"

"He loves her. Doesn't understand what the problem is."

"Do you remember what you told her the job was?"

"Sure. I told her that the department seemed low on energy, needed a boost in productivity, and I expected her to take charge of the day-to-day operation as quickly as possible."

"Has that happened?"

"Well, no; at least not yet. Her manager feels that she needs more time to 'get her feet wet.' Also, it turns out that she rapidly became the largest producer in the department, so he is reluctant to take her off the line and lessen his chances for improving his numbers."

"So, she hasn't had the opportunity to do any supervising yet?"

"It's only been a month, what does she expect?"

"I guess she expects what you told her."

"And I meant it. But, you know how it is. I knew the manager would probably be reluctant to give over much control at first, but she's good and I didn't want to lose her. She made such a point about wanting additional responsibility. Look, we're trying to expand that department and we need good people."

"So, what you're saying is that you responded to an expressed need on the part of this applicant during the interview with a statement that was not entirely true."

"Come on. It was an interview. The applicant tries to sell me, I try to sell the applicant. She had to know there would be a transition period. Anyway, she probably doesn't even remember what I said during the interview."

"On the contrary, George. I would be willing to bet that she remembers everything you said during the interview, much better than you. A hiring decision is an act of faith between two people. After all, in this modern world, jobs seem to be more durable than marriages. She put herself on the line, expressed needs, shared experience with you, trusted you. She terminated another relationship based primarily on what occurred during that interview. I'm a bit surprised at you because I know that you know all of this."

"You're right. It's just so competitive out there for good people, the temptation to tell them what they want to hear is almost irresistible. It almost becomes wishful thinking: 'get them on board' and hope it works out for the best."

"Well, based on your current frame of mind, I would say that it's not working out too well. What about the one who turns out not to have the necessary technical skills? Who did the interview?"

"The manager."

"The same manager who has just put him on probation?"

"You got it."

"Really, George, what can I say? How does a manager of a highly technical unit hire an individual who can't handle the hardware?"

"It's the same old story. The work load jumped significantly, and they needed someone in a hurry. The employment manager screened several applicants and sent them three that he thought were the strongest candidates. The manager interviewed them and made a choice. Apparently, he neglected to actually test the candidate on the machinery."

"How did that happen?"

"When I questioned the manager about that, he said the candidate's references checked out and he had been employed by a company that uses equipment similar to ours. Also, he seemed to talk knowledgeably about the use of the equipment. It turns out that the candidate had only rudimentary training and had spent the last year on a special assignment that kept him away from the machine altogether. What gets me is, how does a guy take a job that he knows he is going to have trouble with?"

"For basically the same reasons you just laid out for stretching the truth to your prospective—now resigned—supervisor. This employee—because that's what he is now, not a candidate—needed a job. He had made it through the initial screening and was in the home stretch. He sensed what the needs were and played to them. Since nobody thought to ask him to demonstrate his competency with the equipment, he figured he'd pick it up quickly when he got 'on board.' The main thing in his mind was that he needed a job. If you think it's a jungle out there for the employer, imagine what it's like for the applicants. When was the last time you were looking for a job?"

"It's been a while, but if things keep going the way they are, I may get to look pretty soon."

"What about the one who can't get along with his workmates? What's the story there?"

"Again, an error in someone's judgment. This guy is a terrific worker—tireless, technically proficient. But he is European and is used to a somewhat more autocratic management style. As a result, every time he is delegated a little bit of responsibility he turns dictator and starts ordering people around. The rest of the folks don't take too kindly to it."

"Sounds to me like there is the need for a bit of coaching and counseling here."

"I don't know if he would be receptive to advice."

"George, he has got to be at least as unhappy with the situation as everyone else. You are assuming that since the problem is obvious to you and apparently to everyone else in his unit, he understands the problem as well and chooses not to rectify the situation."

"Well, that is the way it appears."

"Give him the benefit of the doubt. Encourage his manager to talk to him or have him come in and you talk to him yourself. Again, I think this is a problem that could have been identified and even dealt with in the interview before he was hired.

"You see, this situation is the reverse of the other one. The manager puts all of the weight on the technical skill. When he tested this guy, he flipped. I don't think the interview went much beyond that point.

"It sounds to me like your management team could use some coaching on interview. There are some very common but serious errors being made on a regular basis. Unfortunate hiring decisions are costly. They waste time, drain human and dollar resources, have a negative effect on morale, and can plague you for a very long time. I would begin by providing them with some basic material. I happen to know of a very good book on interview. . . ."

George and I touched on some of the types of problems that occur regularly during interview and as a result of interview poorly conducted. The employment interview is not a simple matter. There are legal considerations as well as the more common problems of controlling biases, making judgments about the reality of what is being presented, and fulfilling the goals and objectives of the organization. When you hire someone, you are making a decision that will cost several thousands of dollars in a very short period of time. If relocation is involved, it could cost several more thousands of dollars immediately. We begin with the premise that we must give the employment interview the same careful attention that we would give a purchase of the same value or cost.

No single activity has as much impact on the nature, success, and future of an organization as hiring. This chapter will consider the process of hiring both from the point of view of the person doing the hiring and from the point of view of the person seeking the position. Our primary focus, of course, will be on those aspects of the experience that lead to, have an influence on, and affect the outcome of the interview process.

WHY INTERVIEW?

Obviously, there is a great deal of "gut feeling" tied up with a hiring decision. This is an important factor to consider, not something to be avoided. There are those who base all of their judgments on "track record," what the candidate has done before. To still another, the most important aspect is what previous employers and other references have to say about the candidate. Each of these factors, as well as many others, contributes substantially toward making a good hiring decision. The only way to get the benefit of all of these possible indicators is through thoughtful, systematic interview.

To be a good employment or selection interviewer, you do not need to be a psychologist or a trained personnel manager. You do need reasonable intelligence and a high degree of sensitivity. I agree with John Drake who states in his book *Interviewing for Managers* that because ". . . the success of any manager depends upon the depth of talent with which he surrounds himself, it becomes absolutely critical for him to learn to effectively evaluate manpower."[1]

Research concerning the effectiveness of interview as an assessment tool has shown dramatically that untrained or lightly trained interviewers do not make good assessments while skilled interviewers can make assessments with a high degree of accuracy.[2] Drake was able to demonstrate in a concrete study correlating interviewer predictions with actual acquired performance ratings that, following training, a team of interviewers nearly doubled its predictive accuracy. Drake attributes this to the mastering of fundamental principles and the following of procedural steps.[3]

The study is important from two points of view. First, that interview can be an accurate predictor of performance. Second, that interview is a skill that can be learned.

EMPLOYMENT INTERVIEWING AND THE LAW

Many people who seek to solve a problem through interview have had the misfortune to create actually a bigger one. The best estimate is that nearly 70 percent of discrimination cases arise out of something that was said during the interview. Having been burnt once or twice, some interviewers become afraid to ask anything. The Equal Employment Opportunity (EEO) regulations are designed to protect the applicant against certain kinds of discrimination that are illegal. Groups that are most affected by EEO regulations are women, Vietnam veterans, 40- to 65-year-olds, minorities (Black, Oriental, American Indian, or Spanish-surnamed American), and the handicapped.

The federal laws state that decisions about employment cannot be made on the basis of sex, race, color, age, religion, national origin, or handicap. However, the EEO commission recognizes bona fide exceptions. If the job calls for climbing poles, a person with restricted use of limbs would not meet the basic job competency requirement. Not knowing the law does not eliminate your liability. In addition, each state has its own regulations that are available from the state Human Rights Commission.

Avoiding certain types of questions is not always enough. Sometimes information is volunteered that could be the basis for a discriminatory action. A pending marriage or plans for a family volunteered by a female applicant must be answered with a policy statement asserting that the company only hires on the demonstrated ability to do the job. Drake suggests that you always make a note for the file that the candidate volunteered unsought information and was asked to refrain from further disclosures.[4] He goes on to say that candidates will most often appreciate your efforts to comply with the law and will view your company in a very positive light.

The following lists offer some guidelines of general areas of questioning to avoid.

Sex

It is discriminatory if you suggest by statement or question that:

1. A particular job has always been held by members of the same sex.

2. A candidate is not suitable because the job requires travel with members of the opposite sex.
3. A candidate is not acceptable because members of his or her sex do not traditionally aspire to the position available.
4. A candidate is not suitable based on customer, client, or co-worker preferences.
5. A candidate is not suitable because of stereotyped notions about innate characteristics that are sexually determined.
6. Appropriate physical facilities are not available for one sex or the other.
7. A candidate is not suitable because she is female and subject to the following detractions:
   Plans for a family
   Married, single, divorced, separated, widowed
   Children
   Arrangements for care of children
   Husband's reaction to working or travel

Race or Color

It is discriminatory if you suggest by statement or question that:

1. A candidate is not acceptable because he or she is Black, Hispanic, Asian, Pacific Islander, American Indian, or Alaskan native.
2. A candidate is not suitable for stereotypic reasons, such as being a public assistance recipient.

Religion

It is discriminatory if you suggest by statement or question that:

1. A candidate is not suitable because of regular, nonregular, or no attendance at church.
2. A candidate is not acceptable because he or she will miss work to attend religious services.
3. A candidate is not acceptable because of active involvement in any church groups.

Age

It is discriminatory if you suggest by statement or question that:

1. A candidate is not suitable because the pace is too hectic.

2. A candidate is not acceptable because the supervisory and/or the rest of the staff is much younger.

National Origin

It is discriminatory if you suggest by statement or question that a candidate is not suitable because of:

1. The nationality of parents or spouse.
2. Clubs, societies, or lodges of which the candidate is a member.

Handicap

It is discriminatory if you suggest by statement or question that a candidate is not suited because of height, weight, previous illness, or physical ability to handle the job.

There are, of course, some questions relating to these areas that are pertinent and legal. Without risking legal action, you are within your rights to ask a candidate what languages he or she speaks fluently, whether or not he or she is a citizen of the United States and, if not, will the visa permit him or her to work. You are also within your rights to describe the job tasks to a handicapped person and ask if he or she feels capable of doing the job.

These points on legalities are primarily for the interviewer in the United States. If you conduct your interviews in the United Kingdom, Canada, or elsewhere, you must familiarize yourself with the specifics of the discrimination laws in that country. In all instances, however, your best defense against discrimination suits is documentation. Take and keep notes.

THE EMPLOYMENT-INTERVIEW SITUATION

Before tackling the issues involved during the interview process, it is useful to examine some of the perceptions that the participants bring with them to the situation. According to Cohen and Etheredge, the employment interview is "an appraisal process in which the recruiter observes various applicant behaviors that prompt a referral decision."[5] When there are problems in the interview situation, they are usually the result of a misunderstanding of the interview situation by the recruiter, the applicant, or both.

Posner compared the expectations of recruiters, students, and faculty members during interview.[6] He came up with the following findings:

1. Students expect interviewers to provide detailed descriptions of the job to be performed; less than half of the recruiters in this study did so. Conversely, recruiters expected the students to know the job description, as well as have a thorough understanding of skills and abilities routinely used on the job.
2. Recruiters expect interviewees to be well acquainted with life in organizations, and to reflect a positive attitude toward the business world. Most of the students in this study were perceived by recruiters as having a shallow understanding of life in organizations, and to reflect disenchantment with the business world.
3. Recruiters and faculty members expect interviewees to adhere to their personal preferences in all categories related to the employment interview. Unfortunately, recruiters' and faculty members' perceptions of those qualities were vastly dissimilar.
4. Faculty members expect recruiters to embody a humorless, impersonal, non-philosophical, "bottom line" mentality, and often instruct students to prepare for interviews using this misinformation. Faculty members were apparently dismal judges of what students expected from a job, and gave misinformation to recruiters about how to "pitch" their organizations.[7]

The implications of this research are important to both employers and potential employees, particularly those entering the work force for the first time. Students are being given the wrong perceptions of the interview situation. Additional research points out that recruiters' perceptions of candidates are primarily influenced by their attitudes, values, and beliefs. Bias still appears to be the strongest factor in selection.[8] This is not surprising since, according to Posner, less than 60 percent of recruiters receive formal training in interview. Add to this the fact that few companies do an effective job of briefing recruiters about necessary job competencies and have no objective measures of the effectiveness of the interview process, and you have some idea of the difficulties being faced by both recruiters and applicants. Goodall and Goodall summarize their findings regarding the interview situation:

> If we regard the interviewing situation as an important variable in the selection process, we can locate three major areas of potential or real difficulty:
>
> 1. Differences in expectations for the setting of desirable communication skills and reflected attitudes interfere with judgments made during the interview.
> 2. Differences in expectations about the locus of responsibility for interview preparation interfere with judgments made during the interview.
> 3. Differences in expectations about the relative structure of the interview interfere with judgments made during the interview.[9]

In summary, current research indicates that pre-interview perceptual differences, fault finding with preparation on the parts of both the recruiter and the candidate, and the lack of training, objectives, and measures for the interview process all conspire to affect negatively the selection process.

PARTICIPATING IN THE EMPLOYMENT INTERVIEW—THE EMPLOYER'S VIEW

Setting the Scene

We do not always have a choice about where an interview takes place, but when we do we should make the best of it. From the employer's point of view, the employment interview is an opportunity to screen applicants for a current and/or future opening. It is also an opportunity to sell the company in such a way that the chosen candidate will be willing to accept the offer, and the rejected candidates will at least think well of the company. A good rule of thumb is to see each applicant as a potential customer.

Ideally, an employment interview should take place in an environment that is free of distractions, such as ambient noise, phone calls, and other interruptions. If these conditions are impossible to attain in your office, you should consider scheduling an off-site location. Sometimes an off-site location can provide added benefits, such as a neutral ground where both candidate and employer feel freer to speak. Wherever you decide to conduct the interview, the surroundings should reflect as much as possible the impression of your organization you want to create. A sparsely furnished, brightly colored, uncluttered space will tend to project energy, youth, efficiency, growth potential. A plush, panelled, carpeted, subdued color space will project stability, security, traditional values, high-earning potential.

Interviews conducted in a restaurant or bar are not recommended because there are too many distractions, it is difficult to concentrate on the interview and handle food at the same time, and liquor will only impair your judgment. If one of the necessary competencies for the job is the ability to meet effectively over lunch, as with account representatives, a second interview should be scheduled for a luncheon setting if you have enough interest in the candidate to warrant it.

As the employer, the choice of setting is usually yours. Make sure your choice helps you achieve your objectives: get the necessary information and project the appropriate image.

The Opening Game

Having lost one supervisor this month, George, the Personnel Director, is determined to be more careful with his interview style. One of George's recruiters has set up an interview for George with Nancy Jones, his top pick for the job. Although he is running a little late, George takes a few minutes to clear the papers from his desk and make sure that his office is generally in good order. He buzzes his secretary to send Nancy in and tells her to hold all calls during the interview.

Nancy appears in the doorway, glances quickly around the room and moves forward. George comes out from behind his desk, extends his hand, smiles, and greets her warmly:

"Ms. Jones, thank you for coming. I'm George Martin. Please call me George."

"Fine, George, call me Nancy."

"I'm sorry to have kept you waiting, I'm running just a little bit behind today." George moves back behind his desk and indicates a chair in front of the desk for Nancy to sit in.

Nancy sits down, sets her briefcase on the floor, leans back comfortably, and crosses her legs. "That's all right. Actually, I was just a few minutes late myself."

"Jack told me about your interview with him. He was quite impressed."

"That's good to hear. Since that interview, I have thought of several questions, so I'm glad to have the opportunity to meet with you today."

"That's good. I have several questions for you as well. Why don't we proceed this way. In the time we have, I want to get acquainted with you as much as possible. I know you want to become acquainted with me and explore whether or not our company is a good place for you. So, let me begin with some questions first, and then we'll cover your questions. Hopefully, by the time we finish, we'll have all the information we need to make an intelligent decision."

George has played his opening game well. He has set the scene by making sure his office is presentable. He was direct and friendly in his greeting. He established rapport by demonstrating concern for Nancy's waiting time. Finally, he establishes control by outlining the events that will occur during the course of the interview. He is now ready to move into the middle game.

The employment interview does not require a long period of small talk. Once the greeting ritual and rapport-building amenities are out of the way, you should move swiftly to the first line of questioning.

The Middle Game

George has reviewed the materials in Part I of this book and has decided to build his strategy around the basic chain-link sequence. As you recall, this sequence begins with an open question followed by a series of probes, closed questions, and a mirror. He wants to derive information about Nancy's supervisory ability. In order to make sure his questions are effective, George has reviewed a list of qualities that he felt were necessary for a supervisor to have. Drake provides a list put together by a group of 43 managers who were asked to list factors considered important in order to make judgments about candidates for supervisory positions.[10] They produced the following list:

Analytical skills
Self-confidence
Poise
Stability
Persistence
Maturity
Ability to communicate
Technical know-how
Ambition
Educational background
Quantitative skills
Job interests
Relevant job experiences
Social perceptiveness
Goals and objectives
Energy
Ability to organize oneself
Drive
Cooperativeness

According to Drake, "The managers were saying, in effect, that they could predict the candidate's job success if they were able to learn about all these items. However, they also doubted that all these topics could be meaningfully explored during a typical interview.[11]

The most important factor for determining your line of questioning is the available job. Always begin with a concrete list of the competencies—the knowledge, skills, and perceptions—needed to handle the tasks and responsibilities of the job. These are your "need to know" items. A second category of much less importance consists of the "nice to know" qualities of the applicant. These are often more interesting than the "need to know" items and pose a danger of eating up time and throwing you off the track.

Making sure you cover the competency questions is so important that you should have them written down—if not the entire question, at least a list. Remember, competencies are not just a demonstration of technical skill. George's European employee had a high level of technical competency but lacked competency in the style of interpersonal skills needed to be successful in his office. In order to cover all of the necessary competency requirements and to structure your middle game to cover as many of the predictors of job success as possible, Drake suggests four broad categories:

1. Intellectual skills and aptitudes.
2. Motivated characteristics.
3. Personality strengths and limitations.
4. Knowledge and experience.[12]

Intellectual skills and aptitudes can be estimated based on past success in school or on the job, how well the candidate organizes thoughts, how well he or she thinks under pressure. Motivation is determined through an understanding of the candidate's interests, aspirations, and energy level. Personality strengths and limitations are determined by discovering the applicant's interpersonal skill and ability to cope with work demands. Knowledge and experience derive from the candidate's training and job experience.

Using the four categories, you can now begin to frame some open questions with which to begin your interview segments. Let us see how George is doing with Nancy:

"Nancy, I notice from your application that you attended Oberlin College in Ohio."

"That's right."

"Having been born and raised in the northeast, how did you decide on Oberlin?"

"Actually, it's because I was born and raised in the northeast that I went to Oberlin. I had the feeling that I was not getting a clear view of what was actually going on in the country. Also, I felt I could get more attention at a smaller midwestern school than on a large campus."

"What do you mean by 'attention'?"

"I had this notion that it would be easier to establish relationships with professors and with the other students as well. I had visited some of the local campuses and they seemed so large and impersonal."

"Impersonal?"

"Yes, you know, everybody does their own thing. A lot of the students hold down jobs and squeeze school in between. I had the impression that nobody took time to make friends. As I look back on it, I guess I overreacted, but I still think I made the right decision."

"Making friends, getting along with people, building relationships, these things are important to you?"

"Yes."

"So, what you're saying is that you chose Oberlin because you felt the atmosphere was more conducive to building relationships and making friends?"

George has done well in his opening sequence. Following the chain-link model, he began with an open question, ". . . how did you decide on Oberlin?" He followed with two consecutive probes, "What do you mean by 'attention'?" and "Impersonal?" He then asked a closed question, ". . . these things are important to you?" and finished with a mirror, "So, what you're saying is. . . ." Through this line of questioning, he begins to build an understanding of Nancy's intellectual ability, her personality traits, and what motivates her. George decides to examine Nancy's intellectual abilities in more depth. He begins again with an open question:

"Nancy, you indicate that your grade point average was quite high, 3.6, I believe. Tell me what went into achieving that average."

"A lot of hard work. A lot of hours. Particularly with subjects that I wasn't very good at."

"In retrospect, do you feel the hard work was worth it?"

"Yes. I loved my years in college. Those were very happy times. I also feel that I got a good education and I wouldn't be the same person without that experience."

"You mentioned before that there were some subjects which you weren't good at. Can you tell me more about that?"

"Language and psychology. Both were requirements. I took French, primarily because I had some notion that I wanted to spend some time in Paris. I had a friend who had gone to Paris for a year during high school and she was able to speak French. It seemed like a great thing to be able to do. I had done reasonably well with Spanish in high school, but the demands were so much greater. Also, I discovered that French was much more difficult. I had a tendency to put off doing the work because I wanted to devote most of my time to my science courses, and then I would have to scramble to catch up."

"And psychology?"

"It wasn't that I didn't enjoy aspects of psychology, but the reading was so heavy. The worst thing about psychology was that it met at 8:00 in the morning. I would usually be up late studying, so I was a basket case when the alarm went off at 7:00."

"So, you're not a morning person?"

"Well, I've had to adapt since I'm in the work world. I just pace myself differently. I'm much more conscientious about getting enough rest. Good grief! Hearing myself talk about it, I sound like I flunked out! I still managed to pull Bs in both of those subjects."

"If you had it to do over again, what would you do differently?"

"I suppose I would rearrange my priorities somewhat; spend more time on psych and French and less on science."

"Why?"

"Because, as it turned out, the science never developed into anything. I couldn't find a job in science with a bachelor's degree. I couldn't afford graduate school, or so I thought, and I was anxious to get out into the world."

"Do you still have an interest in science?"

"Only as a hobby. I try to follow the latest developments, particularly in genetics. Biology was my favorite."

George has drawn out more information on Nancy's intellectual ability. He is also discovering more personality traits. As you can tell, George is effectively controlling the interview. The candidate is doing most of the talking, thereby providing the opportunity for George to gather the information he needs to make a selection decision. Nancy appears to be comfortable or at

least willing to be self-disclosive about her interests and experience at college. George has probed effectively and has asked a closed question to focus on Nancy's current relationship with science, "Do you still have an interest in science?" He can finish this sequence with a mirror:

"So, you feel that the work world has caused you to make some adjustments in your interests and the way you structure your time, but do you feel that you have adapted effectively?"

"Yes."

"What do you find particularly rewarding in your current job?"

George moves on to another category, and by the end of the sequence, he will find out what motivates Nancy and what her goals and aspirations are. When George feels he has enough information in all four categories, he will move the interview to the final phase, the end game.

The End Game

As you recall, the main objectives of the end game are summarizing and projecting outcomes. An effective closing segment allows the participants, and particularly in this case the candidate, to ask questions or to make statements that will clarify, confirm, or delete an impression made earlier. George recalls that Nancy said at the outset that she had some questions, and he had agreed to return to them later. He begins with a standard closing ritual:

"Well, Nancy, I think I have just about everything that I need." George lays his pencil on the note pad and leans back in the chair. "You mentioned earlier that you had some questions. Have we covered them?"

"Yes, I believe we hit upon just about everything I had in mind. I am a bit concerned about the starting date."

"Why is that?"

"Well, if I were to come to work here—assuming it's going to take some time yet for you to make a decision—in order to start on the first of next month, I couldn't give proper notice to my current employer."

"That's a good point, Nancy. First of all, I plan to have this decision made as soon as possible, probably by the end of this week. But, assuming that the time gets tight, I'm not locked into that starting date. We can make accommodations so that you can give notice."

"One other thing. . . ."

"Yes?"

"As I think back on the interview, I feel that I may have given the impression that I have difficulty getting to work in the morning. I just wanted you to know that I have very rarely been late or absent in my current position, and I'm sure my employer will verify that."

"I appreciate your clarification of that point. Anything else?"

"No, I think that covers it."

"Okay, Nancy. I have a few more candidates to see during the next two days, but you will hear from me by Friday either way."

"I'd appreciate that." They both rise and move toward the door.

"Thank you for coming. I have enjoyed our talk."

"Thank you. I have, too. I'm looking forward to hearing from you."

George has handled the end game well. He gave the proper closing signals, created an opportunity for Nancy to question or clarify, and maintained a good rapport right to the end. Most importantly, he summarized future expectations and gave Nancy a definite response date, something dear to the heart of anyone who has ever been on the job-seeking end of the employment interview. Let us have a look at this situation through Nancy's eyes to determine some basic principles to follow when you are the job seeker.

PARTICIPATING IN THE EMPLOYMENT INTERVIEW—THE CANDIDATE'S VIEW

There are two overriding concerns for the job seeker during interview. First, you must appear interested in the job. Second, you must project that you are a person with whom the boss can get along. In their book *How to Get the Job You Want*, Donaho and Meyer polled a large number of professional interviewers, including managers and supervisors, and discovered:

> One common complaint about applicants emerged time and time again—NOT that the applicant lacked experience or training; but that he showed a "lack of interest and enthusiasm both in the interview being conducted and in the job being discussed." Despite the desire of the candidates and the obvious importance of the interview, applicants persistently conveyed the opposite impression: "I'm really not very interested and really don't care."[13]

In order to be successful with interview, you must participate fully in the process. In the same way a prospective employer might prepare for an interview by reading your application, checking your references, and weighing your qualifications against the job description, you must also prepare. Find out whatever you can about the company, the position applied for, the person with whom you will interview. Always assume that the person across the desk is a skilled interview participant. Try to anticipate the kinds of questions you will be asked. Rehearse. Ask yourself questions about your résumé and give the answers out loud. Never rehearse "in your head." You will not feel secure with your answers until you hear them verbalized. Also, verbalization helps fix your responses in your memory so that they will be more forthcoming when the situation arises.

Use your knowledge of the interview structure. Employ rapport-building behavior in the opening game to complement the behavior of your counterpart.

Often, as in chess, the game is won or lost in the opening moves. Understand your role as the participant with the greatest pressure for self-disclosure. You must be responsive without rambling and consistent without being studied. The employer's role is to set the scene, establish control, and direct the line of questioning. Your role, according to Donaho and Meyer, is ". . . to be alert, to be patient, to listen and to react."[14]

Obviously, you want to do whatever you can to influence the hiring decision. Hollandsworth summarizes what appear to be the most important characteristics associated with favorable hiring decisions. These include appropriateness of answers to questions, fluency of speech in providing answers and in asking questions, and the perception of composure.[15] Other research also points to the fact that the job seeker with superior communication skills has a distinct advantage. Additional factors that influence hiring decisions are grade point average, work experience, appearance, extracurricular activities, location preference, and academic accomplishments.[16]

Steps for Preparation

When you are preparing for interview, there are some steps you can follow.

Step One: Know Yourself. As a job seeker, you need to sell yourself and your qualifications. In order to do this effectively, you need to see yourself as a "product." The key to successful job-seeking strategy is to match the employer's needs with the benefits you provide. In addition, a thorough personal inventory will save you from making some job-selection errors, such as accepting a job that is incompatible with your needs, aspirations, and temperament. You can conduct your self-inventory by asking a few basic questions: What do I need from a job? What do I want from a job? What are my strengths? What are my weaknesses? What have I done or need to do to control or minimize my weaknesses?

The following is a checklist that provides some specific questions for your consideration:

1. How much money do I need?
2. Have I completed my education or do I plan to continue now or later?
3. What kind of work do I enjoy doing?
4. Do I prefer to work alone or as part of a team?
5. Am I attracted to a large corporate environment or would I be happier with a small company?
6. Do I want high visibility or to be left alone to do my job?
7. Do I want a great deal of responsibility?
8. Do I want to work inside or outside?
9. Do I enjoy traveling?

10. Would I rather work with machines or people?
11. Which part of a task do I enjoy most? Planning? Organizing? Doing the task?
12. How are my communication skills?
13. What is special or unique about me? About my background? Training? Experience?
14. What have been my greatest successes?
15. What have been my greatest failures? How did I handle them?
16. What are my physical capabilities? Limitations?
17. What do I want for myself in the future?
18. Whom do I admire? Why?
19. What do I believe people feel about my appearance?
20. What does "success" mean to me?

Step Two: Know the Employer. As we discussed earlier, research shows that employers expect applicants to be knowledgeable about the company and the industry it serves. You do research on the employer not only to demonstrate your knowledge and seriousness but also to determine if the company is right for you. Here is a checklist to guide your investigation:

1. Do I know anyone who is now working or has worked for this company?
2. What is the company's history?
3. What does the company produce or service?
4. How well is the company doing?
5. Who are the company's competitors?
6. What is the company's reputation in the industry? As an employer?
7. What is the opportunity for advancement?
8. What are the working conditions? Safe? Comfortable? Convenient?
9. What are the benefits? Insurance? Retirement?
10. Does the company pay competitive salaries? Are there additional compensations like stock options, discounts, housing?
11. What type of training does the company provide?
12. What are the company's prospects for growth?
13. Where is the company located? What is the cost of living?
14. Does the community provide the necessary life-style elements for my family's happiness and well-being?
15. Is there any reason to believe that my family would not be accepted there?

The answers to some of these questions may be hard to find prior to the interview. Unanswered research questions should be converted to questions for you to ask the employer during the interview. There are several resources you can turn to in order to gather much of this information. Talk to current employees if that is possible. Take a trip to the company if the distance or cost is not prohibitive. Get a copy of the most recent annual report. Investigate the materials available in your own hometown library. *Thomas Register of American Manufacturers*, the *Macmillan Job Guide to American Corporations*, and *25,000 Leading American Corporations* all provide rankings, locations, sales, products, assets, and the like. *Standard and Poor's Register* and *Moody's Industrial Manual* as well as back issues of several periodicals, including *The Wall Street Journal* and *Fortune Magazine*, will provide additional details about stockholders, employees, and how well the company is doing.

Step Three: Know the Business. A prospective employer will be impressed with your sincerity when you demonstrate your knowledge of the company. However, he or she will be doubly impressed if you demonstrate a knowledge of the type of business the company is engaged in. Find out what the key issues of the industry are. The following is a checklist to help you discover those issues:

1. What are the latest developments?
2. What is the impact of technology? Automation? Robotics?
3. What is the current labor situation?
4. How is the business being affected by imports?
5. What is the competitive situation?
6. Is there any legislation pending that will affect the industry?
7. Do you have any firsthand experience with the product or service?

Again, the best resource for such information would be the general business magazines as well as "trade" publications that devote their entire content to industry concerns and advertising.

Step Four: Know the Situation. The most important factor in getting to know the situation is anticipation. In a sense, you have to enter a fantasy, a role play. You need to create a likely scenario for the interview. While it is most often not possible, it helps to know something about the person who will conduct the interview. It is, as I have mentioned, always better to assume that you will be dealing with a skilled interview participant and prepare accordingly. As with the other steps in readiness, you can follow this checklist to help you with your rehearsal:

1. What are you going to wear? Choose carefully. Dress and grooming will go a long way toward making either a positive or negative impression.
2. What will you use to take notes?
3. Do you have additional résumés? Samples of your work?
4. What answer will you give to a question about your experience? Train-

ing? Education? Interest in the business? Your greatest success? Why you left or want to leave your current position? Where you would like to be five years from now?

5. What questions are you going to ask during the interview? Compensation? Benefits? Starting date? The company's future? The community?

If you rehearse your answers to these and other questions several times out loud, the answers will come more readily to mind during the stress of the interview. You will appear more poised, verbal, organized, interested, and generally communicative—the most important qualities in a selection decision. Donaho and Meyer summarize the preparation phase this way:

> If you understand the purpose and types of employment interview you are engaging in, and if you follow the steps of preparation, you will direct your energies toward more constructive means of developing confidence in the employment interview. You will be more confident because you will be more competent to participate and more committed to fulfilling your informational and persuasive objectives. You will be a more interested and active participant in the employment interview, and thus you are more likely to get the position which is right for you.[17]

Fielding the Question

To be effective at fielding questions, you must be solid in your interview technique. Technique, as you recall, is a command of the various types of questions. The first step in framing an effective response is to recognize the type of question being asked and to make a judgment about the purpose of the question. The most difficult questions to field are open questions. An open question requires an extended or expanded response. They are essential to the interview process because they provide the greatest opportunity to give and receive information. They also give the respondent a chance to demonstrate intelligence, sensitivity, organization, and general communication competence. In the following vignette, Jason Reeves, a young certified public accountant (CPA), is interviewing with Jackson Stone of Clay, Mortar and Stone, a midsized but prestigious accounting firm. Greetings have been completed, coffee has been served, and we eavesdrop on the beginning of the middle game:

STONE: Well, Jason, I am quite impressed with your high scores and recommendations. Frankly, I'm surprised you're not beating down the doors of some of the larger firms in town. Can you tell me about your interest in CMS?

REEVES: I had a feeling we would cover that issue, Mr. Stone, and I'm glad it came up early. If I may, I'd like to answer in two parts. First, I have applied to some of the larger firms, and I would be dishonest if I implied that they were without attraction for me. On the other hand, one of the most appealing things about CMS, from my point of view, is its smaller size. I feel that my opportunities to become involved with more important aspects of various projects would be greater at a smaller but highly successful firm like CMS. For example, I know you have the Friendly Oil account and that Friendly is in the midst of a three-party merger. Contracts are an area of high interest for me, and I feel that CMS would be more likely to give me more responsibility sooner than a larger firm.

STONE: Now, hold on there! What makes you think that if we took you on, you would immediately start working on merger contracts?

REEVES: I believe I could be an asset to CMS in the contracts area, particularly with the opportunity to work with Mr. Clay, who I believe is one of the best contracts accountants around. Of course, I wouldn't expect to start assuming contract responsibility right away. I do feel, however, that I can develop more rapidly at CMS than at one of the larger firms.

Jason demonstrates a variety of attributes in his answer to Mr. Stone's question. He shows an ability to organize his thoughts and segment a problem, important qualities in an accountant. He takes the opportunity to present Mr. Stone with information he has about the company, showing interest in the firm. He builds rapport by being complimentary toward CMS in general and the managing partner, Mr. Clay, in particular. He is aggressive about his goals and self-confident about his ability.

The prospective employer is also going to want to know how you will fit in with the organization. You need to be prepared to respond to questions designed to discover personality traits and professionalism. Use the following list as a guide:

1. What do you consider your greatest success on your last job?
2. What was your biggest failure?
3. If I called your last supervisor, what do you think he/she would say about you?
4. What do you see yourself doing five years from now?
5. How do you feel you respond to pressure?
6. Why did you leave your last position?
7. What job activities do you like best? Dislike?
8. What was your most difficult problem on your last job? How did you solve it? What would you do differently today?
9. What is it about this job that appeals to you?
10. How do you feel about this industry?
11. What do you see as the main areas where you need help in order to handle this job effectively?

12. Are there any things that we have not talked about that you feel may help me to get to know you better?

When you field questions of this type, there are several things to consider. You must assume that the employer has a specific purpose in asking the questions. Do not answer too quickly. Take some time to consider your response. What type of question is it? Is it job related? Personality related? Organize your response. Think about what you will say first, second, etc. A well-organized response gives the impression of intelligence, coherence, and maturity. What do you think the employer wants to hear? What is the truthful response? Are they compatible? If you are interested in the job, do not be afraid to be self-disclosive. If you are not sufficiently self-disclosive, you will diminish your opportunity to get the job. If you are self-disclosive and still do not get the job, you have not really lost anything in concrete terms. Tell the employer what he or she wants to know as long as you can determine that the information sought is pertinent to the hiring decision. If a question does not seem to be relevant, do not hesitate to ask for an explanation of the relevance. If a question goes beyond the limits of job relatedness, do not answer it. Such questions may be a test.

In the following exchange, Jason Reeves fields some hard questions from Jackson Stone:

STONE: Jason, I see you worked for a year and a half as a clerk at Accounting, Inc.

REEVES: That's correct.

STONE: Can you tell me why you left?

REEVES: Yes. The experience I had at Accounting, Inc. was very valuable. It was my first job with an accounting firm, and because it was a large firm handling diversified accounts, I really got an overview of the business. After I had been there a year, I felt ready to make a firm commitment to accounting as a profession. I knew I had to pass the CPA exam, and I began studying at night and on weekends. This was frustrating for me, so I decided to leave Accounting, Inc. to study full time. I had put some money away that carried me until the exam three months later. I enrolled in a course, passed the exam, and here I am.

STONE: Would you go back to Accounting, Inc.?

REEVES: I haven't closed my mind to any options at this point.

STONE: Do you think they would take you back?

REEVES: I left in a very cordial manner. I believe that if they had a position, they would take me back.

STONE: If I called your supervisor, Mr. Krieger, what do you think he would tell me about you?

REEVES: Mr. Krieger was always very supportive of me. I consider that we had an excellent relationship. He would probably say that I was conscientious, eager to learn, and ambitious. I believe he was sorry to see me go.

STONE: Let's discuss that ambitious streak for a minute. You seem very eager to get ahead, and that's commendable. But what's going to happen if you can't move fast enough to suit you?

REEVES: Mr. Stone, I can appreciate your concern. I am ambitious and eager to move ahead as you said. But I am also realistic. I am interested in CMS because you handle the type of clients that appeal to me. I realize there are limitations on how fast I can move. However, when I am ready for additional responsibility, I feel the opportunity will come more quickly with CMS. In the meantime, I still have a great deal to learn, and the learning itself is a great challenge.

Jason Reeves did a good job of responding to the aggressive style of Jackson Stone. Stone wants to see how the candidate thinks on his feet and responds to pressure. These are probably qualities he perceives as essential for dealing with the clients he has. He also wants to learn as much about the candidate as he can before he makes an investment of time, money, and development. Jason responds assertively and positively. He meets the questions head on without hedging. He acknowledges what is true about him, his ambition and eagerness, but tempers it with his understanding of the reality of the situation. He finds another opportunity to show knowledge about CMS and to be complimentary.

SUMMARY

In this chapter your attention has been focused on the dynamics of the selection interview. While the selection interview is only one step in the job search process or recruitment process, it is a vital step. As the job seeker, you will need other tools, such as a résumé and well-constructed application letters. As the employer, you will need well-written and enticing advertisements, good job descriptions, and a manpower plan. Nevertheless, it all comes together at the interview. No single activity has as much impact on the nature, success, and future of an organization as hiring. Untrained interviewers do not make good hiring decisions. You do not need to be a psychologist to conduct an effective selection interview. You need intelligence and sensitivity.

This chapter also covered some of the things that by law you cannot ask during an interview. The federal laws state that decisions about employment cannot be made on the basis of sex, race, color, age, religion, national origin, or handicap. Errors on these issues can be costly both in dollars and in the damage done to the reputation of the organization.

We examined some of the perceptions that the participants bring with them to the interview situation. Recruiters expect applicants to be familiar with life in organizations and to reflect a positive attitude toward the business world. When there are problems in the interview, they are usually the result of a misunderstanding of the interview situation by the recruiter, the applicant, or both.

The chapter also takes a look at the interview process from the points of view of both the recruiter and the job seeker. The recruiter or employer needs to know certain things about the applicant or candidate in order to make a reasonable hiring decision. The items boil down to discovering two things: Can the candidate do the job and will the candidate do the job? The recruiter skilled in interview strategy will use more open questions and probes than other types of questions. The questions must be designed to elicit information on the four main predictors of job success: intellectual skills and aptitudes, motivated characteristics, personality strengths and limitations, and knowledge and experience.

From the job seeker's side, there are two overriding concerns: You must appear interested in the job, and you must project that you are a person with whom the boss can get along. An applicant's success during interview is directly related to the amount and depth of the preparation before interview. Conduct an honest self-appraisal, ask yourself some difficult questions, and rehearse before the interview takes place. The most important characteristics associated with favorable hiring decisions include appropriateness of answers to questions, fluency of speech, and the perception of composure. If you are interested in the job, do not be afraid to be self-disclosive. If you are not sufficiently self-disclosive, you will probably not get the job. If you are self-disclosive and still do not get the job, you have not lost anything in concrete terms.

Questions for Study and Discussion

1. How does the employment interview affect the total organization?
2. What do you need to be a good employment interview?
3. What kinds of questions can you not ask?
4. What do applicants expect from recruiters?
5. What do recruiters expect from applicants?
6. What is the most important factor for determining a line of questioning?

Suggested Activities

1. Using the classified section of a local newspaper, select a job advertisement that specifies in detail the competencies needed for the job.
   a. As the employer, develop a list of questions that you need to ask in order to determine if a candidate has the appropriate background.
   b. As the candidate, create a life history that provides the qualifications for the position.
   c. In role play, conduct interviews and make a hiring decision.

Notes

1. John D. Drake, *Interviewing for Managers*, rev. ed. (New York: AMACOM, 1982), 4.
2. E. E. Ghiselli, "The Validity of a Personnel Interview," *Personnel Psychology* 4 (1966): 389–394.
3. Drake, *Interviewing for Managers*, 8–10.
4. Ibid., 232.
5. B. M. Cohen and J. M. Etheredge, "Recruiting's Main Ingredient," *Journal of College Placement* (Winter 1975): 75–77.
6. B. Z. Posner, "Comparing Recruiter, Student, and Faculty Perceptions of Important Applicant and Job Characteristics," *Personnel Psychology* 34 (1981): 329–339.
7. This summary of Posner's findings appears in Donna Bogar Goodall and H. Lloyd Goodall, Jr., "The Employment Interview: A Selective Review of the Literature with Implications for Communications Research," *Communication Quarterly* 30, no. 2 (Spring 1982): 116–123.
8. H. D. Tschirgi, "What Do Recruiters Really Look For in Candidates?" *Journal of College Placement* (December 1972–January 1973): 75–79.
9. Goodall and Goodall, *Communication Quarterly*, 118.
10. Drake, *Interviewing for Managers*, 19–20.
11. Ibid., 20.
12. Ibid., 21.
13. Melvin W. Donaho and John L. Meyer, *How to Get the Job You Want* (Englewood Cliffs, N.J.: Prentice-Hall, 1976), 67.
14. Ibid., 68.
15. J. G. Hollandsworth, R. Kazelskis, J. Stevens, and M. E. Dressel, "Relative Contributions of Verbal, Articulative, and Nonverbal Communication to Employment Decisions in the Job Interview Setting," *Personnel Psychology* 32 (1979): 259–267.
16. H. D. Tschirgi, "What Do Recruiters Really Look For in Candidates?" 75–79.
17. Donaho and Meyer, *How to Get the Job You Want*, 91.

6

The Appraisal Interview

Key Concepts

- Giving credit where credit is due
- Setting standards by example
- Positive discipline
- Appraisal as a process

> Another, less legitimate, reason for appraisals and interviews is to make the personnel system look like a personnel system. A personnel manager who collects and files 6000 appraisals a year probably appears to have more of a system than someone who collects and files no appraisals. A personnel manager who can proclaim that everyone in his company except the president has a semi-annual appraisal interview with his supervisor is a personnel manager with a future. Personnel systems are often judged by volume and activity, and appraisal is one element that usually generates plenty of both.[1]

Appraisal is perhaps the most widely misunderstood and abused form of interview. This is partially because it is often dreaded by at least one of the participants and sometimes both. With all of the resistance or, I should say, in spite of all the resistance, appraisal interviewing has grown to be a major force in the work place.

This chapter begins with Johnson's quote on the less legitimate reasons in order to highlight that there are some very legitimate reasons for regular, ongoing, frequent, and high-quality appraisal. Performance appraisal serves the goals and objectives of the individual. It provides touchstones of achievement and development. It helps to shape and nurture career goals, define direction, or redefine direction for one who needs guidance. Performance appraisal also serves the goals and objectives of the organization since it has a direct relationship to productivity. It allows the organization to develop a cogent plan, provide motivation, and assess training and development needs.

The legal necessity for providing a standard performance-appraisal process to be applied equally to each employee has led to some elaborate performance-appraisal forms. One of the ways that performance appraisal can be ineffective is when the emphasis is placed on the form instead of the process. Although there are almost as many variations of these forms as there are companies, most of them deal with the same major categories:

1. A description of the job task or responsibility.
2. Key actions, plans, or expectations for accomplishing the tasks and responsibilities.
3. An evaluation of how effectively the employee has measured up to the key actions, plans, or expectations.
4. A future plan for correcting faults, attaining growth and development, receiving new tasks and responsibilities, and establishing a time frame for accomplishing the new objectives.

Some organizations develop rating schemes that are directly tied to compensation. In fact, performance appraisals are inextricably tied to compensation. This is particularly true when appraisals are done only once or twice each year. When the process of appraisal is ongoing and frequent, it becomes less compensation bound. Whether money is involved or not, an evaluative judgment must be made. Is the employee performing below the standard expectation? At the expected level? Above the expected level? In spite of the terms used, these are the questions with which you are confronted during an appraisal.

APPRAISAL AS INTERVIEW

Regardless of the purpose, appraisal takes place within the context of interview. As such, it is governed by the same principles as any other interview situation. It is a structured and purposeful conversation requiring the active participation of both parties. When difficulty occurs, it grows out of the potential for conflict that is always present in the appraisal situation. The manager who is skilled at appraisal will employ nondefensive skills and conflict-resolution techniques to facilitate the interview. This will have an impact on the technique and strategy used during interview.

The basic notion of appraisal is to provide a vehicle for informing a staff member how his or her performance measures up to or exceeds the established standards. Growing out of this notion are three specific elements of appraisal: reward, motivation, and discipline. It is possible for a single appraisal interview to contain all of these elements. It is also possible for one of the elements to be the primary purpose of the interview.

The need for performance appraisal can be summarized in this way: It is a need inherent in the employer-employee relationship, and the effective use of appraisal benefits both parties. As Johnson says:

> The employee has a legitimate need to know how his performance compares with his supervisor's expectations. It is not merely a matter of idle curiosity, but a true need, an essential link of communication between employer and employee. . . . In the absence of specific feedback on performance, some serious problems may develop. The employee may be forming undesirable work habits, but he may assume quite erroneously that the supervisor's silence means approval. . . . The employer—specifically, the supervisor—needs to carry out the essential process of communication between employer and employee. If the employee is doing less than satisfactory work and his performance is correctable, the supervisor needs to convey this in the appraisal interview and arrange for improvement. If the employee's work is satisfactory, the supervisor has a stake in that person's future and will use the appraisal interview to promote continued satisfactory performance.[2]

Appraisals are conducted for five specific reasons:

1. To evaluate performance.
2. To give feedback.
3. To assess the capacity of employees.
4. To establish goals for employees.
5. To affect personnel actions.

APPRAISAL AS PROCESS

It is useful to think of performance appraisal in terms of goals—both goal setting and goal evaluation. Both parties in the appraisal interview bring certain goals with them. On one side, there are the goals of the organization. On the other, there are the goals of the individual.

In order to be successful, the organization must maintain an overall plan for the work force. There must be employees occupying positions who have the competency to fulfill the tasks and responsibilities of the job. The organization must also ensure that enough employees are receiving the right measure of experience, training, and encouragement to develop into future managers. The appraisal process enables the organization to make ongoing assessments of and adjustments in the work force. These assessments and adjustments may result in the need for providing guidelines or even discipline and termination. Overall, the organization seeks, through appraisal, to maximize the potential of the work force, thereby enhancing or increasing productivity.

The individual, in order to be successful, needs a regular and ongoing understanding of how he or she is measuring up to the standard. The individual's goal is to get valid feedback. The employee needs to make plans also, and these plans will be based on knowledge of what future expectations may be. Employees also have an appraisal of how well they have performed, and they are seeking, through the appraisal process, a confirmation of their perception. Finally, they are seeking additional compensation as the tangible evidence that they are performing well.

With two sets of goals operating in the same situation, the potential for conflict is very high. First of all, the money issue is always volatile. An employee always wants more money. Very few of us go through life feeling that we are being overpaid for what we do. The manager may be limited in terms of how much can be given or may feel that performance does not warrant an increase. There may also be a discrepancy about the job tasks and responsibilities. The employee may be working according to a different set of guidelines, perhaps from a previous manager. Guidelines in the form of objectives, key actions, and responsibilities may not have been effectively stated. Another source of conflict arises from the employee's need for valid feedback while resisting a differentiation of opinion on performance. These potential areas of conflict can easily push the interview participants into an adversary relationship.

Arguments are less likely to occur when there is frequent contact and ongoing opportunities for appraisal. Under these conditions, there is ample opportunity to clarify and confirm guidelines and expectations. When there is little contact, resentment and hostility have an opportunity to build up. These pent-up feelings can be triggered by the appraisal situation. Lack of skill in conducting the interview can also be a major source of conflict. Insensitive, overly aggressive, defensive, or hostile behavior on the appraiser's part will undoubtedly engender a like response in the other party. A poorly conducted appraisal, even if it does not become an argument, can do much damage to an employee's outlook, feelings toward the manager, and general productivity.

Christopher Wood of Coopers and Lybrand points out in his seminar on performance appraisal that there are two primary purposes for the appraisal process: to evaluate performance and to develop people. If you look at the focus of these two purposes, you see that they head off in opposite directions. When we evaluate performance, we are concerned with the past. When we develop people, we are concerned with the future. This split focus must somehow be held in balance during the appraisal interview. The two purposes also have an effect on the role behavior of the participants. When the manager is evaluating, he or she is a judge. When development is the purpose, the manager is a teacher, counselor, or advisor. Meanwhile, the employee responds to evaluation as an advocate and to development as a student. Wood highlights these dichotomies in Table 6.1.

Table 6.1

Main purpose	Focus	Manager's role	Employee's role
Evaluate performance	Past performance	Judge	Advocate
Develop People	Future performance	Teacher, counselor, adviser	Student

Again, we see the constant potential for conflict. If the appraisal process is to be successful, the conflict must be minimized. A certain amount of conflict is inevitable and healthy in that it may clarify some clouded issues and bring new facts to light. Too much conflict will have negative results. How do we minimize conflict? By mastering the nondefensive skills of active listening.

Active Listening as a Nondefensive Skill

The skillful manager will indicate from the outset an interest in the employee's opinions and concerns. The work of Jack Gibb was mentioned in Chapter 3, but it is worth restating and reexamining further. Gibb observed group interaction for eight years and reported that defensiveness is one of the major barriers to interpersonal communication. He defined defensive behavior as behavior "which occurs when an individual perceives threat or anticipates threat."[3] He continues to say that speech which appears to be evaluative is likely to cause defensiveness. Nonverbal behavior, such as shaking the head, sighing, or appearing skeptical, can evoke the same defensive response.

Assuming we must evaluate as part of the appraisal process, how can we diminish the potential for defensiveness? Stewart and D'Angelo give six suggestions for listening to diminish defensiveness:

1. Be generally positive.
2. Postpone specific evaluations.
3. Limit negative evaluations.
4. Own your evaluations.
5. Keep your evaluations tentative.
6. Actively solicit responses.[4]

Stewart and D'Angelo point out that being positive means acceptance of the notion that people have intrinsic worth in spite of the behaviors or attitudes we find objectionable. If managers listen from a positive point of view, employees will have less of a tendency to react defensively.[5]

Postponing specific evaluations is difficult when you have reviewed the record and determined the message you want to deliver. Prejudgment is an integral part of appraisal. Indeed, it is part of the manager's preparation. Even so, effort must be made to hold back positive or negative feedback until the employee understands clearly what is being evaluated. Making judgmental statements early on in the interview will tend to limit the interaction. This is counter to one of the main purposes of appraisal, which is to enhance or to improve communication.

Negative evaluations are inevitable during appraisal. What you say, or how you direct your negative comments, makes a big difference in the outcome. Limit your negative observations to behavior. Never speak negatively about the person being evaluated. Consider the difference in the following statements:

"Nancy, I'm afraid you simply do not possess any of the instincts necessary to do this job."

"Nancy, I'm concerned about the way this job is going for you. You don't seem to have taken hold of it."

The first statement is a personal attack and will probably draw a defensive reaction. The second statement may also create some defensiveness, but it invites Nancy to speak about job performance rather than herself.

Stewart and D'Angelo explain what they mean by "own your evaluations" this way. "It also helps to reduce defensiveness when you identify your evaluations as just that: *yours* and *evaluations*.[6] Statements like, "Most of our people here don't do that" or "Do you think that was a good idea?" may appear to be neutral, but they are highly evaluative and are generally perceived as such. You should explicitly verbalize your evaluations in first-person terms:

"John, you are consistently late coming to work, and it's causing problems for me and your fellow workers."

"Jean, I thought we had an understanding of how to handle this. In my view, it's gone badly and I'm frustrated and angry with you."

You need to be equally specific when the evaluation is positive. Cite the instance or behavior that exemplifies the positive response and be personal and direct:

"Marsha, I like the way you have taken hold of this job. You really straightened out that mess with accounts receivable. I know you worked hard and it paid off. Keep up the good work."

Keeping your evaluations tentative means considering your own perceptual biases and not generalizing beyond the behavior being evaluated. Stewart and D'Angelo put it this way: " . . . your evaluations of persons and attitudes can easily be wrong, so it's fairest to keep them tentative and open to change. We believe you can be more firm in your evaluations of another's *behavior*. But the trick is to keep your firm evaluations limited to behavior."[7]

Poor employee performance could be the result of a variety of factors, any of which might be dealt with in a constructive manner. To assume that an employee is lazy if the rate of work is slow or that an employee who is chronically late doesn't care about the job goes beyond the boundaries of sound evaluation. Have the employee respond to open questions about the behavior. Put yourself in the position of one trying to understand rather than being aggressively critical:

"John, your sales figures are way off for this month. What do you think is causing this to happen?"

This leads directly to the last suggestion for listening to diminish defensiveness, the active solicitation of responses. This is not an easy suggestion to follow, since asking for responses carries with it the assumption that your evaluation may be altered by an appropriate response:

> It's usually pretty difficult to be genuinely open to change after you've evaluated someone's behavior or ideas negatively. It's easy to feel as though you've made a public commitment to a point of view and that you'd look like a fool if you were to change your mind. It's hard not to feel the need to defend your evaluations—and along with it, your self-respect.[8]

At such times it is helpful to remember the goals and objectives of the evaluation process. Appraisal is linked to productivity through motivation and direction, and all are dependent on effective interpersonal communication. Soliciting responses most often will not change your evaluation of a particular behavior, but it may change your evaluation or perception of the individual. Stewart and D'Angelo see willingness to accept the possibility of change as a major step toward good communication:

> Asking for responses to your evaluations also shows a win/win rather than a win/lose attitude. In other words, this kind of perception checking reveals your genuine willingness and ability to share some of your humanness and to be aware of the humanness of the other. The other person might have changed since you perceived whatever you're evaluating. He or she might be conscious of the behavior you're noticing and have good reasons for continuing it. . . . The point is, communication that involves negative evaluating should be mutual and interdependent, as should any other human communication. . . .[9]

In summary, active listening, when employed as a nondefensive skill, will tend to reduce the potential for and the degree of conflict during the appraisal interview. It helps you focus your attention on behavior rather than attitude and promotes a climate within which communication can take place.

The Work Plan

For appraisals to be effective, the participants must agree on what is being appraised. A manager must prepare work plans for the staff that fit both the goals and objectives of the organization as well as the experience, competence, maturity, and specialized knowledge of the employee. An employee needs to be sure he or she can make a commitment to the work plan as prepared. If not, the plan must be "negotiated" until the employee is logically and emotionally involved with the success of the plan. In her book, *What to Do About Performance Appraisal*, Marion S. Kellogg says that there are probably as many variations to work planning as there are managers:

> But in general a manager should (1) be sure the employee has basic information about the business, about the department goals his work will support, about any assignments the manager has already decided he will handle, and about the probable ground rules for manpower and money; (2) discuss the employee's goals, regardless of their origin, to be sure that both manager and employee agree on their meaning, agree that they should be accomplished, and agree on what will constitute successful accomplishment; (3) review together the major steps for accomplishment of the goals so that needed resources are identified and agreed to, the timetable looks reasonable, and the timing will fit the goals of the total organization. This activity, when documented, becomes the broad plan for the employee's work.[10]

The work plan sets the standard by which the employee is measured during the appraisal process. But, more than a simple measure of performance, the work plan takes into account the employee's development as well. Kellogg continues:

> Ultimately what an employee and his manager agree to do represents a psychological contract between them. If the work package requires the employee to add to his knowledge, develop his skills, fill an experience gap or undertake a desired behavior modification, the groundwork for the employee's development is established. And the manager's guidance will contribute not only to organization results but to employee growth as well.[11]

The work plan and subsequent appraisal interview may be tied together by an appraisal form. If a form is used, it should focus on limited, attainable objectives. Johnson expresses concern about the use and abuse of appraisal forms:

> The appraisal form itself is at bottom of the many appraisal interviews that accomplish very little. The form itself may be an exhaustive tome attempting to deal with too much, or it may be misused by the appraiser.[12]

It is beyond the scope of this text to delve into the construction of appraisal forms. In the hands of a skilled interviewer, even a bad form can provide the basis of a good outcome. In the hands of a poor interviewer, even the best form will produce negative results. The following exchange with a manager who is a skilled appraiser shows the connection between the appraisal interview and the appraisal form:

CAROL: Listen, Martin, I really appreciate your staying late this evening to do this appraisal with me. We've both been on the road so much I thought we'd never touch base.

MARTIN: I'm glad we're getting it over with, too. I'm tired of worrying about it.

CAROL: Why are you worrying about it?

MARTIN: Oh, come on, Carol, I haven't exactly been given the star treatment lately, and I think I'm doing a better job than I think you think I am.

CAROL: Whoa! Hold on a minute! I'm having enough difficulty sorting out that last sentence, let alone your interpretation of my thinking. Let's back up. Was it my entire first sentence that inspired such an attack or only a few specific words?

MARTIN: All right. I'm sorry. I didn't mean to snap at you. But, damn it, I don't believe that my work is recognized.

CAROL: Can we set an agenda for this discussion that will make sure we cover all of your concerns?

MARTIN: Good idea.

CAROL: How about this? Let me share with you where I feel the strengths and concerns of your performance are. We'll take each item point by point, referring to the appraisal form when it's appropriate. I think you'll be somewhat surprised, because based on your initial reaction, you seem to be assuming that the appraisal is generally negative. While I do have some concerns to discuss with you, I do not consider this a negative appraisal. If at any point you feel that the picture I have of your efforts is inaccurate, set me straight. Okay?

MARTIN: Okay.

In the opening game, Carol attempts and finally succeeds in establishing rapport. Martin, although a subordinate, appears quite comfortable with Carol and willing to be outspoken. He is defensive. Carol uses her nondefensive skills, resists the temptation to continue pursuit of the "I'm doing a better job than you think" issue, and refocuses on the opening-game objectives: rapport, control, and a clear outline of expected events.

To help herself control the direction of the interview, Carol has to answer these questions, either before or during the interview:

1. Does Martin understand the tasks and responsibilities of the job?
2. Do both she and Martin interpret these tasks and responsibilities the same way? Do they share the same spectrum of priorities?
3. What criteria will she use to measure the performance behavior exhibited by Martin?
4. To what extent are other factors, including herself, responsible for both the positive and negative aspects of Martin's performance behavior?
5. Are her expectations beyond the scope of this job? This person?
6. Is Martin's performance satisfactory or not?

Carol begins the middle game with a positive statement and an open question:

CAROL: Let's begin with the Spring Catalog project. I thought that came out beautifully. How do you feel about it?

MARTIN: It was a bear! I thought I would croak when the backgrounds on the first shooting came back green. Some of the positioning was awkward. But aside from that, I thought it looked pretty good.

CAROL: You're being modest. The catalog is excellent and so far the response has been very encouraging. You really took that job on. I know you put a lot of overtime in on this one, and you remained calm and disciplined throughout all of the tedious layout work.

MARTIN: Well, thanks, Carol. I'm happy to hear the response is good. I didn't expect any figures for another week.

CAROL: These are preliminary, but they are strong. If it holds up, we have a real winner. In retrospect, what would you do differently in managing that project?

MARTIN: Differently, I don't know . . . I liked the way all of the vendors performed. . . .

CAROL: How about your staff?

MARTIN: They were okay . . . although I think they were overstressed a lot of the time.

CAROL: What makes you say that?

MARTIN: Well, they complained a lot. There was a lot of bitching on this job. Some of those folks had been on the road for five of the previous seven weeks. I guess they were feeling burnt out.

CAROL: What did you do about it?

MARTIN: I tried not to pressure them—ended up doing a lot of extra work myself.

CAROL: That's my concern, Martin. Your technical performance on this project was excellent. Your management performance was disappointing.

MARTIN: I couldn't push them, Carol.

CAROL: Managing doesn't mean pushing, although that may be a part of it. This was an extremely important project. The success of this catalog has direct impact on the entire organization, including your staff. I know the work load has been heavy. But we're all in the same boat. You let some of your people evade their responsibility.

MARTIN: You're right. But the darn catalog was so important, I didn't want to drain my energy with hassles.

CAROL: What would you do now?

MARTIN: I'll tell you one thing. I'd start earlier and have the entire staff in on some aspect of the planning.

CAROL: Good.

MARTIN: I think if they bought in to the project more—had a stake in it creatively—they would have been more enthusiastic. You know, I have a problem giving orders. I'm just not comfortable telling people what to do. So, I probably come across a bit tentative, unsure, and they exploit that.

CAROL: I think you're on the right track. What can I do to help you with that problem?

MARTIN: I'm not sure. I like the way George works with his staff. He seems to pile the work on, but everyone takes it good naturedly.

CAROL: George is very skillful at delegation. You may be confusing giving orders with delegating. There are many similarities, but delegation carries with it decision-making authority. George's people feel that they have a proprietary interest in the work they do. George gives them a large measure of autonomy and authority over what they do.

MARTIN: I'd be a nervous wreck! You know me, Carol; I have to have my hands on everything.

CAROL: Delegating doesn't mean that you don't monitor progress or maintain quality control. These are important management functions. I appreciate and admire your technical expertise and your stamina, but these are not the criteria by which managers are judged. How would you feel if we arranged some management training for you?

MARTIN: That would be great! Can we find the time?

CAROL: Let's make time. I think you have the qualities to be an excellent manager, and I think training would be a good investment for you, for me, and for the company. I have some catalogs here that list some courses and seminars available in this area. Why don't you take them home with you, look through them, and let's meet again at 10:00 tomorrow morning to set something up, okay?

MARTIN: Sounds good to me.

CAROL: Also, maybe we can arrange for you to work with George on something so that you can observe and "pick his brain."

MARTIN: I'd like that, too.

CAROL: All right, Martin, let's see where we are. My evaluation of your performance on the catalog project is very high and you are to be commended for a fine job. I would like to see you begin to develop more quickly as a manager. In this area, your performance is below expectation. To accomplish this, we are going to establish a development program, including formal management training and exposure to management within the organization that is effective. I will be monitoring your progress carefully, and we will have another formal review in six months. I want to be sure you understand that I believe you can do the job. You have my sincere support for your development, and I'm sure you have a long and successful career with us. Ten tomorrow?

MARTIN: Ten tomorrow . . . and thank you again for your support.

As I have said before, you may conduct a thousand appraisals in your lifetime and never have one come out exactly as this one. However, all of the elements of a good appraisal are contained within this example. The pattern of criticism is supportive since Carol begins with strong assertions about what is right in Martin's performance. She uses a strategy of open questions followed by probes to force Martin to focus on his own deficiencies. She offers her blanket assistance to help Martin overcome his problem areas. Between them they develop a plan with which both can live and a realistic time frame within which progress can be measured. The closing summarizes the events and makes a strong statement of support.

The statement of support is particularly important. Unless you intend to terminate an employee, you must always leave him or her with the feeling that you believe they can succeed. This final impression has a very strong and lasting effect. The employee who senses your belief will work very hard not to erode your confidence or change your opinion. An employee who senses your skepticism or disinterest may be just as likely to fulfill your expectations and fail.

Notes for the Appraised

When you are the object of appraisal interview, you have rights. As with all interview, you are seeking information. You have a right to know on what grounds and by what standards you are being judged. You have a right to clarify or dispute judgments made about you that are untrue or ill informed. You have a right to know what the outcome of the appraisal will be. You have a right to express your personal goals and objectives as well as your future plans and to determine if they are in line with the company's plans for you. In order to exercise these rights, you need to be well prepared for the appraisal interview.

The following ten points will help you maximize your participation in the appraisal:

1. Keep good records. Memos, letters, directives, general comments, congratulations, records of phone conversations, and the like, all add up to make a clear picture of how you are performing—or not performing—within the context you have been placed.
2. If there is an appraisal form, write one for yourself. Even if your organization does not use a form, it is helpful to write out an appraisal for yourself. It enables you to anticipate areas of concern and questions

that may be raised about your performance. Also, having been over the issues will make your responses more cogent and direct.

3. Be assertive but not defensive. This is a tough order to follow, but it will serve you well if you can manage it. Do not count on your appraiser being an expert in using nondefensive skills. Remember, the appraisal interview is not always comfortable for the appraiser either. Often, a show of reasonableness on the part of the appraised will cause the appraiser to be more open and cooperative as well.
4. Resist the temptation to predetermine the outcome of the appraisal. If you believe an appraisal is going to go badly, you may project that attitude and make it come true. In the midst of criticism, there may be some very positive opportunities that will be missed if you are not listening for them.
5. Take the appraisal very seriously. Indicate that you feel the appraisal is a significant part of your job. Arrive on time. Be well dressed.
6. Insist on a development plan. If your superior is critical of some aspects of your work behavior, clarify and confirm the standards by which your work will be judged in the future. Through what means will both you and the organization seek to bring your performance up to standard?
7. Be responsive. If you are asked to state your opinion of your performance, do so. Be realistic without being too hard on yourself or self-serving. Focus on accomplishments and behavior on the job.
8. Never blame others for your shortcomings. If someone or something in the job environment is interfering with your performance, discuss the matter in job-specific terms. Do not say, "Judy doesn't like me and hides the data." Rather, talk of the difficulty, "I'm having a problem getting my hands on the data when I need them."
9. Follow up. If you have been asked to provide information or schedule an additional meeting, do so in a timely fashion.
10. Follow through. If questions or concerns about your performance have been raised and a development plan has been prepared, throw yourself into it. Make it work. This is not the time for pride. You can make tremendous gains in the eyes of your superior and the organization as a whole if they perceive that a plan that they developed actually worked.

SPECIAL FORMS OF APPRAISAL

While it is hoped that appraisal will mostly provide positive results and the strengthening of the relationship between the employee and the organization, sometimes performance behavior requires corrective action. One type of corrective action is *discipline*, which is stronger in tone and intent than normal appraisal, but it still reaches for positive change. The other, *termination*, seeks to protect the organization from further harm because of unacceptable job behavior.

Discipline

Let us begin with a basic principle. Discipline is an application of power. Use it with discretion. As supervisors or managers, you still report to a boss. As such, you probably feel many of the same pressures and constraints you have always felt, but there are now people very close to you who have these same feelings about you. In a very real sense, you have acquired power.

Some people run from power because it carries responsibility. Others abuse it by exercising it randomly, without sensitivity, and too often. The successful supervisor or manager exercises power sensitively and with discretion. The key to all well-disciplined organizations is control. Controls must be established in advance in order for discipline, when necessary, to be effective.

This brings us to the second basic principle. The most effective controls are employee centered. Whenever we think about establishing controls, the concept of discipline comes into play. Children need discipline in order for them to establish acceptable limits of behaviors. Psychologists tell us that children demand discipline. They want to understand their limits because knowing how far they can go creates security for them. Even as adults, we never outgrow that need. In our jobs we are uneasy when we are not sure what is expected of us. While we may not agree about the necessity for certain rules, we are still more comfortable knowing what the rules are. We are then free to conform or rebel, but at least we know where we stand.

Discipline can be used to teach or punish. You may have to use discipline both ways. The aim of discipline is to get the employees to comply with the established rules of conduct. When discipline is used to teach, it is preventive or positive discipline. When it is used to punish, it is corrective and negative discipline. You will encounter some situations where corrective discipline is unavoidable, but in general it is positive and preventive discipline that supervisors and managers hope to achieve. This view asserts that it is your function to train employees to develop self-discipline in work habits and in on-the-job behavior. Self-discipline is employee centered. It places a large proportion of the responsibility for discipline on each individual employee.

This brings us to the third basic principle. Your behavior sets the pace for all discipline. A climate must be established that makes it possible for employee self-discipline to occur. The supervisor or manager establishes the climate. You must know the rules and the reasons for them. You must monitor your own personal conduct. When you violate a rule, you must be subject to the same corrective discipline as any employee. A good working climate, favorable to employee self-discipline, occurs when the employee perceives these elements:

1. Swift action is taken when misconduct occurs.
2. The supervisor or manager is successful at developing stronger ties between the employees and the company.
3. The supervisor or manager exhibits and insists upon high standards of performance.
4. There is consistency in the application of standards.
5. The supervisor or manager is very specific about his or her expectations.
6. The supervisor or manager gives the impression of being genuinely interested in the employee's problems, both on and off the job.

Almost all of these behaviors are dependent on good two-way communication between you and the employees that you supervise. If you have open lines of communication, you will rarely need to apply corrective discipline. When an employee feels that he or she is able to communicate with the supervisor, interest develops in the common goals of the department. Employees believe that they are a part of a common effort, and a feeling of mutual respect develops. You open lines of communication by applying the following principles:

1. Be as accurate as possible when passing along information. Accuracy enhances the supervisor's credibility.
2. Make reasonable demands, and be sympathetic with an employee's reasons for not being able to meet certain demands.
3. Treat those under your supervision with common courtesy. Do not be patronizing or abusive. Avoid embarrassing an employee in front of his or her peers.

If the employees under your supervision feel that you are reasonable, accessible, and generally concerned about them, open lines of communication will develop. These open lines of communication will ultimately create a more positive work atmosphere and increase productivity.

Sometimes corrective discipline is unavoidable. Perhaps you have just been placed in charge of a department where discipline has been lax or maybe there are one or two individuals whose behavior is disruptive to other members of the department. How well you handle corrective discipline can set the tone of your relationship with the employees you supervise. While the specific objective of a corrective action is to reestablish control over the offending individual, the overall objective is to establish or maintain a climate of employee-centered, positive discipline.

Respond to a corrective situation like a concerned administrator, not like an angry parent. First, determine the nature and degree of the offense. Second, check the company rules and policy guidelines regarding the range of disciplinary actions at your disposal. If you overreact, you stand the possibility of being overruled from above. Third, weigh the current offense against the basic factors in the employee's record:

1. Has his or her conduct been generally good?
2. What is his or her length of service?
3. Are there any other violations? What penalties were administered?
4. How does the offense relate to the generally accepted interpretation of company policy in your department?
5. Are there mitigating or aggravating circumstances connected to the offense?

Corrective discipline will be most effective if the employee is left with the feeling that having paid the penalty, he can start clean and that he has not done permanent or irreparable damage to his relationship with the company. An effectively applied corrective action can set an employee on the right track and provide positive benefits for both the employee and the company. An ounce of offense does not deserve a pound of cure.

The reasons why employees develop disciplinary problems are many and varied, as are the types of offenses. Some problems are caused by conditions in the employees' personal lives. An employee may break a rule because of a work-related problem he or she cannot solve. You must always take into account the severity of the offense when giving the employee a penalty. Some supervisors dislike confrontation because it seems severe, but in actuality the reprimand is the least severe type of discipline. It is also the most used of the potential disciplinary actions. The ability to deliver an effective reprimand should be treated as an important part of a supervisor's administrative skills. A reprimand can be oral or written, and it can be used for violations such as the following:

1. Not putting in full working time or disrupting other employees trying to work.
2. Careless handling of equipment and materials.
3. General insubordination. You can only maintain the respect of your department when you are in control of everyone.
4. Not following safety practices.

Each employee needs to be considered individually before a reprimand is given. Factors such as the employee's personality, the severity of the violation, and the surrounding circumstances will help shape an appropriate reprimand.

Before a reprimand is administered, the supervisor should know why the offense occurred.

When you administer a reprimand, you must remain calm and objective. You should not be guided by personal feelings. You must follow through on your reprimand with periodic checks on the employee's behavior. Remember, when you deliver a reprimand, you are the company talking. Do not confuse giving reprimands with giving orders.

In the following scene, Tom gives Debbie a reprimand for taking too many personal phone calls:

TOM: Debbie, I've noticed you've been spending a lot of time on personal phone calls lately. Is there something wrong? A problem I should know about? Maybe there's something I can do.

DEBBIE: Well, yes, there is a bit of a problem, but really I don't think it's anything you could possibly help with. You see, my husband and I just hired a new baby sitter for our son, and she does call me a lot. But you know how it is when someone's learning a new job, right? She calls to find out where things are or what to do if he gets fussy . . . that kind of thing. And besides, I kind of like to keep in touch with her, just to make sure everything's okay.

TOM: Of course, I can understand that you want to make sure everything's okay at home and that Joey's getting the right kind of care. But Debbie, these calls from your sitter are causing problems in the office. Your productivity is starting to fall. You're letting business calls go unanswered because you're tied up with your sitter or you're expecting others on the staff to cover for you. Debbie, it's not just a service problem; it's beginning to cause a morale problem as well. You know our policy is that personal phone calls should be restricted to breaks or lunchtimes unless, of course, it's an emergency. That's why the work gets done and everyone does their fair share. You're going to have to limit your personal calls to breaks. Do you see any ways you could do this and still be satisfied things are going smoothly at home?

DEBBIE: I really have been meaning to do something about it, something to cut down the interruptions from home. I was thinking . . . maybe I could put together a list of instructions for the sitter, things she needs to know or do. I suppose I should have done it before, but I'll definitely do it tonight. And I'll ask her not to call me unless it's an emergency, of course. That'll be okay, so long as I can call her on my breaks or at lunch. Would that be okay?

TOM: That'd be fine. I'm very pleased with your solution. This is what we'll do. I'll monitor your calls this week. Then you and I'll get together one week from today to see how it's working. I'm sure that your solution will take care of both problems: your problem with the sitter and our problem in the office, and you'll be the productive worker you've always been in the past, right?

DEBBIE: Right.

Tom handles the situation well. He gets directly to the point and identifies the behavior with which he is displeased. Each step of the way he uses open questions to encourage Debbie to suggest and "buy in" to a solution. He ends, as he should, with a vote of confidence in Debbie's ability to surmount the problem, correct the offending behavior, and return to being a productive employee.

In conclusion, discipline is power. Discipline is part of your supervisory and management responsibility. Discipline should be predictable, immediate, consistent, and documented. Discipline starts with orienting your employees to the rules of work, such as starting on time, what time is lunch break, and what time is quitting time. Reinforcement of work rules is important, particularly at staff meetings and at other appropriate times. Issuing first a verbal warning, followed by a written warning, and ultimately by a final warning, is the order in which discipline should progress. Each progressive step—verbal, written, or final—must be documented. Be sure to include a time frame for reviewing the behavior again, and along with that review, make a promise. If the behavior changes for the positive, you will applaud the employee. If the behavior does not change and is still unacceptable, you will take the next progressive action. Do not promise to act and then not act. If you make the promise, carry it out. Above all, document your actions at all stages.

Termination

The termination of an employee is the most serious disciplinary step any manager can take. As a manager, you are responsible for the overall effectiveness of your operation. Sometimes, for a variety of reasons, it becomes necessary to terminate the employment of one of your staff. The most common reasons for terminations are:

1. Inadequate job performance.
2. Personnel reduction.
3. Frequent absenteeism or tardiness.
4. Insubordination or disruptive behavior.
5. Reorganization.

All terminations require attention to the basic concepts of documentation, timing, and appropriate word choice. The concept of documentation cannot be stressed too strongly. You must document in great detail all steps leading to and including the termination of an employee. Obviously, the type and amount of documentation will differ among termination for reorganization or personnel reduction, termination for job performance, and termination as the result of a disciplinary problem.

The documentation for reorganization and headcount should include:

1. All money for salary, vacation, or expense reimbursement owed to the employee.
2. All money from loans, travel advances, or other sources owed by the employee to the organization.
3. Most companies require the completion of a personnel action authorization indicating the date of termination, the last day worked, the last day that the employee is to be paid plus vacation due.

Documentation for inadequate job performance, frequent absenteeism, and discipline problems should include a precise description of the nature of the problem; the dates of the problem (that is, when the actions actually occurred); and specific steps that you have taken in the form of warnings, appraisals, goal setting, and directives to correct the problem.

An employee whose behavior or job performance is creating a negative response is entitled to a fair and reasonable opportunity to adjust his or her behavior according to your specific standards. Be sure your documentation supports your action. It is unethical, unfair, and legally unsupportable to terminate an employee for poor performance when that employee has only positive appraisal information in his or her file. You must follow these steps leading to termination:

1. Give a verbal warning. This outlines the behavior to be corrected, the time in which you will observe it, and the actions that you will take next.
2. After a verbal warning, if no improvement is noted, you may follow it up by a written warning.
3. After the written warning, you may take the final action, which ultimately may be termination.

Again, documentation is critical. Think through the seriousness of the offense. Has the employee had an opportunity to correct his or her behavior and meet your standards? If the answer to this question is yes, then termination may be warranted.

The following example demonstrates a verbal warning. The manager, Julie, and her employee, George, exchange some information and enter into a verbal warning:

JULIE: George, it's become apparent that you're having some problem getting to work on Mondays and Fridays. Is there a reason you can discuss with me?

GEORGE: I was out last Friday because of my teeth. You know, I've been having some work done.

JULIE: George, during the last two months, the record shows that you have been absent two Fridays and two Mondays. In one instance, you were out both Friday and the following Monday. Is there something I can do to help your attendance?

GEORGE: Well, I'm having a few problems, but I've got it pretty well straightened out now.

JULIE: Okay, George, I'm happy to hear that. I just want you to understand that the performance of this office depends on everyone working and making their best effort. If there's a problem, with your teeth or anything else, which will affect your ability to be on the job, please let me know. I'll be monitoring your attendance, and we will have another discussion in four weeks.

In the preceding example, the manager makes no accusations and does not state any suspicions or conclusions. Instead, she speaks only to the facts—what the record shows. She next states her expectations for the employee as part of the office team. Finally, she clearly states what action will be taken and when there will be further discussion.

When the period stated in the verbal warning is over, you have two possible courses of action. If the behavior has improved, reinforce the change with praise. If the behavior has not changed, issue a written warning. A written warning should read as follows:

> Dear George:
>
> As per our discussion on July 29, I have been monitoring your attendance record. I am sorry to see that you have been absent on one Friday and on one Monday during the month. Despite my request to be informed of any problems, I have not heard from you. I would be pleased to hear any explanation you may have. Please understand that any further absences within the next month will result in immediate termination.

If the letter initiates a discussion, listen attentively and reiterate the warning in the letter. You have established the guidelines. Do not allow yourself to be put on the defensive.

At the end of the month, you once again have two possible choices or courses of action. If the employee has adhered to the guidelines, reward with praise. If the negative behavior has continued, schedule a termination interview. You must have no doubt about your decision. When you engage in a termination interview, this is not the time to weigh options. If you are not

definite, do not do it. The result will be an argument resulting in the loss of creditibility for you.

The following example demonstrates a termination interview:

JULIE: George, I've called you in today because we need to resolve a problem.

GEORGE: Uh, gee, I really meant to tell you. I'm sorry about Monday, but my mother-in-law was sick, my wife had to get to work, so I had to stay with the kids.

JULIE: I realize, George, there are special problems when both family members work. However, we have had ample time to resolve or at least address these problems. I warned you on July 29th that your attendance was creating problems for the overall effort of the office. I reiterated this to you last month in my letter of August 29th. You will recall that I stated that any further absences would be cause for termination. I regret to point out, George, that Monday was it.

GEORGE: You . . . you're firing me?

JULIE: In this envelope you will find a check covering all of the money the company owes you to date. You will also find a memorandum that details each of the amounts that make up the total.

GEORGE: I don't see why we can't work this out. You've never been sympathetic to my problems. I've never had this kind of trouble with the last manager.

JULIE: George, I wish you all the best in the future. I think if you work through your difficulties and apply yourself, you can develop into a good worker. I'm sorry this had to happen. It is a business decision, and in my judgment, it is best for the office that we sever our relationship.

Julie, correctly, was specific, swift, and businesslike. She did not hesitate or digress or get into an argument on a personal level. She kept the exchange to a minimum, further avoiding the possibility of any errors in word choice that could instigate legal action.

Appropriate word choice must be employed at every stage. Stick to business language. Relate all negative criticism to job performance. Never mention race, color, creed, sex, age, national origin, or discuss family or family members or other employees as reasons for termination. Again, be brief and businesslike.

Let us summarize the main points. All terminations require attention to three main points: documentation, timing, and word choice. Document everything. There is no such thing as too much documentation. Give a reasonable span of time within which you provide first a verbal, then a written warning. Each time, give specific goals or objectives for the employee to achieve. All discussions should center on the accomplishment of those objectives. Keep

the termination interview short, low key, and to the point. Have all the necessary paperwork completed before the interview, and above all, be sure.

Termination is neither an easy nor a pleasant task. Unfortunately, it is occasionally necessary. As a manager, you must become effective with termination procedures. A botched termination in the long run can cause the company more problems and cost more money than keeping the employee.

SUMMARY

This chapter positions the appraisal interview as an essential tool of organizational productivity. Used skillfully, appraisal can develop, motivate, and build important relationships between managers and employees. The best appraisal focuses on behavior as well as the employee's nondefensive active listening skills, and it creates a climate within which both participants feel they have profited from the experience. The manager profits from the opportunity to develop and motivate an employee. The employee profits by receiving direction and establishing new goals. Both parties should come away with a clear understanding of what the standards are and a plan to achieve them.

Questions for Study and Discussion

1. Why do both employers and employees resist performance appraisal?
2. How does performance appraisal serve the goals and objectives of the organization?
3. What are the five specific reasons to conduct a performance appraisal?
4. How does performance appraisal "develop people"?
5. Why is it important to focus your negative evaluations on behavior?
6. What is meant by the phrase "active listening"?
7. Outline the progression from reprimand through termination. What are the essential steps at each level?

Suggested Activities

1. In groups of three or four, develop a list of activities, documents, and other materials you need to have in order to prepare effectively for a performance appraisal:
   a. As the manager.
   b. As the employee.

Notes

1. Robert G. Johnson, *The Appraisal Interview Guide* (New York: AMACOM, 1979), 5.
2. Ibid., 3–5.
3. Jack R. Gibb, "Defensive Communication," *Journal of Communication* 11 (September 1961): 141.
4. John Stewart and Gary D'Angelo, *Together: Communicating Interpersonally* (Reading, Mass.: Addison-Wesley, 1975), 199.
5. Ibid., 201.
6. Ibid., 204.
7. Ibid., 205.
8. Ibid., 206.
9. Ibid.
10. Marion S. Kellogg, *What to Do about Performance Appraisal*, rev. ed. (New York: AMACOM, 1975), 63.
11. Ibid., 64.
12. Johnson, *The Appraisal Interview Guide*, 11.

7

The Journalistic Interview

Key Concepts

- **Being Prepared**
- **Building Rapport**
- **Persistence**
- **Accuracy**

REPORTER: Mr. Jones, may I have a few minutes of your time?

JONES: Are you with the press?

REPORTER: Michaels of the World Gazette. Mr. Jones, you are a principal in the Conner case, and . . .

JONES: I'm not sure I should talk to you.

REPORTER: Why is that, Mr. Jones?

JONES: I don't think a lot of publicity will help this case, and if I talk to you, then everyone will be after me.

REPORTER: This is an important case. The public has a right to know what's going on.

JONES: I have a right to my privacy. Besides, publicity may prejudice the outcome of the case.

REPORTER: Mr. Jones, the case is going to be extensively covered anyway. You may as well benefit from the publicity that will come out of it.

JONES: If I talk to you, how do I know you will not distort what I say?

Few things in life stir as much ambivalence as being approached by the press for an interview. On the one hand, it is a signal that you are important, "have arrived," are central to an important issue or event. On the other hand, by granting an interview, you become public property, subject to scrutiny and evaluation by total strangers. Fortunately, human nature being what it is, the potential for glory is generally a stronger motive than privacy. Otherwise, we would have very few interviews to print.

First, let us put the journalistic interview into context with other types of interview. Information seeking is still the objective, but much greater pressure for self-disclosure is placed on one participant, whom we will call the *subject*. Both participants will undoubtedly ask questions during the exchange, but the subject will usually be confined to clarifying and confirming questions while the journalist uses the full range of questioning techniques available. This type of interview carries a responsibility with the action. Since what you are acquiring will eventually turn up in print, you need to be fair, accurate, and consider the consequences. John Brady, editor of *Writer's Digest* and the author of *The Craft of Interviewing*, positions the journalistic interview this way:

> In interviewing, you will have a modest feeling of power. Not the power of manipulation, but the power of knowledge—of holding a handmade key to a secret room of the subject's mind. The feeling is ephemeral, but sturdy and true. Afterward, when the interview is in print, you will realize that the secret has ended, but has touched other lives.[1]

PREPARING THE SUBJECT

In all but exceptional circumstances, you will need an appointment to conduct a journalistic interview. You need to identify yourself and what information you seek. You need to show up on time and appear well dressed and civilized. Brady suggests writing or phoning at least one week in advance. This gives the subject the opportunity to collect his or her thoughts, do research, or otherwise be better prepared to give a full response.[2]

When you phone a subject, be prepared to identify yourself fully, put forth your purpose directly and concisely, and tell the subject where he or she fits in. Specify the amount of time you need, and be prepared to complete your interview during the time allotted.

Writing for an appointment follows the same basic format. Fully identify yourself and your purpose. Sell your idea to the subject. Indicate that you are flexible as far as appointment dates. Use attractive professional-looking stationery with a letterhead and a good typewriter.

PREPARING YOURSELF

A rule of thumb that journalists use asserts that ten minutes of research needs to be done for each minute of actual interview time. You are in much better shape if you are overprepared than if you are caught without enough material or background information on which to base your questions. Brady warns that you can never be quite sure how a particular subject is going to react. He gives several illustrations of reporters caught with more time than anticipated and too few questions, such as the following:

> Associated Press correspondent Eugene Lyons once had an interview with Joseph Stalin, which he was told would last two minutes. "At the end of two minutes I found that Stalin was in no hurry," recalls Lyons, "and there I was without a program of interrogation. I remained in Stalin's office nearly two hours and forever after would reproach myself for having failed in the excitement of the thing to ask significant questions."[3]

The purpose of research is to provide you with the necessary information to frame significant questions. Although the subject may be favorably impressed with your knowledge, the purpose of research is not to impress or intimidate. Your subject will be more willing to talk when you show that you have cared enough to spend some time and effort familiarizing yourself with events and issues that are important to the subject.

Research for interview begins where all research usually begins—the library. Obviously, your approach will vary with the topic of the interview, but a good general place to begin is with an encyclopedia. Encyclopedias give historical information on almost any subject. Try both the *Britannica* and the *Americana* because coverage differs, as does the quality of articles on the same subject. Specialized encyclopedias are also available in various fields. Almanacs are a wealth of statistics on various topics, and statistics are useful for questioning a number-conscious world. Depending on your subject, you might find other compilations of statistics helpful, such as the *Statistical Yearbook of the United Nations*, *Statistics Sources*, and the *Rand McNally Commercial Atlas* (for economic data).

When researching personalities or events, nothing is as effective as the newspaper indexes. The *New York Times Index* is your best source because the *Times* provides more in-depth coverage of daily events than other papers. Searching the indexes of the *Wall Street Journal*, *Christian Science Monitor*, *National Observer*, and the *Washington Post* will provide you with articles from varying points of view and will add dimension to your understanding of a subject or issue. Magazine articles are also an important source for the journalist. Guides like *The Readers' Guide to Periodical Literature*, *The Social Sciences Index*, *The Humanities Index*, *The Business Periodicals Index*, and the *Applied Science and Technology Index* provide a range of articles on a variety of subjects at different levels of scholarship. Biographical information on famous people can be found in the *Biography Index*, *Current Biography*, *Who's Who in America*, and the whole host of other Who's Who titles.

Librarians are a great resource. They have the first-hand knowledge of the resources in their library and where to find them. A research librarian can cut hours off of your research time by going directly to the needed materials. Interlibrary loans can be arranged when materials are located in a different branch or a different library across town or across the country. The librarian will also know where the elusive cache of government pamphlets is stored; how to access information through the new computer systems; which issues are bound, at the bindery or still in single-copy form; where the newspapers are; where the microfilms of the newspapers are; and many other things you would never think of until you had begun your research.

While we have covered only some of the basics of journalistic research, the importance of doing such research cannot be stressed enough. Research will build confidence in your knowledge of the subject. It will enable you to frame intelligent questions. It will make it easier for you to demonstrate to your subject that you are interested in the same events or issues and cared enough to put in time to find out about them. Finally, doing research and knowing your subject will help you establish rapport.

ESTABLISHING RAPPORT

Quoting psychiatrist John Rich, Brady says, "Forming a rapport is a prerequisite for anything other than the most superficial work."[4] Brady goes on to give guidelines for beginning the interview:

> How do you go about it? Everything matters. Even unspoken communication can influence the replies one gets during an interview.
>
> When meeting someone for the first time, it's usually best to be a little formal at the outset. Never be familiar. A cautious interviewer will not even sit down until he has been asked. Other taboos include gum chewing, smoking (without asking permission), and handling things in the subject's office or home. In short, don't take liberties or make assumptions that a guest would not be expected to make in your own home.[5]

Each interview subject will respond in a unique manner. Your success depends on your ability to assess the situation correctly at the outset. If you perceive that the subject is reluctant to talk or appears suspicious of you, take the lead and talk steadily for a period of time. This gives the subject the opportunity to observe you and make some judgments. Your research can help you here. The more you know about a subject, his or her likes and dislikes, the more opportunity you have to open with talk that is likely to strike a responsive chord. Brady says:

The point is this: be flexible, and be ready for anything at the outset. Chances are good that the subject will be in the midst of some activity when you arrive; few people are simply sitting around waiting to be interviewed. Take the subject's mind off the interview by talking about unrelated matters which may interest him. For all but the busiest subjects, small talk is a smooth icebreaker.[6]

When one is sharing intimate aspects of their lives or expounding passionately on their beliefs, it is easy to lose objectivity. If you are interviewing a celebrity, you are in danger of being too much of a fan and distorting the truth. You may become protective or soft on the subject. Too much rapport of the wrong kind can trigger a loss of objectivity with a resultant loss of accuracy.

Close Listening

We have discussed the importance of listening at other points in this book, and it is safe to say that all suggestions for good active listening are appropriate for the journalistic interview. The emphasis for the journalist is on accuracy. Once rapport has been established and the subject is talking, do very little talking yourself. Do not interrupt and maintain a neutral response pattern. Use probes such as "uh-huh," "mmm," "I see," nods of the head, or other appropriate gestures. There is a tendency in all interviews, not just the journalistic type, to begin framing your next question before the subject is through answering the last one. To listen really closely, you must train yourself not to think of another question but to concentrate on what the subject is saying all the way to the end. In this regard, your mirror segments may be closer together as you continually clarify and confirm the information you are receiving.

Phrasing Effective Questions

Brady quotes Michael J. Arlen from *Living-Room War*, a collection of television writings on the tendency of journalists to ask "how do you feel" questions:

> I mean, the "how-do-you-feel" stuff would be okay if it led anywhere, if it were something people could respond to . . . but in a professional interview what it really amounts to is a sort of marking time while the reporter thinks up some real questions, or maybe while he hopes that this one time the Personage will actually include a bit of genuine information in his inevitably mechanical reply, which the reporter can then happily pursue. . . .
>
> Sometimes . . . I have this picture of the last great interview: The polar icecaps are melting. The San Andreas Fault has swallowed up half of California. . . . The cities of the plain are leveled. We switch from Walter Cronkite in End-of-the-World Central to Buzz Joplin, who is standing on a piece of rock south of the Galapagos with the last man on earth, the water rising now just above their chins. Joplin strains himself up on tiptoe, lifts his microphone out of the water, and, with a last desperate gallant effort—the culmination of all his years as a TV

newsman—places it in front of the survivor's mouth. "How do you feel, sir?" He asks. "I mean, being the last man on earth and so forth. Would you give us your personal reaction?" The last survivor adopts that helpless vacant look, the water already beginning to trickle into his mouth. "Well, Buzz," he says, gazing wildly into the middle distance, "I feel really good."[7]

Also to be avoided are questions that are not really questions, such as, "So, Mr. Jones, I'll bet you are really upset that the great mass of the American public sees you as a liar and a thief."

Posing good questions begins with the proper mental attitude. One of the principles of nondefensive listening that was covered in the last chapter is particularly appropriate here. Suspend judgment. Derive questions from your research of the subject and your knowledge of the individual that you are questioning. Focus on issues that you know are of interest to the respondent. Keep a clear view of what you want to get out of the interview. The technique for the journalistic interview calls for an abundance of open and probing questions. The objective is to get your subject to talk, and to talk with some depth on the matters relating to the purpose of your interview.

The good journalist is prepared to move in any direction that presents itself. Once the subject is talking, you do not want to risk stopping the flow by being doggedly assertive about your prepared pattern of questioning. However, you should have a plan and a list of questions that you need to have answered in order to carry out your original plan. A good strategy for the journalist is the funnel sequence. The funnel, you will recall, opens with general questions and gradually focuses on specific details. The following is an example:

REPORTER: Mr. Megabucks, the growth in Dallas has been phenomenal during the last ten years. As a developer, what factors do you feel have contributed most significantly to this growth?

MEGABUCKS: Well, son, I believe the most important factors are the pioneering spirit and free enterprise.

REPORTER: You are a great believer in free enterprise?

MEGABUCKS: Free enterprise is what has made this country great, and don't you forget it, boy.

REPORTER: What does free enterprise mean to you as a developer?

MEGABUCKS: When I see an opportunity—like my Longhorn Plaza development—I go for it. Office space, that's the name of the game today. When that project is finished, it will have two million square feet of office space.

REPORTER: On the issue of Longhorn Plaza . . . there seems to be quite a bit of opposition to that project.

MEGABUCKS: Well, there are always a few people around who insist on standing in the way of progress.

REPORTER: The main objection seems to be the amount of traffic that will be generated in what is basically a residential area.

MEGABUCKS: That parcel is zoned for either residential or commercial use. I can't help it if a lot of people built houses in there. Business is business.

REPORTER: Mr. Megabucks, there is a bill before the city council at the moment that is aimed at restricting zoning to preserve the residential character of several areas, including the Longhorn Plaza area. Do you see this as a threat?

MEGABUCKS: It's no threat to Longhorn Plaza. They can pass any darn bill they want to. They can't make it retroactive. I have the site, the plans, and I'm breaking ground next week.

REPORTER: Are you categorically against zoning?

MEGABUCKS: I believe some zoning is necessary. But by and large, there is too much restriction already.

REPORTER: What if someone wanted to put a trailer park or a junkyard next to Longhorn Plaza?

MEGABUCKS: They couldn't. The area isn't zoned for a trailer park or a junkyard.

The reporter in the preceding scene used a funnel strategy to focus on the Longhorn Plaza issue. He uses broad questions in the beginning to get the subject talking about matters of interest to him. Megabucks knows why the reporter has requested this interview—Longhorn Plaza. The reporter allows him to set the direction of the interview by not bringing up the issue or questioning about it until Megabucks mentions it. The overwhelming majority of the questions are open questions, even when the intent is very specific. The continual use of open questions sets the stage for the closed, sharp, and direct question, "Do you see this as a threat?"

As a reporter, you must always keep the interests of your readers in mind. Certainly, you want to get the facts, the opinions, and the position statements, but you also want to profile the subject, bring the subject to life for the readers. Brady uses my central image of the chess game to describe what the reporter does:

> Above all, the interviewer knows exactly what he wants to get from his interview. He is like a chess player: he does not move a piece—or ask a question—without a purpose, a plan.[8]

There are times, of course, when the funnel strategy is not the best approach to the subject. If there is little time or if what you are after is a broad perspective on an issue or anecdotes based on personal experience, the *inverted funnel* may be effective. The inverted funnel is exactly what it says: You begin with the sharp, specific questions and move on to the more general.

If you were after a story about the thrill and danger of scuba diving, you would not ask your subject, "Tell me about some of your most exciting experiences." Think of what would be of interest to your readers and frame a specific question like, "Have you ever run out of air while you were under water?" The closed question could be answered by a simple yes or no—that is a risk—but in most instances the subject will go on to tell you some interesting experiences surrounding the problem of running out of air. The last question you might ask after several more closed questions like "Sharks?" or "Getting lost?" might be, "Given all of these incidents, how can you recommend this sport to the general public?" Ending with the open question requiring a broader response could elicit an interesting, perhaps a soul-searching, response.

TAKING NOTES

There is probably no really good substitute for taking notes. Even the audiotape or videotape recorder, unless they are set up under studio conditions, can miss an important word or phrase or obscure a piece of communication in such a way as to impair accuracy. There is no doubt that tape gives you more of the reality of the interaction, the inflections, the gestures, the pauses, the stops and starts. But eventually your interview is going to appear in print and these subtleties will be lost anyway, except as captured by your superlative descriptive passages. If your subject is not disturbed by electronic recording and you have the means to use it, go ahead. Some interviewers get overly involved with the technology and lose sight of the main purpose. Regardless of how accurate the depiction of an event may be when captured on tape or film, viewing the event through a lens does not produce the same experience as participating in the event.

Taking notes will help your powers of recall as well as provide you with the references you need for quotes, figures, or other precise information. Take as few notes as possible during the interview. However, immediately after completing the interview, write down the material in as much detail as you can recall. Some subjects will be wary and unresponsive if they see you taking notes. If you sense this is happening or anticipate that it will happen based on your research of the subject, you may have to forgo the note taking and depend on your memory to gather the information. As a general rule, you are better off when you take notes despite the fact that you may have a good memory. As we discussed in an earlier chapter, perception is a participating function and you can be guilty of distortion without even knowing it. Note taking forces you to remain objective.

In addition to notes on what the subject says, you will want to record descriptive elements. What does the setting look like? What is the subject wearing? What other nuances of the experience can be collected and used later to give life and dimension to your story?

Take your notes as quickly as possible. It is a good idea for a reporter to know shorthand or to develop a personal shorthand consisting of abbreviations. It is a good idea to block out parts of a page to contain notes on similar issues. Another approach is to use a separate page for each new topic and flip back and forth as the answers move from one topic to another. As soon as you can after the interview, fill in everything else you can remember that has not already been written down. Then organize the notes in a logical pattern. This may require a rewrite or a photocopy and a cut-and-paste session.

PARTICIPATING IN THE JOURNALISTIC INTERVIEW

The Reporter

Most interviews are done at the subject's convenience. The reporter will want to arrange a time that is both suitable to a normal routine and that allows for enough time to cover the necessary questions. This, of course, is not always possible, and you may find yourself riding with a subject in a cab on the way to an airport or sitting in a neighborhood bar near closing time in the early hours of the morning. When there are time conflicts or when the subject is late, it is the reporter's schedule that has to be juggled, not the subject's. Be sure to leave yourself enough time. The subject should be allowed to talk as freely and for as long as he or she wants. If you indicate at the outset that you have another appointment or are rushed for some reason, the subject will react by shortening what might have been full and useful responses. The subject may also be insulted that you feel that your next appointment is more important than the present one.

If you are going to use recording equipment, make sure that it is working properly. Also, be sure to have note-taking apparatus available as a back-up if the equipment should fail. The most important factor in using recording equipment is getting permission to use it. Some subjects do not want their voices on tape for fear of possible identification; others simply fear being recorded. While not completely endorsing the use of tape recorders, Brady lists seven ways they can be potentially helpful:

> First, the interviewer can ask more questions in less time than the notetaker.
> Second, taped interviews tend to have that crisp ring of truth.
> Third, the interviewer can concentrate on the interview.
> Fourth, a taped interview is reassuring to an editor or publisher if the subject matter is at all controversial.
> Fifth, a tape recorder frees the writer on the road.
> Sixth, when the interviewer's hands are tied, a tape recorder is of real assistance. For instance, if a writer must interview a subject over lunch. . . .
> Seventh, tape recorders can be used for recording lengthy documents.[9]

Keep your questions as short as possible. Do not try to impress the subject with your knowledge of the issue or event. If the question requires some background, make it concise. Even though you have a plan as to where you want the interview to go, do not be afraid to follow a digression if the subject seems interested in it. You can weave your way back on track later, but the subject must not feel controlled. Most important, do not interrupt.

Do not shy away from tough questions. Tough questions are those that delve into the personal side of the subject's life and experience. The answers to tough questions often determine the difference between a mediocre or a very successful interview. When you ask a tough question—say, one regarding income, personal relationships, sexual preference, rumors of illegal activity—you cannot appear embarrassed by your own question. Place your toughest questions toward the end of the interview. Ask such questions with the same tone and intent as the rest of the questions you have asked. Indicate that you expect an answer. If an answer is not immediately forthcoming, you will have to make a judgment as to whether you should persist or let the issue drop.

Be professional, direct, businesslike, friendly when appropriate, interrogatory when appropriate, interested, accurate, and prepared. Keep your attention on getting the information you need for your story without missing a fruitful digression. When you have been granted an interview, do not abuse the privilege, but do not leave without the information you need.

The Subject

Being the subject of a journalistic interview is difficult to meet with indifference. As the subject, you are probably flattered by the notion that someone feels your experience or expertise is worth putting into print. If, however, you are at the center of an unpleasant situation, a tragedy, or a personal problem that has for some reason gained wider attention, you may be understandably reluctant to respond to the probes of a journalistic interview. First of all, if you do not want to be the subject of an interview, you are under no obligation to do so. Yet, if you want to participate, here are a few ground rules to keep in mind.

Remember your position in the event. You are the subject. You are the person with the pertinent information. While you may be pleased that you have been selected for an interview, do not lose sight of the fact that you are the one in control of the information. Often people are awed by the fame of an interviewer, perhaps because of television coverage, and they lose their perspective. You are under no obligation to reveal anything that you may regret seeing in print or broadcast over electronic media. Listen to each question carefully. If you do not understand the question or feel that you require additional background before answering, insist that such clarification or background be provided. Whenever possible, insist that the interview be conducted in a place that is comfortable for you. Weigh your answers carefully. Do not answer abruptly, and feel free to ask what the purpose of any particular question is. You also have a right to know exactly how the material collected from you will be used—where and when it will be broadcast or appear in print.

As the subject of a journalistic interview, you are clearly under greater pressure for a self-disclosure than the reporter. This does not mean that you are passive. You must be an active participant. You exercise control by only answering what you think is appropriate and in words and manner that you determine is proper for the response. Never see yourself as a victim. If you are worried about what a reporter will ask, request that questions be submitted to you in advance. A good subject is cooperative, direct, thorough, and truthful. But remember, as the subject, it is *your* interview. You may respond to questions you did not expect, but be sure that you include everything that you wanted to say. If you are flattered by the attention, enjoy it.

SUMMARY

In this chapter the technique and strategy of the journalistic interview have been examined. This type of interview takes us a step further along our self-disclosure continuum. The burden of response begins to fall even more significantly on one participant—the subject. A good journalist always requests a response. The proper mind-set for the journalistic interview begins with a sincere commitment to accuracy. Adequate preparation can make the difference between acquiring meaningful information and wasting your time—and the subject's time.

Questions for Study and Discussion

1. The chapter stresses that the journalist has a responsibility to be fair, accurate, and considerate of the consequences. Discuss the importance of this, perhaps citing examples from your own experience.

2. What is the purpose of research as part of your preparation?

3. Brady is very critical of "How-do-you-feel?" questions. What is his objection? Assume that you are interviewing someone who has just won a Gold Medal at the Olympics. Write five open questions that cause the person to discuss feelings without actually asking for feelings.

4. The following article was constructed from an interview. Read the article carefully and reconstruct the interview by writing the questions that would logically elicit the information contained in the reported responses of the subject. Then evaluate the technique and strategy. What would you have improved on? Why? How?

INVESTORS AT WORK

Jack Andrews's New Publishing Venture

It's not the first time he has started a magazine from scratch, but it's the first time he has ever done it on his own—the first business of his own.

March was a big month for Jack Andrews of Belmont. With March came the debut of *High-Tech Marketing*, a new national business trade magazine into which Andrews has poured a considerable amount of talent, financial reserve, and reputation. With the help of a single publishing-oriented investor from New York, Andrews has put together a start-up that he hopes will begin to make money in 1986 and that he hopes will keep him permanently off the payrolls of other publishers.

Andrews, a 46-year-old publishing veteran, is a former publisher of *Hospital Care Publications*, *National Druggist*, and *Men's Fashion*.

It was the founding of *Clothes International* in 1982 that really got Andrews going on the road to independent publishing. He was recruited by an investor to handle the start-up, but he says he felt frustrated by his nonequity position with the company. Eventually, he and the founder split apart, and Andrews once again found himself talking to other publishers.

"In July of 1983 I can recall saying to my wife that if I took a certain job which I was considering at the time, I would recommend that the company launch a new magazine combining the interests of high technology products with marketing," says Andrews. "My wife very casually said, 'Why don't you do it yourself?' And that was it. I really couldn't give a reason why not and I started working on it right away."

To launch a new magazine these days requires start-up capital of at least $500,000 and often many times more. Andrews, with a home and three teenagers to provide for, had no such funds available on his own. His financing came from a long-time associate in New York who operates a publishing service business. "He and I had worked together indirectly before, and we had built up a mutual respect for each other's work," says Andrews. The arrangement called for the investor to have a controlling interest in the paper, in return for contributing most of the needed start-up funds, a portion of which are in the form of loans to the company. Andrews, also with a major equity position, would serve as full-time publisher at an initially reduced salary. Total capitalization will be between $500,000 and $750,000, according to the publisher.

Andrews and his financing partner faced two immediate risks. The first is inherent with any publishing venture—it is all but impossible to forecast accurately the financial growth of the business. A publisher's market for readers and advertisers can only be broadly described as potential sources of revenue. The art of projecting sales and earnings for a product as nonessential as a magazine is usually just that—an art.

Also, Andrews faced a major challenge in that he was committing himself to the start-up of a new magazine without the most essential ingredient: an editor. Andrews had no editor in mind as he planned his start-up, and he eventually had to shop for that future key man for his publication by advertising in other newspapers and magazines. Luckily, he found a person whom he thinks is a perfect fit in Janet Marshall.

"I am not an editor, and I know that finding an editor is a pivotal step. We had to solve that problem or we would never succeed," Andrews explains. "But I didn't want to cancel the entire project just because I did not personally have an editor in mind. It was a risk that we had to take and it seems to have worked out OK."

Fortunately, Andrews did not face the same challenge in building a sales staff. He would start out handling all of the sales work himself. It was only a few weeks ago, in fact, that he hired his first sales person. "I feel very comfortable selling, and although I had never before even met a single one of our advertisers, I knew I would be able to handle that end of the job," he said.

Technology Journal was conceived last July. The magazine got the green light, in a sense, when Andrews struck his deal with a backer in August. He rented an office on September 23 with, at that time, one additional employee. And it was to be five more months before Andrews could send out his first invoice to begin to establish cash flow. During those months the costs mounted steadily: salaries, rent, postage, printing costs, market research, travel to visit advertisers all over the country, and countless other expenses. Andrews spent $5,000, for instance, subscribing to the 160 magazines that he could identify in the "high technology" field. These he had analyzed and, working with a service company, cataloged every single advertiser as a company engaged in marketing in the field. That list would form the basis for his own controlled mailing list that today numbers 10,000.

The first issue of Andrews's magazine came out with 50 pages of advertising, but that was not a true measure of selling success because the publisher had offered advertisers an introductory package giving large discounts for signing up for the nine issues of 1984. Advertisers would get the discount in the first few issues and they could cancel participation in future issues at any time. Sounds like a give away? "That's the way we had to do it," said Andrews. "It's very hard to get advertisers to commit themselves for something they haven't seen. How can you sell them space in a magazine that doesn't even exist?"

The second issue of *Technology Journal* came out with 47 ad pages, and the third had 55 pages. For these issues, the amount of discounting was less, so Andrews believes that he may be on the road to success. The single largest category of advertisers thus far has been the media companies, particularly publishers of technology-oriented magazines who are offering Andrews's readers a marketing outlet for their products.

"If the advertising keeps coming in, I think we'll do pretty well," said Andrews. "I'm still projecting that we'll turn profitable sometime in 1986, and if all goes well after that, we could pay back our original investment—some of the start-up capital was in the form of borrowed capital from the investor—by the end of 1986."

Andrews say he takes great pride in the fact that this is his own start-up, and that his wife (who has a job of her own) and his family have been very supportive. "The only thing that bothers me sometimes, aside from the uncertainty of knowing whether or not we'll be successful, is the relatively poor reputation of this publishing business. It's well known that nine out of ten new magazines fail, and it seems that a lot of people can get into the business fairly easily. It's kind of like the restaurant business. It bothers me that a lot of people right away say something like, 'Oh, not another magazine.' But I guess as long as they don't refuse to hear my story, that's something that I can live with."

Notes

1. John Brady, *The Craft of Interviewing* (New York: Random House, Vintage Books, 1977), 4.
2. Ibid., 7.
3. Ibid., 37.
4. Ibid., 49.
5. Ibid., 49–50.
6. Ibid., 52.
7. Ibid., 69–70.
8. Ibid., 71.
9. Ibid., 140–141.

8

Investigation, Interrogation, and Cross-Examination

Key Concepts

- Cross-Examination of Witnesses
- Leading Questions
- Collapsing the Lie Structure
- Using Nonverbal Communication

The following excerpt is from *Inherit the Wind*, by Jerome Lawrence and Robert E. Lee.

DRUMMOND: Look, Mr. Brady. These are the fossil remains of a prehistoric marine creature, which was found in this very county, and which lived here millions of years ago, when these very mountain ranges were submerged in water.

BRADY: I know. The Bible gives a fine account of the flood. But your professor is a little mixed up on his dates. That rock is not more than 6000 years old.

DRUMMOND: How do you know?

BRADY: A fine Biblical scholar, Bishop Usher, has determined for us the exact date and hour of the Creation. It occurred in the year 4004, B.C.

DRUMMOND: That's Bishop Usher's opinion.

BRADY: It is not an opinion. It is literal fact, which the good Bishop arrived at through careful computation of the ages of the prophets as set down in the Old Testament. In fact, he determined that the Lord began the Creation on the 23rd of October in the year 4004 B.C. at, uh, at 9 a.m.!

DRUMMOND: That Eastern Standard Time? *(Laughter)* Or Rocky Mountain Time? *(More laughter)* It wasn't Daylight Saving Time, was it? Because the Lord didn't make the sun until the fourth day!

BRADY: *(Fidgeting)* That is correct.

DRUMMOND: *(Sharply)* That first day. Was it a 24-hour day?

BRADY: The Bible says it was a day.

DRUMMOND: There wasn't any sun. How do you know how long it was?

BRADY: *(Determined)* The Bible says it was a day.

DRUMMOND: A normal day, a literal day, a 24-hour day?

(Pause. Brady is unsure.)

BRADY: I do not know.

DRUMMOND: What do you think?

BRADY: *(Floundering)* I do not think about things that . . . I do not think about!

DRUMMOND: Do you ever think about things that you *do* think about?

(There is some laughter. But it is dampened by the knowledge and awareness throughout the courtroom, that the trap is about to be sprung.)

DRUMMOND: Isn't it possible that first day was *25* hours long? There was no way to measure it, no way to tell! *Could* it have been 24 hours?

(Pause. The entire courtroom seems to lean forward.)

BRADY: *(Hesitates)* It is . . . *possible. . . .*

(Drummond's got him. And he knows it! This is the turning point. From here on, the tempo mounts. Drummond is now fully in the driver's seat. He pounds his questions faster and faster.)

DRUMMOND: Oh. You interpret that the first day recorded in the Book of Genesis could be of indeterminate length.

BRADY: *(Wriggling)* I mean to state that the day referred to is not necessarily a 24-hour day.

DRUMMOND: It could have been 30 hours! Or a month! Or a year! Or a hundred years! *(He brandishes the rock underneath Brady's nose) Or ten million years!*

DAVENPORT: I protest! This is not only irrelevant, immaterial—it is *illegal*!

(There is excited reaction in the courtroom. The judge pounds for order, but the emotional tension will not subside.)

DAVENPORT: I demand to know the purpose of Mr. Drummond's examination! What is he trying to do?

(Both Brady and Drummond crane forward, hurling their answers not at the court, but at each other.)

BRADY: I'll tell you what he's trying to do! He wants to destroy everybody's belief in the Bible and in God!
DRUMMOND: You know that's not true. I'm trying to stop you bigots and ignoramuses from controlling the education of the United States! And you know it!

(Arms out, Davenport pleads to the court, but is unheard. The judge hammers for order.)

JUDGE: *(Shouting)* I shall ask the bailiff to clear the court, unless there is order here.
BRADY: How dare you attack the Bible.
DRUMMOND: The Bible is a book. A good book. But it's not the *only* book.
BRADY: It is the revealed word of the Almighty. God spake to the men who wrote the Bible.
DRUMMOND: And how do you know that God didn't "spake" to Charles Darwin?
BRADY: I know because God tells me to oppose the evil teachings of that man.
DRUMMOND: Oh. God speaks to you.
BRADY: Yes.
DRUMMOND: He tells you exactly what's right and what's wrong?
BRADY: *(Doggedly)* Yes.
DRUMMOND: And you act accordingly?
BRADY: Yes.
DRUMMOND: So you, Matthew Harrison Brady, through oratory, legislation, or whatever, pass along God's orders to the rest of the world! *(Laughter begins)* Gentlemen, meet the "Prophet from Nebraska!"

(Brady's oratory is unassailable; but his vanity—exposed by Drummond's prodding—is only funny. The laughter is painful to Brady. He starts to answer Drummond, then turns toward the spectators and tries, almost physically, to suppress the amused reaction. This only makes it worse.)

BRADY: *(Almost inarticulate)* I . . . please . . . !
DRUMMOND: *(With increasing tempo, closing in)* Is that the way of things? God tells Brady what is good! To be against Brady is to be against God!

(More laughter.)

BRADY: *(Confused)* No, no! Each man is a free agent. . . .

DRUMMOND: Then what is Bertram Cates doing in the Hillsboro jail? *(Some applause)* Suppose Mr. Cates had enough influence and lung power to railroad through the State Legislature a law that only *Darwin* should be taught in the schools!

BRADY: Ridiculous, ridiculous! There is only one great Truth in the world. . . .

DRUMMOND: The Gospel according to Brady! God speaks to Brady, and Brady tells the world! Brady, Brady, Brady Almighty!

(Drummond bows grandly. The crowd laughs.)

BRADY: The Lord is my strength. . . .

DRUMMOND: What if a lesser human being—a Cates or a Darwin—has the audacity to think that God might whisper to *him*? That an un-Brady thought might still be holy? Must men go to prison because they are at odds with the self-appointed prophet?

(Brady is now trembling so that it is impossible for him to speak. He rises, towering above his tormentor, rather like a clumsy, lumbering bear that is baited by an agile dog.)

DRUMMOND: Extend the Testaments! Let us have a Book of Brady! We shall hex the Pentateuch, and slip you in neatly between Numbers and Deuteronomy!

(At this, there is another burst of laughter. Brady is almost in a frenzy.)

BRADY: *(Reaching for a sympathetic ear, trying to find the loyal audience that has slipped away from him)* My friends . . . Your Honor . . . My Followers . . . Ladies and Gentlemen. . . .

DRUMMOND: The witness is excused.

BRADY: *(Unheeding)* All of you know what I stand for! What I believe! I believe, I believe in the truth of the Book of Genesis! *(Beginning to chant)* Exodus, Leviticus, Numbers, Deuteronomy, Joshua, Judges, Ruth, First Samuel, Second Samuel, First Kings, Second Kings,. . . . .

DRUMMOND: Your Honor, this completes the testimony. The witness is excused!

The characteristics of the investigative interview vary in degree, not in kind, between the various types. The preceding scene, famous for its theatricality and brilliant construction, is based on the actual cross-examination of William Jennings Bryan by Clarence Darrow at the "Scopes Monkey Trial." What distinguishes this as cross-examination is the circumstance within which it takes place. The courtroom setting establishes the event as cross-examination. If the same scene between these two men took place elsewhere, it might have been interrogation. In this chapter we will examine the characteristics of investigative interviewing and sharpen our strategies for employing investigation when it is called for. We will distinguish three types: investigation, interrogation, and cross-examination.

INVESTIGATION

Investigation means the systematic questioning of persons who have knowledge of an event or persons involved in the event or circumstances surrounding an event, including documentary or physical evidence. As an investigator, you should form no preliminary judgments about the person being investigated or the event itself.

With investigation we move further along the self-disclosure continuum. In this case the respondent or witness is dramatically limited in his or her information-collecting opportunity. Even with the journalistic interview, there was considerable opportunity to question the reporter and limit responses. In investigation, the respondent may be required to answer regardless of feelings.

The Uses of Investigation

The most obvious use of investigation is associated with law enforcement agencies. When a crime has been committed or suspected, an investigation ensues that depends heavily on investigative interview. Sometimes journalists employ investigative techniques to uncover criminal activity or other kinds of newsworthy items. Lawyers also use investigative interviewing to gather facts for the defense or prosecution of a case. Welfare agencies investigate potential fraud. Adoption agencies need to investigate in order to develop an accurate profile of potential parents. Parents themselves become investigators when their son or daughter is three hours late coming home. Investigative interviewing is used variously by arbitrators, clergy, accrediting boards, discipline committees, congressional committees, and a host of others. Each of us engages in more investigative activity than we are aware of. Whenever we need accurate information from someone about a situation or event—particularly if the situation or event has disturbing overtones, like an accident, crime, or breach of discipline—we use investigative interview strategy.

Characteristics of the Investigative Interview

The investigative interview is closed in style. It is highly directive and gives few opportunities to stray from the main purpose. The investigator is clearly in control from the outset. You must establish this control strongly in the opening game. Effective investigation also exhibits a tight structure of questioning, although not necessarily obvious to the respondent. The answers acquired should be detailed, in some cases quantifiable, and useful as comparisons with other methods of data collecting. An example follows:

MR. JONES: Stanley, I called you in because I need your help in solving a mystery. [Orientation]

STANLEY: A mystery, Mr. Jones?

MR. JONES: Yes. You are aware that we are the only people assembling and distributing the XB47 widget? [Leading]

STANLEY: Of course, I helped set up the assembly line six months ago. What's this all about?

MR. JONES: We've got a problem, Stanley. A load of XB47's showed up on the open market out of Hartford. [Fact statement]

STANLEY: What? We don't have an outlet in Hartford.

MR. JONES: Not only showed up, but at $2 a piece cheaper. [Additional fact statement]

STANLEY: How could that happen?

MR. JONES: That's what I'm hoping you can help me with. There's a leak in our supply system somewhere, and that's your responsibility. Let's put our heads together and come up with some answers. [Orientation]

STANLEY: I can't believe that one of my guys is ripping off widgets.

MR. JONES: When you were on vacation last month, Sam covered for you, right? [Leading]

STANLEY: Yeah, but Sam . . . I mean, he's been here ten years.

MR. JONES: Where else could they come from? Your department logs everything that leaves the warehouse. [Closed]

STANLEY: Except the rejects.

MR. JONES: The rejects? [Closed probe] These widgets in Hartford were up to standard. [Fact statement]

STANLEY: Well, quality control takes substandard widgets off the line. Maybe some good ones got mixed in.

MR. JONES: Who double checks the widgets? [Closed]

STANLEY: No one. When QC says "out," they get sent to a holding area for meltdown.

MR. JONES: So, what you're saying is, it's possible these widgets came from the rejects? [Mirror]

Mr. Jones is on to something. He has used good investigative skills to focus Stanley's attention on the problem. He begins by soliciting Stanley's aid because Stanley is in charge of the department where the problem appears to be occurring. He quickly establishes control with a closed lead, "You are aware that we are the only people assembling and distributing the XB47 widget?" He follows immediately with a fact that contradicts the established belief, ". . . a load of XB47's showed up on the open market out of Hartford." This tight structural pattern creates great pressure to respond. Stanley, even if guilty, doesn't want to be accused, "How could that happen?" The attempt

to relieve the pressure by throwing the ball back fails when Jones returns it, "That's what I'm hoping you can help me with."

Why interview Stanley unless there is suspicion that he is guilty? Because he is close to the circumstances and has information that can be correlated with other methods of investigation. The strategy here is the selection of a leading question followed by a contradictory fact followed by a closed question or series of closed questions capped by a mirror, which ends the segment.

Preparing for the Investigative Interview

The following steps are good advice for a variety of interview situations and are crucial for investigation:[1]

1. Collect all necessary records and materials that are currently available. This will enable you to develop your strategy and avoid diluting your effect or wasting time asking obvious questions.
2. Based on your available information, develop specific objectives. What do you want the interview to accomplish?
3. Create a list of questions and arrange them strategically. It is important that you direct and control the progress of the interview. Prepared questions will keep you on track and keep the interview moving.
4. If the interview will not take place in your office or another place familiar to you, find out as much as you can about the setting.
5. Make sure there will be no distractions or interruptions. The effectiveness of an investigative strategy depends a great deal on the momentum it creates. Interruptions make opportunities for respondents to develop evasive or untruthful answers.
6. Be prepared to take notes. The taking of notes positions the interview as a serious event. If the respondent is inclined to provide information, more detail will be provided and answers will be more carefully drawn if notes are being taken.
7. Be sure of your own frame of mind. Are you in the right mood to conduct this interview? You need objectivity to listen carefully and evaluate the responses. Regardless of what the respondent says or does, you cannot respond emotionally.
8. Suppress your suspicions. Make no prejudgments. Focus your attention on your objectives and your strategy.

Participating in the Investigative Interview

The Investigator The opening game still requires rapport building. The more you put the respondent at ease, the more information you will get. Orientation must be focused on your need to acquire information about a particular set of circumstances, event(s), or person(s), not on the individual being questioned. Assuming you are not questioning a guilty party, you need to build trust. Explain why you need the information, how it will be used, and whether or not it will remain confidential.

The middle game requires continual maintenance of control. While some open questions may be effective for broad-ranging investigative interviews, you will use more leading, probing, and closing questions to accomplish specific information objectives.

There are some special requirements for the closing, particularly if the investigation is to be ongoing. Use the following five points as a guide:

1. Give the respondent a short summary of what was accomplished.
2. Give the respondent an opportunity to make any statements or ask any questions.
   A chance to alter any previous information.
   A chance to make additions or deletions.
   "Is there any additional information you would like me to know before we end this interview?"
3. Indicate the next step to be taken.
   Will there be additional interviews?
   Do you have all the information you need?
4. Do not expect to finish the interview with a neatly wrapped package with a solution all worked out. Leave the door open for further interviews.
5. Encourage the respondent to call if she/he has any questions.

The Respondent It is not often pleasant to be the subject of an investigation. Most people today seem to shun the notion of coming forward to offer information on an accident or crime they may have witnessed. The reasons usually cited include the time and inconvenience and a fear of reprisal on the part of the criminal. I will not stand in judgment of anyone's actions in favor of the safety of themselves and their families. That remains a matter of individual conscience. However, inconvenience is not a good excuse. As a citizen and a member of a civilized community, you should provide, within your ability to do so, information that may help to bring an issue into focus or aid in the determination of truth.

Every situation does not require you to respond in the same way. Consider who the investigator is: a family member? clergyman? officer of the law? If you find yourself involved in an investigation that concerns legal issues, do not hesitate to exercise your right to have a lawyer present. A lawyer can advise you of the liabilities involved in answering certain questions and can protect you from incriminating yourself. However, all investigative situations do not take place in a legal setting. In those instances careful, thoughtful responses can be given freely.

I emphasize the words *careful* and *thoughtful* because some respondents get caught up in their own self-importance as being the key to a mystery, and they begin to embellish and interpret the actual facts and observations. This can be very damaging to the investigation because it obscures the real issues with superfluous or fictitious observations. Answer as truthfully and specifically as you can. Where you are unsure, be candid about your confusion. Remain as detached and unemotional as possible. Listen to the questions carefully, and have the investigator repeat or rephrase questions that are unclear to you. If you disagree with a leading question, ask that it be stated another way. If you sense you are being accused of something, stop answering all questions and consult an attorney.

INTERROGATION

Interrogation is the questioning of suspects and of uncooperative witnesses for the purpose of obtaining evidence or proof of significant omissions to previous testimony. It allows the respondent an opportunity to volunteer facts that might put existing evidence in a different light. The interrogator has already made a preliminary judgment. Interrogation tests the validity of that judgment. The pressure for self-disclosure on the part of the respondent is intense while almost nonexistent for the interrogator.

The Uses of Interrogation

As with investigative interviewing, interrogation takes place in a variety of settings, but law enforcement agencies are the primary users of the strategy. The term *interrogation* conjures in some minds images of torture, brutality, and psychological assaults. Certainly, history provides us with enough real examples to substantiate these images. We will not examine such extreme strategies but will focus on the more acceptable practice of extracting information through the use of skilled questioning strategy.

Characteristics of Interrogation

Like the investigative approach, interrogation is highly structured with emphasis placed on leading, closed, and mirror questions. However, while the tone of the investigative interview is neutral and spirited inquiry, interrogation is skeptical and aggressive. An example of interrogation is presented in the following exchange:

DETECTIVE: Where were you last night? [Closed]
SUSPECT: Around.
DETECTIVE: Around where? [Probe]
SUSPECT: Just around.
DETECTIVE: You were seen in the vicinity of Joe's Pawn Shop. [Factual observation]

SUSPECT: So, I was seen. So what?

DETECTIVE: Listen. I pulled your record. You've done two felony stretches already. You missed your last two appointments with your parole officer. Maybe we'll send you back up. You don't want to go back up, do you? [Leading]

SUSPECT: Why can't you leave a guy alone? I didn't do anything.

DETECTIVE: Somebody broke the window at Joe's and grabbed some watches. We think it was you. We've got somebody who makes you at the scene. [Factual statement]

SUSPECT: So, I was around there. I didn't break any window.

DETECTIVE: You were around there but didn't do anything? [Mirror] You want to do some hard time? [Closed] You better eat those watches. If they turn up anywhere, we'll know about it, and it's going to lead right back to you. You want to do 20 years for a few watches? [Closed]

SUSPECT: What if the watches got returned? [Open]

In the preceding scenario, the detective uses closed and leading questions mixed with facts or speculation that focuses the suspect's attention on the potential consequences. This is a power strategy used to effect change in the respondent's behavior. In describing power strategy, William J. McEwen says:

> What distinguishes the "power" approach is its customary focus on specific types of punishments and rewards: economic, political, and moral. . . . Power strategies usually emphasize the differences between the change proponent and the potential adopter in terms of reward control. The approach assumes that those with lesser power, of whatever type, will usually comply with the changes advocated by those with the greater power.[2]

McEwen points out that having the power is not enough. You must communicate the fact of your power to the subject.

> Acutally possessing some amount of power may be insufficient, however. The potential adopters must *perceive* the change proponent as actually having the sort of control over economic, political, moral, or physical rewards that has been claimed. It does no good to threaten an employer with a strike, a county school system with a cut in appropriations, or a mugger with a black eye, if such powers are not at your disposal, or if the potential adopter does not feel you are capable of carrying out the threat.[3]

Participating in the Interrogation Interview

The Interrogator The same basic preparation takes place for interrogation as outlined for investigative interviewing. The only difference is that you have made a judgment that you hope the interrogation will support. Your basic information now becomes evidence to support your judgment. You will want to direct carefully the interview, and so you should prepare a list of questions and facts arranged in a power sequence. Rapport building is not a primary issue in interrogation unless you are working as a team with another interrogator in the classic "good guy-bad guy" routine. In this approach one interrogator is overtly hostile and threatening while the second appears friendly and sympathetic. The respondent may be encouraged to talk to the "good guy" to avoid the wrath of the "bad guy." Do not abandon all attempts at establishing rapport, but if the situation calls for interrogation, it probably has passed beyond the friendly stage into an adversary relationship.

Again, concentration and careful listening play a large part in the success of interrogation. Royal and Schutt list seven signs to look for in determining if a respondent is withholding information:

1. Attempts to evade any question.
2. Vague answers.
3. Physical actions and appearance that contradict what is being said.
4. Conflicting information received at different points during the interrogation to the same or similar questions.
5. Information from other sources indicating that he/she has other knowledge.
6. Circumstances placing the respondent in a position to know certain information.
7. Inconsistencies: respondent knows some things, therefore should know other things that happen at the same time in the same place.[4]

It is sometimes effective to get the respondent thinking about how the situation appears from your side. Try open questions like, "What would you think if a person refused to talk about a situation?" The implication is that silence or evasiveness could be interpreted as guilt. If a respondent is totally unwilling to talk, switch to topics on which he or she is willing to talk freely. Once the respondent is talking, try another line of questioning to get at your information. When a question is evaded or unanswered, reframe the question and continue to press until you get the answer you want. Again, the respondent must be continually reminded of the consequences of not responding truthfully. The alternative consequences must be made to appear the more attractive of the two options, as in, "There is no pleasant way to resolve this problem, but if you cooperate with me and admit what you've done, it will go easier on you." Also, never allow yourself to be put on the defensive or let yourself become involved in a discussion that is irrelevant to the information that you want.

Distortions and lies are best handled by poking holes in the structure on which the fabrication is built. Point out enough inconsistencies and the entire structure will crumble, leaving the respondent with two options: silence or truth. The five points that follow provide some guidelines for handling distortions of fact or lies:

1. Confront the individual making the assertion with open and frank disbelief.

2. Do not confront with terms such as, "You're a damn liar."
3. Phrases to use in a challenging circumstance:
   Tell me more, this is extremely interesting to me, for I had heard it differently from someone else.
   Are you sure that you couldn't be mistaken? After all, I had the feeling that. . . .
4. Let respondent know that you are not going to let him get away with fabrication, but at the same time give him a face-saving way to get out of the situation.
5. If the respondent will not retract his/her statement, do not pursue the issue. However, do not imply in any way that you are accepting the story. In this situation the following phrases are useful: "Well, let's drop the subject; we can come back to it later, after we have had time to do some more investigation of the facts."

In summary, interrogation is an effective method of confirming prior judgments by extracting information from reluctant or hostile respondents. It is not for amateurs. There are legal boundaries that cannot be crossed without doing serious damage to an investigation. It is hoped that the guidelines and suggestions provided above will sensitize you to some of the factors operating in the interrogation interview. They are no substitute for adequate apprenticeship with a seasoned professional.

The Respondent There is little, if any, justification for committing crime or withholding or distorting the truth to thwart an investigation. My comments here are limited to one issue, that is, you have rights when you are being interrogated and should not be subjected to methods or strategies that violate these rights. If you are being arrested, it is the obligation of the arresting officer to inform you of these rights, as stated in the Miranda decision.

The Fifth Amendment to the Constitution of the United States provides that no person shall be compelled to be a witness against him/herself. In other words, no one can be compelled to make incriminating statements. When such statements are introduced as evidence, proof that the statement was voluntary must be submitted.

Courts have held that a sharing of voluntariness means that the accused was aware of the right not to make a statement. Some type of rights warning is generally required.

The U.S. Supreme Court, in *Miranda* v. *Arizona*, delivered a strict rights advisal. However, the Miranda warning requirement pertains only to custodial interrogation, that is, after arrest.

1. You have the right to remain silent and refuse to answer questions. Do you understand?
2. Anything you do say may be used against you in a court of law. Do you understand?

3. You have the right to consult an attorney before speaking to the police and to have an attorney present during any questioning now or in the future. Do you understand?
4. If you cannot afford an attorney, one will be provided for you without cost. Do you understand?
5. If you do not have an attorney available, you have the right to remain silent until you have an opportunity to consult with one. Do you understand?

CROSS-EXAMINATION

At the outset, I want to acknowledge my dependence in this section on the work of Francis L. Wellman. His book *The Art of Cross-Examination* first appeared in 1903 and subsequently in 4 editions and 50 printings. The serious student of cross-examination may whet the appetite here, but should read Wellman's book in its entirety. Wellman helps us understand the nature of cross-examination this way:

> No cause reaches the stage of litigation unless there are two sides to it. If the witnesses on one side deny or qualify the statements made by those on the other, which side is telling the truth? . . . . The opinions of which side are warped by prejudice or blinded by ignorance? Which side has had the power or opportunity of correct observation? How shall we tell, how make it apparent to a jury of disinterested men who are to decide between litigants? Obviously, by the means of cross-examination.[5]

While the courtroom is the most obvious place to find cross-examination, it is not the only place. With the rise of arbitration in labor disputes and other matters of disagreement among commercial enterprises, cross-examination has found wider usage. However, there are certain characteristics common to all cross-examination situations. Your interview of a respondant, whom we will call a witness, is to some degree in response to a previous interview of the same witness that you have observed. Cross-examination is necessary when a witness has said things that are materially damaging to your side of the issue. It is also the logical response when a witness has made an impression on a jury or arbitrator that is against you. Every witness should not be cross-examined. You need to consider if you can bring out some new facts that would shed a favorable light on your side of the issue. A witness who is truthful and candid need only be asked straight and specific questions, as you would in any investigation. "If, however," Wellman says, "there is any reason to doubt the willingness of the witness to help develop the truth, it may be necessary to proceed with more caution, and possibly to put the witness in a position where it will appear to the jury that he could tell a good deal if he wanted to, and then leave him. The jury will thus draw the inference that, had he spoken, it would have been in our favor."[6]

Skilled cross-examiners are keen observers. They can sense whether a witness has made an honest mistake or is purposely telling a lie. Cross-examination in each case would follow a different line. There is a difference between discrediting testimony and discrediting a witness. Wellman knows the value of reading nonverbal cues:

> A skillful cross-examiner seldom takes his eye from an important witness while he is being examined by his adversary. Every expression of his face, especially his mouth, even every movement of his hands, his manner of expressing himself, his whole bearing—all help the examiner to arrive at an accurate estimate of his integrity.[7]

Unless a witness is an out-and-out liar, he or she has probably come to court to tell the facts and circumstances as he or she believes them to be. Any attack on the witness's view of the truth is certainly going to meet with resistance and hostility. Add to this the fact that juries tend to be sympathetic to witnesses, and you can see the necessity for approaching the cross-examination with care. Wellman suggests using a conciliatory tone and common courtesy to relieve the witness's tension about being cross-examined and fear of you. The key is to draw the witness into a discussion of the testimony that points out the weaknesses and inconsistencies. There will be times when you have to take a harder line, as when the witness evades or refuses to answer a question. Wellman tells an anecdote concerning one of Lord Russell's cross-examinations:

> Once when cross-examining a witness by the name of Sampson, who was sued for libel as editor of the *Referee*, Russell asked the witness a question which he did not answer. "Did you hear my question?" said Russell in a low voice. "I did," said Sampson. "Did you understand it?" asked Russell, in a still lower voice. "I did," said Sampson. "Then," said Russell, raising his voice to its highest pitch, and looking as if he would spring from his place and seize the witness by the throat, "why have you not answered it? Tell the jury why you have not answered it." A thrill of excitement ran through the court room. Samson was overwhelmed, and he never pulled himself together again.[8]

Wellman goes on to summarize the characteristics a good cross-examiner exhibits during the interview.

> Speak distinctly yourself and compel your witness to do so. Bring out your points so clearly that men of the most ordinary intelligence can understand them. Keep your audience, the jury, always interested and on the alert. Remember it is the minds of the jury you are addressing, even though your question is put to the witness.[9]

Wellman's final point highlights a characteristic that is unique to cross-examination: It takes place before an audience. The outcome of the interview will be determined in some measure by how you present yourself as well as how you ask questions and the answers you receive.

Participating in Cross-Examination

The Cross-Examiner Keeping in mind the point made immediately above, think of yourself as a member of the jury. Try to see the evidence through their eyes. Avoid the temptation to play to an audience in order to make a reputation for yourself. Think only of winning your side of the case. After all, that is usually why you are being paid.

In the opening game, make particular effort to establish rapport and put the witness at ease. Aside from the research and investigative material you have brought with you, you have been carefully listening to and watching the witness while he/she is being questioned by the opposition. If you have detected an inconsistency or other weak spot in the testimony, go right to that point as you move into the middle game. Does the witness have a direct interest in the outcome of the case? Did the witness actually observe the incident with the detail provided or were some of the details brought into focus through the examination of counsel? If the witness was in a position to observe the facts correctly, does the witness have the intelligence or knowledge to absorb and interpret the facts correctly? How recently has the observation of the facts taken place? Answering these questions forms the basis of your strategy. This strategy is emphasized by Wellman, as seen in the following statements:

> All these considerations should readily suggest a line of questions, varying with each witness examined, that will, if closely followed, be likely to separate appearance from reality and to reduce exaggerations to their proper proportions. It must further be borne in mind that the jury should not merely see the mistake; they should be made to appreciate at the time why and whence it arose.[10]

Unless you have observed a weak point in the testimony, do not ask the witness to repeat what he has just said in hope that an inconsistency will appear. More likely, the testimony will make an even stronger impression on the jury the second time. Always in your tone of questioning, indicate that you believe the witness is telling the truth and that you want to be fair. Inconsistencies must be drawn out by inference since witnesses are afraid of self-contradiction and will go to great lengths to conceal it. Wellman warns that if you induce a witness to provide a contradictory statement, do not pounce on it and make the witness repeat it. Chances are the witness, now put on guard, will correct the statement and diminish its effect. Point out this contradiction in the summation.

Try not to ask questions, particularly critical ones, unless you are reasonably sure of the answer. The following example illustrates this point:

LAWYER: *So, it is your opinion that Mr. Jones was not intoxicated.*
WITNESS: *That's right.*
LAWYER: *And yet you say he was staggering about and knocking things down in the store.*

WITNESS: Yes.
LAWYER: Well, if he wasn't drunk, why was he staggering around?
WITNESS: Insulin shock.
LAWYER: Insulin shock? What credentials do you have to make such a diagnosis?
WITNESS: I am a diabetic.

Through research and investigation, find out all that you can about a witness who will be cross-examined. If you are uncertain about an answer, do not ask the question. You can sense when you are on a dangerous track when the line of questioning is proceeding obviously and easily toward a discrepancy and the witness is making no attempt to slow or alter the process.

The cross-examiner should use the entire arsenal of questions available. Success in a cross-examination often depends on the ability to move quickly from one type of question to another as opportunities arise. One factor, however, that distinguishes the technique of cross-examination from other types of interview is the regular and continuous use of mirror questions. The mirror forces the witness to examine and confirm his or her own testimony while highlighting the progress of the interview for the jury. In the following segment of cross-examination attributed to Abraham Lincoln, the witness has testified to having been present at the scene of a murder and has positively identified the accused as the murderer. Lincoln uses a combination of mirror, leading, and closed questions to point out a major discrepancy in the testimony:

LINCOLN: And you were with Lockwood just before and saw the shooting? [Mirror]
WITNESS: Yes.
LINCOLN: And you stood very near to them? [Mirror]
WITNESS: No, about 20 feet away.
LINCOLN: May it not have been 10 feet? [Leading]
WITNESS: No, it was 20 feet or more.
LINCOLN: In the open field? [Leading]
WITNESS: No, in the timber.
LINCOLN: What kind of timber? [Closed]
WITNESS: Beech timber.
LINCOLN: Leaves on it are rather thick in August? [Leading]
WITNESS: Rather.
LINCOLN: And you think this pistol was the one used? [Leading]
WITNESS: It looks like it.
LINCOLN: You could see the defendant shoot—see how the barrel hung, and all about it? [Mirror]
WITNESS: Yes.
LINCOLN: How near was this to the meeting place? [Closed]
WITNESS: Three-quarters of a mile away.
LINCOLN: Where were the lights? [Closed]
WITNESS: Up by the minister's stand.
LINCOLN: Three-quarters of a mile away? [Mirror]

WITNESS: Yes—I answered ye twiste [you twice].
LINCOLN: Did you not see a candle there, with Lockwood or Grayson?
WITNESS: No! What would we want a candle for?
LINCOLN: How, then, did you see the shooting? [Closed]
WITNESS: By moonlight!
LINCOLN: You saw this shooting at ten at night—in beech timber, three-quarters of a mile from the light—saw the pistol barrel—saw the man fire—saw it 20 feet away—saw it all by moonlight? Saw it nearly a mile from the camp lights? [Mirror]
WITNESS: Yes, I told you so before.

The interest was now so intense that men leaned forward to catch the smallest syllable. Then the lawyer drew out a blue-covered almanac from his side pocket—opened it slowly—offered it in evidence—showed it to the jury and the court—read from a page with careful deliberation that the moon on that night was unseen and only arose at one the next morning.[11]

While some cross-examination can take days or even weeks to complete, many cross-examinations are extremely short. In an article for the *New York Times*, Irving Younger, a law professor and Washington attorney, recounts a cross-examination that consisted of four questions. Defending the *Washington Post* against William P. Tavoulareas, the president of Mobil Oil Corporation, in a libel case, Younger cross-examined a trucking executive about what a dynamic executive Mr. Tavoulareas was. The witness had stressed that he did not depend on Mobil for business and was a completely independent and unbiased admirer. Here is their exchange:

YOUNGER: Mr. Hoffman, did you just get into Washington just about an hour ago?
HOFFMAN: About an hour and a half, I would think.
YOUNGER: Did you come up from Florida?
HOFFMAN: No, I did not.
YOUNGER: Where did you come from?
HOFFMAN: Indianapolis.
YOUNGER: How did you get from Indianapolis to Washington?
HOFFMAN: On a Mobil corporate jet.[12]

Unlike most other forms of interview, a cross-examination tends to end abruptly. When you have uncovered the information or discrepancy you were seeking, simply dismiss the witness without a formal end game. On occasion, you might want to thank a witness for cooperating or, failing to get the answer you want during the normal course of cross-examination, you might recall the witness quickly after just dismissing him and casually ask a crucial question as if it were just a matter-of-fact issue. The confusion of being dismissed and recalled in rapid succession sometimes puts a witness off guard and the answer is provided without hesitation.

In summary, you have only two options in the cross-examination interview: discredit the testimony or discredit the witness. Cross-examination strategies are difficult to employ, are effective and exciting when they work, and are disastrous when they fail. Your best apprenticeship is at the side of an experienced trial lawyer. But you have to start somewhere. Younger recounts his first big break as a fledgling federal prosecutor in New York City. He was sitting in to watch a more experienced prosecutor examine a witness in a fraud case:

> Kevin gives me a jab in the ribs and says, "You conduct the direct examination," first news I had that I was going to do it. . . .
>
> Oh boy, I went from thinking, "This is the greatest stuff I ever saw," to, "Why am I here, I don't want to do this." You can imagine the fright, my heart was pounding and I was praying I would remain continent, that's how scared I was.
>
> Finally I managed to say, "What is your name?" And as I ask him that question, his eyes grow as wide as saucers, and the whites of his eyes turn up, and over he goes, out cold and unconscious.
>
> It's a good thing he went . . . because otherwise I might have gone first.[13]

The Witness I suppose the first thing to remember when you are the object of cross-examination is that you are usually under oath. As such, you are obligated to tell the truth or face prosecution yourself. Again, it is not my purpose to help you evade punishment if you are guilty of a crime or otherwise feel compelled to cover up or distort the truth. There are, however, circumstances when any of us may be called on to be a witness because we have some special knowledge of people, places, or things that have a bearing on a particular case. For these circumstances I offer the following suggestions:

1. Answer the questions as directly and completely as possible. If you do not understand a question, ask the cross-examiner for clarification.
2. Avoid the temptation to embellish the truth. If the subject you are asked about happened some time ago and you have difficulty remembering, say so. Filling in from your imagination only distorts the issue and could cause a miscarriage of justice.
3. If for some reason you find a question particularly disturbing, ask the judge if it is necessary for you to answer it. Do not always depend on counsel to be sensitive to your needs or feelings, even if he or she is on your side of the issue.
4. Try to relax and think through your answers. Do not allow the cross-examiner to bully you into saying something you do not believe or do not mean. Keep your composure. Remember, much of what the cross-examiner does is to impress the jury. You have little to gain by entering into a battle of wits.

5. Listen to the mirror questions. Is that what you said? Is that what you meant? If the mirror seems distorted, clarify or correct the words and interpretation of your meaning.
6. Listen for inconsistencies in your own testimony. It is possible through cross examination that you will remember things or realize discrepancies that shed a new light on the facts as you originally interpreted them. In such an instance, do not stick doggedly to your original position simply to avoid embarrassment. The cross-examiner, having uncovered the inconsistency, will keep hammering at it anyway. No one, least of all members of the jury, expects you to have a perfect memory. Besides, there is a natural empathy for the witness which places the jury on your side.

SUMMARY

This chapter has explored a special form of interview—interview that is designed to compel a subject to provide information. Three types were discussed: investigation, interrogation and cross-examination. We covered some of the uses and characteristics of each and looked at them from the points of view of both the investigator and the subject. In its most common manifestations, the form appears to be closed, structured, and dependent on some of the less common questioning techniques, such as leading and mirror questions in abundance and succession. This form places intense pressure for self-disclosure on the part of the subject, often with the threat of legal sanction.

Questions for Study and Discussion

1. Many successful trial lawyers subscribe to the theory that you should never ask a question in a cross-examination to which you do not already know the answer. Discuss the reasons for this. When would you knowingly violate this rule?

2. The difference between investigation and interrogation has more to do with the attitude of the questioner. What defines the difference?

3. The chapter has focused on this form as a relatively closed and controlled form of interview. When and in what circumstances might you use an open technique for investigation?

4. The following is a reprint of a script from a broadcast of CBS-TV's "60 Minutes." It makes certain allegations about a doctor's misuse of MediCal, California's Medicaid program. The reprint of these materials does not mean that I believe these allegations to be true. Its use is intended to sharpen our skills of investigation, interrogation, and cross-examination.

The names of the people involved have been changed. Read the script and respond to the following questions and suggestions:

a. Examine Wallace's technique and strategy. What form of investigation does he tend to use?
b. Assume you have the opportunity to cross-examine Dr. Hendler. What questions would you ask? How would you arrange your questions in a series?
c. You are interrogating Dr. Rubin. Have another person play the role and apply your strategy.

MIKE WALLACE: The Los Angeles grand jury has for months been hearing testimony in a criminal investigation conducted by the MediCal Fraud Unit of the California attorney general's office, an investigation into the activities of one Dr. Edward Rubin and his associates. Now, the State of California spends more than $4 billion every year on MediCal—that's what they call Medicaid out there. It's medical treatment for folks who couldn't otherwise afford health care, and it's paid for by you and me, the taxpayers. The money goes to doctors and hospitals, clinics and labs. And the doctor Edward Rubin who is the object of that investigation by the MediCal Fraud Unit in California is typical, we are told, of those physicians nationwide who've been building empires on these public medical dollars. Rubin has been doing it for almost as long as the programs have been in existence, and his medical and financial practices have been under scrutiny by federal and state authorities for years. Nonetheless, he continues to operate, and we wondered why and how. Our story begins in downtown Los Angeles at the Washington-Main Medical Clinic, across the street. That is the hub of the health empire of Dr. Ed Rubin. That is where his office is. We arrived here about an hour ago to try to see Dr. Rubin, and we went to the front door, the entrance. This is what occurred.

The clinic that advertises it is open 24 hours a day was suddenly shut tight, at least to us.

(Man locks the door on Wallace) What's that?

The clinic that is licensed to serve the public was locked—iron gates drawn across the entrances. It's obvious that they just don't want "60 Minutes" coming into the Washington and Main Clinic. Why? Perhaps because they thought we would find what Dr. Joe Hendler found. He worked for Rubin for eight months and was an eyewitness to the way that medicine was manipulated to make big money.

DR. HENDLER: People came in, and they went out in one of two directions—with lots of lab tests or into the hospital. Or lots of medicine, because I believe Ed had a piece of the pharmacy action as well. They also had lots of X-rays, because I believe Ed had a piece of the X-ray action as well.

WALLACE: Rubin also owned the hospitals that most of his clinic patients were sent to.

DR. HENDLER: Every morning, one of the technicians would bring around a mimeographed form, and on top of it would say, "A Friendly Reminder." And then would be the . . . listed the hospital names that Ed was involved in at the time. They changed often enough.

WALLACE: You mean, like. . . .

DR. HENDLER: Imperial Hospital, Beverly Hills Doctors Hospital. . . .

WALLACE: Stanton?

DR. HENDLER: . . . Stanton Hospital.

WALLACE: Um-hmm.

DR. HENDLER: And here would be: "Number of Beds—100. Number of Patients—46. Number of Empty Beds—54." It didn't say fill those beds up. . . .

WALLACE: But the message was. . . .

DR. HENDLER: . . . but the implication was clear.

WALLACE: Now, Dr. Rubin knew, and his doctors and nurses quickly learned, that MediCal would pay only if the symptoms of potential hospital patients were described as serious, urgently needing attention.

You go to the clinic. You have a headache.

DR. HENDLER: You go to the hospital, and they write down "suspected meningitis," and they do more tests than anyone would need for that diagnosis. Then the patient gets sent home. Hallelujah, no meningitis! Tension headache. Meningitis suspected; none found.

WALLACE: Hallelujah? A bill for perhaps a thousand dollars, paid by MediCal. And that, says the California Attorney General, was typical.

In this room at the California Attorney General's office are half a million documents, seized by the MediCal Fraud Unit, involving Dr. Rubin, his patients, his clinics, and hospitals. It is reported that Rubin's various medical enterprises have collected as much as $20 million from MediCal, another $12 million from Medicare. And the investigators here believe that as much as 40 percent of all that—40 percent—may have gone for fraudulent or unnecessary care and services.

For four years this woman was a nurse in one of Dr. Rubin's hospitals. She, as well as Dr. Hendler, was willing to tell us on the record what other Rubin nurses and doctors told us privately.

NURSE: MediCal will only pay for certain illnesses written down in certain ways, so you have to know how to word things correctly. If a mother brought a baby into the emergency room and it had an ear infection . . .

WALLACE: Yes.

NURSE: . . . the baby would be admit . . . admitted to the hospital with a diagnosis of acute otitis media, which is an acute ear infection.

WALLACE: We've heard that the word "acute" was one that was frequently. . . .

DR. HENDLER: Good word. Good word. . . .

WALLACE: Yes.

DR. HENDLER: . . . used.

WALLACE: Expensive word to the taxpayers.

DR. HENDLER: Probably so.

WALLACE: Did none of the doctors ever object?

NURSE: Oh, yes, there were days when, in a 24-hour period, say, somewhere between 15 and 20 patients were admitted. A responsible physician would come in the next day and discharge all of those patients that had been admitted in the previous 24 hours.

WALLACE: And?

NURSE: And those patients would go home, and all those tests would be cancelled. And the doctor would soon disappear.

WALLACE: What she means is the doctor would soon lose his job.

What percentage of the patients, would you estimate, are admitted to hospitals unnecessarily out of Washington and Main?

DR. HENDLER: Minimum 80 percent.

WALLACE: It was also common practice, we learned, for Dr. Rubin's mother, who was in charge of the money at Washington-Main, it was also common practice for the woman known as Mama Rubin to ask patients who forgot their MediCal I.D. to give her partial payment in cash up front. Sometimes that money was refunded to them later when they produced their MediCal I.D. But frequently, according to Gail Yockley, who worked under Mrs. Rubin for four years, frequently the clinic kept the cash and still billed MediCal for the full amount.

Miss Yockley, are you absolutely sure about this double billing?

GAIL YOCKLEY: That's right.

WALLACE: Didn't you ever say anything about it to the people, for instance, to Mama Rubin? Say, "Ma . . . Mrs. Rubin, look, that . . . that poor person gave you $15 in cash."

YOCKLEY: Oh, are you kidding? You wouldn't do anything like that to Mama Rubin, because it was like you know what was being done, Mama Rubin knew what was being done; they were doing it, they'd been doing it, and they were going to continue doing it.

WALLACE: Gail Yockley, Dr. Hendler, and others had told us that MediCal patients, Medicare patients, indeed, patients with any kind of insurance, were given many more expensive tests and procedures than patients who paid cash. We sent two persons to the Washington and Main clinic to find out about that. Each complained of lower back pain. Each saw the same doctor. There was just one difference: Kathy paid cash, Lionel used his MediCal card.

KATHY: The first question I was asked literally was, "Do you have insurance?" I said no. And by the time that my chart got back to the examining room, it was marked in red "Not Insured."

WALLACE: So the difference, apparently, between you is that you're a cash patient. They didn't run tests on you. They just gave you a reasonable. . . .

KATHY: Right, and I think that was due to the fact that it said "Not Insured" at the top of the chart.

WALLACE: And as far as you're concerned, blood test, X-rays, urinalysis, two visits . . . all paid for by MediCal?

LIONEL: All on MediCal.

WALLACE: Kathy's visit cost $23 in cash. Lionel's visits, X-rays, and tests cost the taxpayer $240 in MediCal and Medicare money. And remember, they both went in complaining of the identical ailment—lower back pain.

This is Dr. Edward Rubin. He ignored our letters and telephone calls requesting an interview. Nevertheless, we did manage to photograph the silent Dr. Rubin coming to work.

Dr. Rubin, I wonder if I could talk to you just for a moment, sir. Dr. Rubin?

Shortly after Dr. Rubin disappeared inside the clinic, I came out and got back into the van where we had been staking him out for the past few days. Once inside the van, an employee of Dr. Rubin handed me a note inside here that said, "Call Mr. Dalton." Mr. Dalton, it turned out, was Dr. Rubin's attorney, and he and I negotiated the terms under which Edward Rubin would come out of his clinic and let himself be photographed.

My understanding is that your attorney says that until these legal matters are over, you don't want to talk, and he's advising you not to talk about it. Is that correct?

DR. RUBIN: Yes, he's . . . yes.

WALLACE: If this is where Dr. Rubin makes his living, this is where he lives, under the palms of Beverly Hills. While we were out here, we learned that he had just put that house on the market for $1,950,000, but was willing to take a million six. We could not find out whether he was planning to move to more lavish or more modest quarters.

The Rubin millions are generated, as we have said, in places like this—Stanton Hospital. Now, according to this memo from the California Department of Health, the percentage of MediCal business at Stanton increased by 331 percent from 1974 to '76, after Dr. Rubin and his partners bought the hospital. The emergency room is the golden door, for most of the MediCal patients here come in that way. But it's not just the money that intrigued us; it was the quality of medical care.

The quality of the doctors?

DR. HENDLER: Awful.

NURSE: There were one or two good ones. The rest of them were all losers.

WALLACE: Roberta Gordon was 30 years old when she was brought to the Stanton Hospital emergency room by Dennis Stillwell, then her boyfriend, now her husband. She was doubled over in pain and was diagnosed, correctly, as suffering from a tubal pregnancy. Then began the nightmare for Roberta, the wife Dennis calls "Bob" for short.

DENNIS STILLWELL: Bob's breathing stopped, just completely stopped, and so for a while was without oxygen to her system and, you know, especially to the brain. That might have . . . not that might have happened if I.V.'s had been started or if Bob had received blood. And as you know, what happened is that the laboratory technician, he left. From the time of coming in and seeing the emergency room physician till the time she was operated on, it was four hours.

WALLACE: In pain?

STILLWELL: Right.

WALLACE: With no blood transfusions, no intravenous feeding?

STILLWELL: Right.

WALLACE: The result? Roberta suffered severe brain damage that has left her unable to speak.

The doctor who admitted Roberta Gordon that night is this man, Jerome Rehman. He was head of the emergency room at Stanton for more than a year. The only picture we could get of him is this mug shot taken when he was booked on criminal charges in 1962.

You, Bobby, knew that his . . . his license had been revoked after he'd been convicted of and served a jail term for conspiracy . . . quote . . . "to commit acts injurious to the public health, and for performing unnecessary surgery and tests for profit?" *(Roberta shakes her head.)* You didn't know that.

After that conviction, Dr. Rehman's license to practice medicine was taken away in 1968. That license . . . he is a Doctor of Osteopathy . . . was restored in 1974, before he signed on at Stanton. Rehman left there in 1977. Now he's head of the emergency room at this hospital in Cerritos Gardens, California. When we found him there, he didn't want to talk to us.

The only way Roberta Gordon can "talk" is with the help of an electronic communicator, and we asked her to tell us who she holds responsible for what happened to her.

(Roberta punches message into communicator . . . hands tape to her husband . . . who hands it to Wallace.)

(Wallace reads tape.) "All of the people involved in the hospital."

Roberta Gordon sued Stanton Hospital and Dr. Rehman. Before the case could go to court, they settled. She received a lump sum of $300,000 plus $2,000 a month for life.

As we said earlier, Dr. Rubin has been at this game for a long time. He has owned Washington-Main Clinic since 1961. He was one of the first to see the potential windfall in California's prepaid health insurance. Tom Moore has known of Dr. Rubin since those days. Moore was then an assistant director of health for California, with direct responsibility for those prepaid plans.

I have here a memorandum from the Department of Health Care Services here in the State of California way back in 1970. Quote: "The most salient aspect of the meeting with Dr. Rubin was his apparent expectation of very significant profits from the project." Why has he survived?

TOM MOORE: Well, physicians don't like to talk about other physicians. They are not likely to . . . to go to the public or go to a law enforcement agency and ask for action against one of their own members.

WALLACE: It is said that one of the reasons that Dr. Ed Rubin has prospered for so long is that he has friends in high places, friends described in this confidential report prepared by California's Department of Justice; friends that include California State Senator John Briggs, who got a $77,000 insurance contract from Rubin; and former California State Senator and Lieutenant Governor Mervin Dymally, whom he rewarded, according to this report, with campaign contributions amounting to $13,000.

One of the many politicians who became aware of Dr. Rubin's activities as far back as the early 70's is Senator Edward Kennedy. He sent two of his investigators to California back in 1971 to take a look at Dr. Rubin. And this never-published 157-page report is only part of what they found. "It is quite apparent," said the Kennedy report back in 1973, "that a substantial portion of the income generated by Dr. Rubin enterprises can be attributed to improper and excessive utilization policies found in Rubin facilities."

You got to wonder about why Senator Kennedy apparently, or somebody in his office, put the quietus on this report.

MOORE: Well, it'll be a good question to ask him.

WALLACE: We wanted to, but Senator Kennedy refused our repeated requests for an interview; refused to tell us why he never held hearings, and why the report was never made public, though it had cost upwards of $75,000 to produce that report.

We also asked another Presidential hopeful, Governor Jerry Brown, to talk to us about his fellow Californian, Dr. Edward Rubin. He declined and refused to talk to us about why he twice vetoed a $125,000 appropriation for nine more MediCal investigators.

MOORE: He never supported strong surveillance or monitoring efforts by the state. In fact, he said one day, somewhat proudly, to the papers in Sacramento that he doesn't believe in government as a manager. Well, that pretty well says it.

WALLACE: Again, Dr. Joe Hendler.

DR. HENDLER: I said to Ed, "There's a lot of money in medicine, Ed. Can't we make money doing good medicine? Do we have to make money this way?" And he would always say, "Well, let's fix it up." I wish I could tell you, Mike, that he'd say, "Ah, the hell with it. I want to practice bad medicine." He never said that.

WALLACE: We were not surprised that Dr. Edward Rubin didn't want to talk to us, but frankly we did wonder why it was impossible to get any responsible public official, state or federal, executive or legislative, to come forward and explain why Dr. Rubin is still practicing the brand of medicine he practices; why they would not talk to us about what some of them privately describe as the biggest case of MediCal fraud in California, the biggest case of Medicaid fraud in the United States. Be that as it may, a Los Angeles County grand jury commences an investigation of the Rubin matter beginning November 1st.

Notes

1. Adapted for this purpose from a checklist for interviewers in James M. Schiff, "Interviewing for Results," in Richard C. Huseman, Cal M. Logue, Dwight L. Frishly, eds., *Readings in Inter-Personal and Organizational Communication*, 2d ed. (Boston, Mass.: Holbrook Press, 1974), 347–350.
2. William J. McEwen, "Communication, Innovation and Change," in Gerhard J. Hanneman and William J. McEwen, eds., *Communication and Behavior* (Reading, Mass.: Addison-Wesley, 1975), 212.
3. Ibid.
4. Robert Royal and Steven Schutt, *The Gentle Art of Interviewing and Interrogation* (Englewood Cliffs, N.J.: Prentice-Hall, 1976), 87.
5. Francis L. Wellman, *The Art of Cross-Examination*, 4th ed., rev. (New York: Macmillan, 1962), 27.
6. Ibid., 29.
7. Ibid.
8. Ibid., 35.
9. Ibid., 35–36.
10. Ibid., 41.
11. Ibid., 74–75.
12. Stuart Taylor, Jr., "A Lawyer Relishes Role of Showman," *The New York Times*, August 27, 1982, A10.
13. Ibid.

9

Salesmanship—The Persuasive Interview

Key Concepts

- Motivation
- Rapport Building as Strategic Planning
- Knowing When Enough is Enough
- Closing as a Process

It is possible that some of us can get completely through our lives without being the object of an investigation, without being interrogated, or without being cross-examined in a court of law. None of us, however, can escape from another form of interview—the persuasive interview. I have grouped the information in this chapter under the heading of salesmanship because, although it is not as lofty a term as persuasion, salesmanship is what we discuss. It matters little whether the setting for interview is the used car lot, the broker's office, or the clergyman's study; if the intent is to alter one of the participant's attitudes, values, beliefs, or actions, somebody is selling.

Selling is an extremely simple process when stripped to the bare essentials. The following is an example:

(Person enters a store.)

SALESPERSON: Can I help you?
CUSTOMER: Yes, I need a gizmo.
SALESPERSON: I have a gizmo.
CUSTOMER: I'll take it.

SALESPERSON: Here it is. That will be $10.
CUSTOMER: Here is $10.
SALESPERSON: Thank you.

This simple transaction contains the elements that lie at the core of every selling situation. One person, the customer, has a need for something. He or she seeks out a source for that need. The other person, the salesperson, is able to provide what the customer wants. The customer leaves with the need satisfied while the salesperson has been compensated—in this case by money—for having been able to satisfy the customer's need. This simple temporary symbiosis takes place millions of times every day in a multitude of settings. Often, however, it is cloaked in some very complicated apparel. Motives, attitudes, and barriers of various kinds can interfere with the direct and simple need-satisfaction transaction. We must hang on to the notion, no matter how complex the situation appears on the surface, that underneath it all lies this simple transaction.

There is nothing particularly new in the area of salesmanship, or persuasion either, for that matter. We still quote Aristotle and use his terminology when we are analyzing a persuasive message. We will not replay Aristotle here since the purpose of this chapter and this book is pragmatic, not analytical. In 1938, E. C. Tolman put this transaction in theoretical form and expressed it as a mathematical equation, $P = f(n, exp. v)$. That is:

> The particular performance or choice an individual makes (P) depends on the amount of effort he or she is willing to expend (f) in addressing
>
> 1. The motivation at the time (n: need);
> 2. The extent or probability that an action or attempted action will lead to a goal or value (exp: expectancy); and
> 3. The importance or satisfaction that goal or value has for the person (v: value).[1]

Effective communication in the persuasive interview affects behavioral change or choice. It must be arousing and relevant to the individual's needs.

MASLOW'S HIERARCHY OF NEEDS

Before we can turn our attention to discovering the specific needs of the person we are trying to persuade, we should have a good understanding of needs in general. Abraham Maslow has arranged a list of needs into a hierarchy. Needs, as Maslow sees them, are bound in an integrated system based on the relative importance of the satisfaction of the needs. Higher-order needs do not develop until lower-order needs are minimally satisfied. Maslow's hierarchy beginning with the most basic need progresses toward more complex and sophisticated needs:

Physiological needs—food, water, sleep, air; basic survival needs.
Safety needs—protection from harm or injury.
Love and belonging needs—warmth, status, acceptance, approval.
Esteem needs—adequacy, self-esteem, competence.
Self-actualization needs—self-fulfillment, ideal and real self in close harmony.
Desires to know and understand—broader understanding and appreciation.[2]

Unless a person's physiological needs are satisfied, he or she will not be concerned with any other needs in the hierarchy. A person who is starving is not going to be a primary prospect for encyclopedias.

MURRAY'S LIST OF MANIFEST NEEDS

Looking at needs as a hierarchical arrangement is not the only way to see them. H. A. Murray defines needs in detail and attempts to distinguish one from another.[3] Murray's list is arranged in alphabetical order:

Abasement. To surrender. To comply and accept punishment. To apologize, confess, atone. Self-depreciation. Masochism.

Achievement. To overcome obstacles. To exercise power. To strive to do something difficult as well and as quickly as possible.

Acquisition. To gain possessions and property. To grasp, snatch, or steal things. To bargain or gamble. To work for money or goods.

Affiliation. To form friendships and associations. To greet, join, and live with others. To cooperate and converse sociably with others. To love. To join groups.

Aggression. To assault or injure. To belittle, harm, blame, accuse, or maliciously ridicule a person. To punish severely. Sadism.

Autonomy. To resist influence or coercion. To defy an authority or seek freedom in a new place. To strive for independence.

Blamavoidance. To avoid blame, ostracism, or punishment by inhibiting asocial or unconventional impulses. To be well behaved and obey the law.

Counteraction. Proudly to refuse admission of defeat by restriving and retaliating. To select the hardest tasks. To defend one's honor in action.

Cognizance. To explore. To ask questions. To satisfy curiosity. To look, listen, inspect. To read and seek knowledge.

Construction. To organize and build.

Deference. To admire and willingly follow a superior. To cooperate with a leader. To serve gladly.

Defendance. To defend oneself against blame or belittlement. To justify one's actions. To offer extenuations, explanations, and excuses. To resist "probing."

Dominance. To influence or control others. To persuade, prohibit, dictate. To lead and direct. To restrain. To organize the behavior of a group.

Exhibition. To attract attention to one's person. To excite, amuse, stir, shock, thrill others. Self-dramatization.

Exposition. To point and demonstrate. To relate facts. To give information, explain, interpret, lecture.

Harmavoidance. To avoid pain, physical injury, illness, and death. To escape from a dangerous situation. To take precautionary measures.

Infavoidance. To avoid failure, shame, humiliation, ridicule. To refrain from attempting to do something that is beyond one's powers. To conceal a disfigurement.

Nurturance. To nourish, aid, or protect the helpless. To express sympathy. To "mother" a child.

Order. To arrange, organize, put away objects. To be tidy and clean. To be scrupulously precise.

Play. To relax, amuse oneself, seek diversion and entertainment. To "have fun," to play games. To laugh, joke, and be merry. To avoid serious tension.

Rejection. To snub, ignore, or exclude. To remain aloof and indifferent. To be discriminating.

Retention. To retain possession of things. To refuse to give or lend. To hoard. To be frugal, economical, and miserly.

Sentience. To seek and enjoy sensuous impressions.

Sex. To form and further an erotic relationship. To have sexual intercourse.

Succorance. To seek aid, protection, or sympathy. To cry for help. To plead for mercy. To adhere to an affectionate, nurturant parent. To be dependent.

Superiority. This need is considered to be a composite of achievement and recognition.

Understanding. To analyze experience, to abstract, to discriminate among concepts, to define relations, to synthesize ideas.

Although any list that attempts to cover the whole range of human needs will be incomplete, Murray's list is very helpful in determining what may be motivating someone in a particular situation. It also suggests areas for exploration when you are trying to motivate someone, as in the persuasive interview. Because they do not relate necessarily to basic survival or other needs on Maslow's list, Murray's needs may be called *indirect* or *manifest*—needs that represent certain aspects or segments of a given motive or in some cases a combination of two or more motives.

Motive Appeals

Monroe and Ehninger use an adaptation of Murray's list to provide a framework strategy for persuasive speakers.[4] They call this strategy *motive appeals.* Using motive appeals, Monroe and Ehninger show how certain combinations of manifest needs become powerful motivators. When acquisition is combined with play and adventure, as with most forms of gambling, the motivation is particularly powerful.

The Motivated Sequence

Although Monroe and Ehninger focus their attention on the problems of public speaking, many of their conclusions have great relevance for the persuasive interview. They begin by looking at the mental processes of a potential listener or in the case of the interview, the participant who is the target of a persuasive message. They conclude that despite listeners' individual differences of temperament and ability, their thought processes in responding to various sorts of specific purposes on the part of the speaker are surprisingly uniform:

> . . . so uniform, in fact, that they provide a practical basis for a standard pattern of speech organization. We shall call this pattern the *motivated sequence: the sequence of ideas which, by following the normal processes of human thinking, motivates an audience to respond to the speaker's purpose.*[5]

Monroe and Ehninger identify five distinct steps in the motivated sequence:

1. Attention.
2. Need.
3. Satisfaction.
4. Visualization.
5. Action.

The steps of this sequence should be used as a tool for planning and as an organizational framework upon which you build the strategy for the persuasive interview. The steps in application will not be applied equally in each interview. Sometimes one or more steps may be developed very briefly because the prospect (what we will call the participant on the receiving end of the persuasion) already understands that a need exists or has no objections to the satisfaction offered for a need. Table 9.1 is adapted from Monroe and Ehninger to pertain to the persuasive interview. It also illustrates how the motivated sequence fits within our scheme of interview organization.

Middle-game issues occupy the greatest amount of space in the model, but this does not always carry through to the actual event. It is possible to spend hours, days, months, or even years establishing rapport to prepare the way for persuasion. The traditional courtship (if anyone does it that way anymore) required a large amount of time for rapport building. The end game can be deceptive also since you can try numerous closes with no success and find yourself continually being dumped back into the middle game.

PLANNING FOR THE PERSUASIVE INTERVIEW

There are two things that are essential if you are going to be effective during the persuasive interview: You must know your subject (or product) and you must know something about your prospect. You need not know a great deal about the prospect personally although many times this can be of great help in establishing rapport and in determining what interests and motivates this person. The main thing you need to know about a prospect is what relationship

Table 9.1

Place in interview	Step	Function	Prospect response
Opening game	Attention, orientation, rapport building	Getting attention, gaining control, building trust	"I want to listen"; "I understand the issue"; "I like this person."
Middle game	Identifying, or establishing need Assess where prospect currently stands on the issue	Describe and develop the problem under consideration Motivate prospect to action	"Something needs to be done [decided, felt]."
	Satisfying need Handling objections	Present benefits of your point of view Locate and satisfy secondary needs	"This is what must be done [believed, felt] to satisfy the need [s]."
	Visualizing Summarizing	Reiterate accepted benefits with visualization of results	"I can see myself enjoying the satisfaction of doing [believing, feeling] this."
End game	Action or closing	Request tangible proof of acceptance	"I will do [believe, feel] this."

he or she currently holds with your point of view, product, or whatever else you are selling.

During the give and take of the persuasive interview, it is usually impossible to prepare a fixed line of questioning. The progression is open and generally fast moving. It is still very helpful to be armed with a list of questions—usually of a fact-finding nature—that will help you initially to uncover needs and other motivational elements like attitudes and beliefs. Fact-finding questions are those that begin with phrases like the following:

How long have you been . . . ?
What has been your experience with . . . ?
Have you found satisfaction in . . . ?
If you could have it your way, how would you change . . . ?
Is there anything that bothers you about . . . ?

The answers to the fact-finding questions will uncover needs and show you how the prospect currently stands with regard to your position. Minnick defines four situational strategies that cover this relationship.[6] These are the goal situation, the barrier situation, the threat situation, and the identification situation. The effective persuader will be able to determine in advance or quickly as the interview unfolds which of the situational strategies is appropriate for the individual subjected to the persuasive message.

The Goal Situation

In a goal situation, the prospect either already desires what we are offering or, it is assumed, will desire it once cognizant of it. When a stranger walks into an automobile showroom, the salesperson already knows something very important about that person—he or she is there possibly to buy a car. The prospect is goal oriented. To urge this person to achieve the goal, you may draw on some of the following ideas for questions and comments during the interview:

1. The goal can produce benefits for the prospect.
2. The goal is among the most significant or important goals the prospect can seek.
3. The goal is deserved by the prospect.
4. The goal is easily obtainable.
5. The goal is necessary for survival.
6. The goal will bring benefits to or is deserved by or is needed by those with whom the audience is identified.
7. The goal will bring long-lasting or permanent benefits.
8. Lesser persons do not seek the goal, but only those who are superior.

Persuasion, of course, runs both ways. If you want to convince someone not to achieve a certain goal, you would use basically the same approach stated in the negative, as shown in these statements:

1. The desire for the goal is unworthy of the prospect; to seek it is irrational, unjust, contemptible; admirable people in the same situation have not been tempted by it.
2. The goal is unnecessary and would not meet a significant or worthy need or would not be long lasting.
3. Other goals are more pressing, more possible to attain, more satisfying, more permanent.
4. The goal would be injurious rather than helpful or pleasant or would produce benefits of a questionable nature or is not what it appears to be.

The goal strategy assumes that a prospect either already desires your product or point of view or can be informed of your product or point of view in such a way as to create the desire for it. The emphasis in this strategy is placed on awareness, the attractiveness of the goal, and its accessibility.

The Barrier Situation

The barrier situation is the most common of the motivational situations. As Minnick puts it, "In a sense we are always separated from our goals, except at the instant of achieving them. . . ."[7] He lists some examples such as the following: a college student who wants a good mark but will not do the work; a man who wants the prestige of a doctor but cannot get through medical school; the musician who will not practice; the athlete who will not train. In the barrier situation, the prospect is also goal oriented, but there is something that gets in the way of achievement. In order to urge the prospect to overcome the barrier and achieve the goal, you may use some of the following ideas for questions and comments during the interview:

1. Increase the desire to get through, over, or around the barrier by increasing the desire for the goal.
2. The barrier is contemptible, unintelligent, unnecessary, or unjust.
3. The barrier works to the advantage of the enemies of the prospect.
4. The person or circumstance that has raised the barrier has allowed others to achieve the goal that the prospect actually deserves.

Again, the strategy can be reversed. If you want to urge a prospect not to surmount a barrier, use some of the following ideas:

1. The barrier is a necessary one.
2. Decrease the desire for surmounting the barrier.
3. Weaken the desire for the goal.
4. Request that the prospect study the barrier more carefully. When action is delayed, the chances that the goal will be achieved are reduced substantially.

Although goal achievement is at the center of the barrier situation also, unlike the goal situation, the prospect is both aware and desirous of achieving the goal but is hampered by some intervening factor.

The Threat Situation

Goal orientation also figures strongly in this situation. The difference is that the prospect has already achieved certain goals. The threat is that they may be taken away. The emphasis here is on combating the threat. In order to urge a prospect to resist and combat a threat, you may employ some of the following ideas for questions and comments during the interview:

1. The threat has the power to harm the prospect if not responded to promptly and powerfully.
2. Great effort can reduce the threat and has done so under similar circumstances.

3. The prospect has the courage, power, and intelligence to resist the force.
4. Others less able than the prospect have combated similar forces courageously and successfully.
5. The means, help, ideas, techniques, and other things necessary for combating the threat are at hand or will inevitably arrive.

Again, in the reverse situation, if you want someone to give in to a threat, shift the strategy in the opposite direction:

1. The threat is superior to the prospect's power to resist and is close at hand.
2. Others, similar to the prospect, have been defeated by the force although they expected to prevail.
3. Help is far away, the prospect is alone.
4. What the force attacks is not worth keeping.
5. Good sense requires that we give up the goal as others have done in similar circumstances.

If you are trying to convince someone through threat, you must be certain that they have goals that they deem worthy of retaining. You cannot threaten people who have nothing to lose.

The Identification Situation

Minnick describes the identification situation as one in which human beings become involved because they identify themselves with others. When we identify with a person or a group, their problems become our problems, their struggles become our struggles, and their failures and successes are experienced as if they happened to us. This situation is built on empathy. It is the same thing we experience when we are rooting for a favorite team. To motivate a prospect to respond through identification, we must accomplish both of the following goals:

1. Convince the prospect that the person or the group is in need, is facing difficulties not of his or her or their own making or fault.
2. Convince the prospect that the person or group is like him or her in background, purpose, attitude, status, hopes, and the like.

This strategy is most often found in fund-raising or patriotic situations such as recruiting for the U.S. Army, Peace Corps, and Vista. As before, it can be reversed:

1. The source of the identification represents attitudes, values, and beliefs that are alien and hostile to the prospect.

2. The need is not great, has been exaggerated, is their own fault, and they should be able to solve it alone.
3. Getting involved would expose the prospect to danger, and the effort would be wasted.

Identification can be a powerful motivator, but it must continually be reenforced. It also works best when the prospect is kept at a distance from the source of the identification so that you can control the perception of the similarities at the expense of the differences.

In summary, a main purpose at the outset of a persuasive interview is to determine where the prospect stands with regard to your persuasive message. In this way the rapport-building phase in the opening game becomes part of your strategic planning for the interview. In the give and take of the interview situation, motivation can shift. It is also probably, particularly in lengthy encounters, that more than one motivational situation will be evident. On a complex issue, the prospect may be goal oriented toward part of it, have a barrier to some of it, and feel threatened by still another part of it. The skillful persuader listens carefully and stays abreast of changes in motivation or uncovers additional needs or concerns.

PARTICIPATING IN THE PERSUASIVE INTERVIEW

The Salesperson

SALESPERSON: Hi, Mr. Sims. I'm Mark Green. I'm glad you could come in today. Did you have any trouble finding the office?

PROSPECT: No, your directions were fine. Also, since my wife was here a few days ago, she steered me in the right direction.

GREEN: I had a delightful meeting with Mrs. Sims. I'm sorry she couldn't join us today.

SIMS: Well, she felt that I should get a feel for this idea on my own although she has been selling pretty hard at home. You must have done some job on her.

GREEN: Actually, Mrs. Sims was quite enthusiastic from the outset.

SIMS: I doubt that you will find me quite as enthusiastic.

GREEN: You seem to have some reservations about Gator Lake. What's bothering you?

SIMS: A lot of things. First of all, I'm not ready to retire; why should I invest in retirement property? Secondly, central Florida! On the edge of the Everglades swamp! Give me a break. I've heard of people buying swamp land when they didn't know any better, but to do it willingly is another story.

GREEN: Oh no! You found me out. Another swamp deal down the drain.

SIMS: All right. You seem more legitimate than that. I'm just not convinced I need to get involved with this.

GREEN: That's fine. Why don't we just spend a short time going over some of the points I covered with Mrs. Sims with particular emphasis on those areas that seem to concern you the most. If it sparks some interest, all well and good. If not, well . . .

SIMS: Well, I'm here. Let's see what this is all about.

GREEN: Mr. Sims, you mentioned several points before which appear to be areas of concern. You said that you were not ready to retire, you had some reservations about central Florida, and were dubious about the quality of the land. Is that right?

SIMS: That about sums it up.

GREEN: Let's talk about the retirement issue first. Gator Lake is not designed as a retirement community. It is true that many of our customers are or soon will be retired, but they represent only a small percentage of the Gator Lake community. The majority of our buyers are people like yourself, still working and energetic and some with children still at home, who are looking for a resort community providing active vacation possibilities with the comfort and security of ownership. Should the time come when you are ready to consider retirement, you will already have established friendships and a life-style that will make such a transition both easier and more pleasant.

SIMS: I just can't see myself hanging around with a bunch of old folks. And I hate golf.

GREEN: I can understand your concern. But I assure you this is not the case. If you would like, I can provide you with the ages of several of our current owners and applicants as stated on their applications. I, of course, cannot release their names.

SIMS: That would be interesting to me.

GREEN: As to your second concern, can you tell me what disturbs you about central Florida?

SIMS: Well, when I think about Florida, I think of the ocean or the Gulf of Mexico. The only thing in between is Disney World.

GREEN: That certainly has been the case throughout the history of Florida's development. It might surprise you to know, however, that in the last ten years, central Florida has been one of the largest growth areas in the nation. Many high-technology industries have been attracted to the area because of the large amount of available inexpensive land and tax advantages of the region. You mentioned Disney World, which is located less than 100 miles from Gator Lake and with Epcot Center is probably the largest private industry employer in the state. These factors—new industry and established large employers—have made the future economic opportunities extremely bright.

SIMS: Yes, but I don't plan to work there.

GREEN: Right. But you probably are interested in the rising property values. Property at Gator Lake can be expected to increase in value at the rate of 10 percent to 15 percent each year, based on past performance of property in the same area.

SIMS: That sounds pretty good.

GREEN: I can show you the figures we have collected on recent property transactions that verify that real estate, not nearly the caliber of Gator Lake, has appreciated over 50 percent during the last five years.

SIMS: Gosh! It is just so hard to believe of that area.

GREEN: Mr. Sims, when you go on vacation, what do you like to do? You've already told me golf is out, so our championship golf course won't impress you. . . .

SIMS: I like to relax; do some swimming, play a little tennis. . . .

GREEN: Well, you probably saw the pictures of our outdoor and indoor tennis courts in the brochures I gave Mrs. Sims. Also, there are some good pictures of the swimming pools. Here, let me give you another set of materials to look at. By the way, do you like to fish?

SIMS: I love to fish. I haven't had much time to do it lately, though. My son really likes it, too.

GREEN: Gator Lake is a cove with a channel leading directly into Lake Okechobee. We are at the edge of the most spectacular fishing grounds in the country. If you haven't seen the Everglades, Mr. Sims, you really owe it to yourself to have a look at what the area has to offer you and your family for both the short and long term.

SIMS: This all sounds very interesting, and I have to admit that the brochures are impressive. But, right now, if I can steal three or four weeks out of my schedule during the year, that's a lot. It's hard to justify carrying the expense of a second home when you spend so little time there.

GREEN: I agree with you totally. That's why several of our buyers rent their homes to vacationing families during the months when they are unable to use the property themselves.

SIMS: Rent?

GREEN: Yes. Gator Lake Management Company will rent and maintain your property for a percentage of the rental fee. This enables you to defray much of the costs of ownership while receiving the tax advantages and depreciation of a rental property. Also, because your property is income-producing, you are eligible to deduct your transportation to and from Gator Lake as well as other travel expenses. I can't guarantee that you will make money on the deal, but the demand for rentals is increasing, and I know of five owners who actually turned a profit on their investment last year.

SIMS: No wonder my wife was jumping up and down. She knew I'd probably go for this.

GREEN: Mr. Sims. I have no doubt that if you could see Gator Lake up close and experience some of the excitement that is being generated by development in central Florida that you would indeed "go for it." We have agreed that Gator Lake is probably not a swamp, that the recreational activities are in keeping with your needs, and that there may be some advantages to renting from cost and tax standpoints. We already know your wife is enthusiastic. Why not let me make an appointment for you to come and see Gator Lake for yourself. Let's say in three weeks or would next month be better?

SIMS: Hold on! I admit that I'm intrigued, but what is this going to cost me?

GREEN: There are a wide range of options depending on the location of the building site and the type and size of structure you select. Mrs. Sims seems to favor our standard three-bedroom unit in an open area but not directly on the waterfront. Today, this unit would cost you $69,500. With a minimum down payment of 10 percent and our special 11.5 percent 30-year fixed-rate mortgage, you can estimate your costs at around $600 per month, less any income you might realize from renting, should you decide to elect that option.

SIMS: The rental would definitely be an important factor. I probably should take a look at this. . . .

GREEN: Mrs. Sims mentioned that you were planning to spend a week in Florida during the next month. I would like to arrange to fly you and your family from wherever you are in Florida to Gator Lake for a day, where you will be our guests for lunch at the club house and can have the opportunity to see first hand the beautiful location and fine workmanship that's creating all the excitement at the Gator Lake community.

SIMS: It looks like it will be Fort Lauderdale the week of the 3rd.

GREEN: Let's make it Wednesday, the 5th. It will break up your week nicely, and the airport isn't too hectic on Wednesdays.

SIMS: That sounds fine.

GREEN: Mr. Sims, in order for me to schedule a plane for you in advance, I will need a $100 deposit, which is refundable to you when you arrive at Gator Lake. If for some reason your plans change, we need a week's notice to alter the arrangements for the plane or to cancel. If you wish, this deposit can be credited toward your contract should you decide to buy property at Gator Lake. Will that be cash or check?

SIMS: How's a personal check?

GREEN: That's fine. Make it out to Gator Lake Development, Inc.

SIMS: Will you be there on the 5th?

GREEN: I may be. I don't know what the schedule is now. If I'm not going to be there, I will have my associate, Tom Drake, contact you before you leave for Florida to introduce himself so you will know someone there. At that time, we will also clarify your flight arrangements.

SIMS: Okay, Mr. Green . . .

GREEN: Mark.

SIMS: Okay, Mark. I'm not sure what I'm getting into, but it seems like it's worth a look.

GREEN: Thank you for coming in, and give my regards to Mrs. Sims.

The preceding scene, although constructed to suit our purposes, contains many of the elements that you may encounter in a real sales situation. The progression moves from resistance to acceptance as we observe Mark Green's use of the motivated sequence and points of various motivational strategies to shape Mr. Sims' perception of Gator Lake.

Green discovers at the outset that Sims is not goal oriented. In fact, he appears to be almost hostile. Green listens carefully to uncover what the main objections are. He uses an open question to see if Sims will volunteer his objections, "You seem to have some reservations about Gator Lake. What's bothering you?" The question uncovers several barriers including retirement, a predetermined idea about central Florida, and the "swamp land" fear. Green maintains rapport-building activity throughout the opening game. He selects his questions and responses carefully, supporting Sims' feelings without agreeing with his premises and avoiding confrontation on any of the issues.

Green moves into the middle game by handling the objections first. He takes one at a time and restates in his own words his understanding of Sims' objection. On the retirement issue, Green selects an identification strategy, "The majority of our buyers are people like yourself, still working and energetic and some with children still at home. . . ." When Sims expresses some skepticism, Green counters with an offer of proof, "If you would like, I can provide you with the ages of several of our current owners. . . ." The central Florida issue is handled with a goal stategy. Green raises Sims' desire for the goal by stating it in the most attractive terms. Sims shows some interest but presents a barrier, "Yes, but I don't plan to work there." Green uses a barrier strategy to counter. He enhances the desirability of the goal by adding a benefit not mentioned earlier, "Right, but you probably are interested in the rising property values. . . ."

Sims' attitude is beginning to shift toward acceptance, "That sounds pretty good." Green shifts to a fact-finding open question to discover additional needs, "Mr. Sims, when you go on vacation, what do you like to do?" Additional needs having been uncovered, Green moves again to the satisfaction step of the motivated sequence. He shows how the benefits of Gator Lake answer Mr. Sims' recreational needs. Sims raises another barrier, "But, right now, if I can steal three or four weeks out of my schedule during the year, that's a lot. It's hard to justify carrying the expense. . . ." Green agrees and supports Sims' concern and then presents the rental benefit. With Sims exhibiting acceptance again, Green moves to the visualization step followed by a trial close, "Mr. Sims. I have no doubt that if you could see Gator Lake up close and experience some of the excitement that is being generated by development in central Florida, that you would indeed 'go for it'." The close is not accepted, and Sims raises another objection, " . . . but what is this going to cost me?" Green provides the information and tries another close, "I would like to arrange to fly you and your family from wherever you are in Florida to Gator Lake for a day. . . ." This time the close works. Green is solidly in the end game. He asks for a commitment in the form of a deposit and summarizes the details of the plan of action.

In addition to the motivated sequence and motivational strategies, the scene points out some other distinguishing characteristics of the persuasive interview. Note, for example, that the salesperson is doing most of the talking. Some of the clusters of responses are very speechlike in form and content. The prospect's responses are very self-disclosive. He is telling of his needs and his objections in addition to seeking information on which to base a judgment. The salesperson is constantly selecting language that moves the prospect toward acceptance.

Closing is extremely important to the overall outcome of the persuasive interview. In this part of the end game, it is crucial that the participant with persuasive intent maintain a firm hold on his or her objective. Too many people, including salespeople, who find themselves in persuasive situations avoid strong closing behaviors. This grows out of two factors. First, if the interview has been generally successful up to the end game, the interview participants have probably established a great deal of rapport. Some persuaders find it difficult to risk this rapport by reminding the prospects that they want something from them. Second, closing brings on the natural fear of rejection. It is quite possible—in fact, probable in a majority of the cases—that your close will be rejected. You must accept this notion at the outset so that you can carry through your strategy to the end regardless of the consequences. Sometimes it helps to remind yourself that you have lost nothing if the close is rejected since you had nothing when the persuasion began. True, you have invested time and energy in the attempt, but that, as the saying goes, comes with the territory.

Closing is a two-step process. When you sense acceptance in the form of agreement statements, positive nonverbal indicators, or other "buying signals," first summarize all of the benefits that have been accepted, as Green does, "We have agreed that Gator Lake is probably not a swamp, that the recreational activities are in keeping with your needs, and that there may be some advantages in renting from a tax standpoint." Then ask for a commitment, "Why not let me make an appointment for you to come and see Gator Lake for yourself. Let's say in three weeks or would next month be better?" Note that the hard decision, that is, whether or not Sims will make an appointment, is made by Green. The easy decision—when—is left for Sims to make. The summary of accepted benefits creates a pattern within which the prospect is responding with yes. When you ask for the commitment, it makes it more difficult for the prospect to say no. If your close does not work the first time, you need not summarize again when you try the next close, unless a long period of time has intervened.

Effective closing is what separates the successful persuasive interview from the unsuccessful one. It bears repeating: Do not be afraid to ask for a commitment. The prospects expect you to ask for something. Do not disappoint them.

The Prospect

The first thing to remember if you are the object of a persuasive approach is that persuasion is amoral. While most people will draw a line between what is ethical and do anything to get their way, you are better served if you make no assumptions about the ethics of the persuader. Your best defense against being sold goods and ideas you would not ordinarily accept is to become aware of the strategic methods outlined above. This itself will not guarantee that you will become immune to motivational strategies nor perhaps should you. Much of the persuasion that comes our way is actually in our best interests. The key is to evaluate each persuasive appeal on its merits and in relation to your needs. If you find yourself to be goal oriented toward a belief, action, or product, make an assessment of your motives. Ask yourself, "What will I really gain (or lose) by adopting the position put forth in the persuasion?" Some other questions to consider are:

1. What will the demands be on my time and resources?
2. What will it cost me in dollars?
3. How will the acceptance of this persuasion affect others with whom I am close (family, friends, associates)?
4. What are the short-term benefits?
5. What are the long-term benefits?
6. What will be the probable outcome if I do not accept the persuasion?

Another important point to consider is that the persuasion is designed to create an impetus toward acceptance. This creates an aura of immediacy. Do not allow yourself to be rushed into a decision. Even if you miss out on a "special price only today," you will be better served later to pay a little more and know you are comfortable with the acceptance. Finally, as a prospect involved in the persuasive interview, you are subjected to the same forces that build rapport as the salesperson. Do not feel that you must accept or buy something simply because this nice person of whom you have grown fond during the course of the transaction has spent a great deal of time and effort persuading you and will be terribly disappointed if you reject the proposal. State your needs as clearly and succinctly as possible. Then listen to and evaluate benefits presented. Consider thoughtfully, and make a decision based on facts. If you are destined to develop a relationship with the other participant, this will happen in spite of, rather than because of, your acceptance of the proposal.

SUMMARY

In this chapter we have discussed persuasion in the interview situation as salesmanship. We have looked at salesmanship as a simple need-satisfaction process that becomes complicated by the vast array of human motives. We examined several ways of determining these motives and how motives influence our acceptance or rejection of persuasion. Salesmanship is a process that moves toward acceptance. This is best stated in Monroe and Ehninger's motivated sequence: attention, need, satisfaction, visualization, action. There are several strategies that can be used when you determine how the prospect stands in relation to your point of view, including the following: goal, barrier, threat, and identification.

We dealt separately with closing as an objective of the persuasive interview. Closing is a two-step process: Summarize the benefits, and then ask for a commitment. Whether you are on the sending or receiving end of persuasion, you cannot avoid it. Understanding its components makes you a more effective practitioner and less of a victim of its power.

Questions for Study and Discussion

1. This chapter states that regardless of the situation or who the participants are, if the interview involves persuasion, someone is "selling." For each of the following settings, list a possible need and a possible benefit for the prospect: automobile showroom, clothing store, lawyer's office, singles bar, clergyman's study, doctor's office.
2. How does Maslow's hierarchy of needs differ from Murray's list of manifest needs?

Suggested Activities

1. Select a product or create one from your imagination. Develop a strategy listing key questions and key points for each of the following motivational situations:

   a. Goal
   b. Barrier
   c. Threat
   d. Identification

Notes

1. E. C. Tolman, "The Determiners of Behavior at a Choice Point," *Psychological Review* 45 (1938): 1–41.
2. A. H. Maslow, *Motivation and Personality* (New York: Harper & Row, 1954), 80–106; also A. H. Maslow, "A Theory of Human Motivation," *Psychological Review* 50 (1943): 370–396; also A. H. Maslow, "Some Theoretical Consequences of Basic Need Gratifications," *Journal of Personality* 16 (1948): 402–416.
3. H. A. Murray, *Explorations in Personality* (New York: Oxford University Press, 1938), 127.
4. Alan H. Monroe and Douglas Ehninger, *Principles and Types of Speech* (Glenview Ill.: Scott, Foresman, 1967), 192–202.
5. Ibid. 265.
6. Wayne C. Minnick, *The Art of Persuasion* (Boston: Houghton Mifflin, 1957), 84.
7. Ibid.

10

The Counseling Interview

Key Concepts

- The helping attitude
- Building trust
- The counselor's role

> To be faced by a troubled, conflicted person who is seeking and expecting help, has always constituted a great challenge to me. Do I have the knowledge, the resources, the psychological strength—do I have whatever it takes to be of help to such an individual?[1]

In the preceding quote, Carl Rogers, the distinguished psychotherapist, asks the central question that all counselors should ask. Note also that Rogers sees the situation as a challenge and a test of his own resources and skill. While most of us are not psychotherapists, we do find ourselves from time to time engaged, sometimes not by choice, in the act of providing counseling to another individual. Counseling, particularly one-to-one counseling, has all of the dynamics of any interview with some important and fundamental differences.

What separates the counseling interview from other types is the purpose of the participants. In a sense the focus shifts away from the normal pattern. The researcher, the reporter, the employer, the investigator all want something from the respondent or participant. The salesperson certainly has a personal objective. It is possible, even desirable, for both parties to gain from the interview, but this is not a primary goal. In counseling, the primary goal is for one participant to help the other, and the lines are clearly drawn. One participant, the counselee, is at the center. He or she is all important, and everything else is incidental. The person to be counseled may have sought us out or have been forced by someone or something to seek counseling. The problem for the counselor is to find out how to best help this person who may even resist or resent the attempt.

The key word is *help*. What does help mean in this context? Alfred Benjamin in *The Helping Interview* grapples with this issue:

> I am not certain I can define "help" satisfactorily to myself. . . . Help is an enabling act. The interviewer enables the interviewee to recognize, to feel, to know, to decide, to choose whether to change. This enabling act demands giving on the part of the interviewer. He must give of his time, his capacity to listen and understand, his skill, his knowledge, his interest—part of himself. If this giving can be perceived by the interviewee, the enabling act will involve receiving. The interviewee will receive the help in a way possible for him to receive it as meaningful to him. The helping interview is the largely verbal interaction between interviewer and interviewee in which this enabling act takes place. It takes place but does not always succeed in its purpose; often we do not know if it has or not.[2]

I believe that seeing counseling as an "enabling act" as Benjamin does is a very useful concept, particularly for those of us who do not engage in counseling on a regular and continuous basis and who need to develop rapidly the proper mind set when the situation does occur. What can we do to enable the counseling to take place in the most effective manner? Certainly, the setting is essential. Also, monitoring our own communication at each major stage of the interview, especially with regard to the questions we ask and the responses we make, will provide us with a framework for the interview. How might we handle hostility, crying, and other disturbing behaviors? These are issues we will explore in this chapter.

THE INTERVIEW SETTING

To the extent that you can control them, all conditions surrounding the interview should facilitate rather than hinder the experience. Try to select an area, hopefully a room or office, which is free of distraction in the form of noise or interruption. The person being counseled has a right to expect your undivided attention. Therefore, an uncluttered desk free of other people's files or other tasks on which you are working is best. Arrange the chairs in a manner that is both suitable for the room and comfortable for you. Some counselors like sitting behind a desk while others prefer two comfortable chairs with a small table between them.

Interruptions of any kind are unacceptable. This includes phone calls, knocks on the door, people who want just a quick word with you, and the like. Counseling is intensely personal, and as such, delicate. Interruptions can destroy a very important moment and thereby jeopardize the outcome of the entire session.

While you cannot be all things to all people, give some thought as to how the counselee will see you. What is your relationship prior to the counseling? Are you a professional counselor, a peer, a boss, a teacher, or a coach? Thinking this through beforehand will help you present the appropriate picture to the person you are counseling. If you are the boss, would it be effective to choose a time and place when you can remove your tie and appear relaxed in order to break down some of the stereotypical barriers set up for this relationship? How long and how well do you know this person? What can you say or do to put this person more at ease? The goal is to provide an atmosphere that makes communication possible.

PREPARING TO COUNSEL

Benjamin cites two internal conditions that he sees as basic to the success of counseling:

1. Bringing to the interview just as much of our own selves as we possibly can, stopping, of course, at the point at which this may hinder the interviewee or deny him the help he needs.
2. Feeling within ourselves that we wish to help him as much as possible and that there is nothing at the moment more important to us. The fact that we hold this attitude will enable him in the course of the interview to sense it.[3]

The willingness to do these things is what builds an aura of trust. Trust in you as a counselor and a belief that you can and will help are essential ingredients in a counseling relationship. Dr. Jerome Frank in his book *Persuasion and Healing* underlines the same elements for the success of the psychotherapeutic relationship:

> The therapist's power is based on the patient's perception of him as a source of help, and it tends to be greater the greater the patient's distress and his faith in the therapist's desire and ability to help him. The attitudes of the therapist that seem to contribute most to the patient's trust in him are a steady, deep interest, an optimistic outlook, and dedication to the patient's welfare. These attitudes enable the patient to talk about any aspects of himself, however shameful they may be, with confidence that the therapist will maintain his interest and concern.[4]

Whether or not to trust the counselor will be the most important judgment made during the initial or opening phase of the interview. This decision is entirely in the hands of the counselee, but it is largely determined by the behavior of the counselor. In the opening game, and throughout, the counselor is under intense scrutiny. Dress, manner, facial expressions, tone of voice, gestures, posture all add up to something for the counselee. After all, for the counseling to be effective, this person must enter into disclosures that are deeply held, and bringing them into the open can create a feeling of extreme vulnerability. In order to come across as trustworthy, several theorists on the matter seem to agree that the counselor must be first knowledgeable and comfortable with himself or herself. Being yourself is very essential to building trust. As Carl Rogers puts it, "In my relationships with persons I have found that it does not help, in the long run, to act as though I were something that I am not."[5] Although you may be called on to counsel a friend, you must maintain your objectivity while you are counseling. To overempathize or oversympathize with the counselee will limit the effectiveness of the counseling. This objectivity also derives from a knowledge of self, as Edinburg, Zinberg, and Kelman note in their book *Clinical Interviewing and Counseling*:

> The counselor's awareness of his own feelings and his acceptance of responsibility for controlling them sharply differentiate him from an ordinary social friend. Friends share their intimacies with each other, taking turns, in a sense, ventilating their feelings and offering temporary relief and support as they hear each other out. In counseling, the client is not expected to know the counselor's problems, let alone assist the counselor with them. Nor is the client expected to guide and correct the flow of the relationship. For these reasons, the client is free to deal with his own difficulties without any sense of burden about the feeling of the counselor.[6]

Edinburg and her coauthors provide what she calls a *working model* that consists of two people who are equal but who have different tasks in the interview. One, the counselee, supplies the subjectivity (the self-disclosure), and the other, the counselor, supplies the objectivity.

A willingness to help, to make the counselee the center of attention, to listen in an active, caring but objective way to what is subjectively offered are the qualities that allow the counselor to create, in Benjamin's terms, the enabling act.

PARTICIPATING IN THE COUNSELING INTERVIEW

The Counselor

The spectrum of possible situations that may involve the counseling interview is so wide that it is unmanageable as far as dealing with each possibility separately. In addition to the variety of settings and the people who may be involved, the reasons why someone is counseled vary greatly. Has the counselee come to you of his or her own accord? Was the counselee sent or referred to you by someone who has power to do so? Are you the initiator of the counseling? Have you been directed to counsel an individual? All of these situations have unique aspects, but they have many similarities as well. It is the similarities on which we will focus, noting, where appropriate, contrasts in approach when they differentiate widely from the norm.

In the opening game, as always, we must concentrate on the development of rapport and the orientation to the matter at hand. If the counselee has come to you, the orientation may differ from the norm because you may not know why this person has sought you out. Even if you have a good idea why the counselee has appeared, you are better served by allowing him or her to state their reason before you take a guess. An example of this situation is given in the following exchange:

JIM: Mr. Jones?
JONES: Yes, Jim, come on in.
JIM: I'm not too early, am I?
JONES: Right on time. Sit down. It's good to see you, Jim, we don't get too many opportunities to talk with you being out of town so much.
JIM: Well, that's kind of what I wanted to talk to you about.
JONES: Oh?
JIM: Yes. I feel like I'm losing touch with what's going on in the organization. On top of which, all this traveling is beginning to cause some problems at home.
JONES: So, you are concerned about how the travel is affecting your life with the company and at home as well.

In this vignette Jones waits for Jim to tell him what the meeting is all about. Then he confirms his understanding of the purpose by closing the segment with a mirror statement. Jones does not imply that he is aware that Jim is there for help. He demonstates a willingness to listen to whatever Jim has to say. Jim may not like the idea of coming to Jones for help or even letting Jones know that there is a problem. For that reason we would not want to say, "What's the problem, Jim?" or "How can I help you?" Although well intentioned, such beginnings tend to make the counselee ill at ease.

In most instances, as Benjamin points out, when a person comes to you for counseling of his or her free will, they will be quite eager to get started. As long as you do not obstruct any expression, you will be rapidly oriented as to the reason.[7] Small talk at the outset can be helpful to let the person know that you are friendly and approachable. Robert Bessell, in *Interviewing and Counseling*, cautions social workers to maintain a freshness of approach even though they may be interviewing continuously for a number of years. The key is to convince the counselee that he is not just another, and probably unwelcome, burden.[8] The other purpose, according to Bessell, of a social chat at the outset is to enable the client (the counselee in social work) to settle down in a strange environment.

However, if the counselor initiates the interview, the obligation for orientation falls to the counselor. Tell the counselee exactly what led you to initiate the interview. If you are a career counselor you may begin with a statement such as, "The results on your aptitude test are in, and I have looked over your other materials, so I wanted to talk to you about some of the types of positions you appear to be best suited for." An acountant might say, "I have gone over your financial picture, and I think we need to discuss some ways you can budget your money more effectively." The hardest thing for some of us who find ourselves in the role of the counselor and the initiator of the interview is to stop talking after we have provided the orientation. Do not deliver a lecture. The person to be helped must "buy in" to the situation every inch of the way. Be certain that the counselee has the opportunity to express himself or herself completely. An example of this follows:

DOCTOR: Mrs. Daniels, sorry to keep you waiting. It seems like everyone in town needs a doctor.

DANIELS: You're always busy. How does it feel to be so popular?

DOCTOR: Sometimes I wouldn't mind being a bit less popular. But I am sorry for the delay. I wanted you to come in today because I have the results of your blood work-up and your GI series, and we need to discuss changes in your diet and your level of activity.

DANIELS: What's the problem?

DOCTOR: There is nothing to be greatly alarmed about, but you are showing a higher cholesterol than you should. Your X-rays show some irritation in the lower section of your stomach that needs to be watched so that you don't develop an ulcer. Otherwise, you appear to be in good health. I want to explore with you some of the reasons we may be getting these results. Are you still experiencing the indigestion since you started the medication?

DANIELS: Not as bad, but it still bothers me . . . particularly at night.

DOCTOR: Can you tell me anything about your diet that you feel might be causing some of these problems?

DANIELS: Well, you know, I'm on the go all the time—the job, the kids. Maybe I don't eat as regularly as I should.

DOCTOR: You feel that the regularity of your meals may be causing some of the problem?

DANIELS: Yes. And what I eat too. I generally grab whatever is in the icebox. I think I had leftover pizza twice this week.

DOCTOR: So, you think what you eat may be a factor as well?

DANIELS: It's not that I don't know better. I know eating like that, or not eating at all, can't be doing me a lot of good.

DOCTOR: Well, Mrs. Daniels, I think that your eating habits are a big part of the problem. You are going to have to make an effort to eat more regularly and sensibly. Perhaps you could prepare something during the week when you have more time that would be easy to warm up and be nutritious at the same time—perhaps a heavy soup or stew. Do you own a microwave oven?

DANIELS: No, But I have thought about buying one. I guess that would make things a lot easier. There are some packaged meals that I like, but they take too long in the regular oven. A microwave might be the answer.

DOCTOR: I think it's worth looking into. In the meantime, I want to go over with you some do's and don'ts about your diet. . . .

The doctor in this interchange has been effective in allowing Mrs. Daniels to focus her attention on her own problem. He offered constructive solutions that the patient appears to accept. He follows up with some direct orders as to meals and diet that will more likely be followed because Mrs. Daniels has participated actively in the analysis and solution to her problem. Note again how the doctor uses mirror questions and statements to confirm to the patient that she is communicating.

The opening game of the counseling interview establishes rapport, states or clarifies the matter that is under consideration, establishes control in the hands of the counselor, and demonstrates the counselor's willingness to listen and help. When these factors have been accomplished, the interview moves into the middle game.

What occurs in the middle game of the counseling interview bears some resemblance to investigation. A problem or circumstance is being examined, and the demand for disclosure is very heavily placed on one participant—the counselee. However, unlike investigation, there is no adversary relationship. Both the counselor and the counselee are on the same side of the issue. Both are striving for objectivity in order to see the situation better. Ironically, the counselor appears to provide the vehicle for the counselee's objectivity by his or her willingness to enter subjectively into the problem—to share the experience, the pain, the frustration, or whatever is the root cause or manifestation of the problem. The counselor's willingness to share this burden further builds trust and allows the counselee to see the issue reflected through a different but sympathetic organism.

Benjamin poses several questions that could be used to evaluate a counselor's performance after the interview, but they also provide important guideposts to look for before the interview begins:

> Did you help the interviewee open up his perceptual field as much as possible? Was he able to look at things the way they appear to him rather than the way they seem to you or someone else? Was he free to look squarely at what he sees and to express it, or did he perceive himself through the eyes of someone else? Did he discover his own self, or did he find a self he thought he ought to be

finding? Did your attitude prevent him from exploring his own life space or enable him to move about in it unhampered by external influences?[9]

In a passage, startling for its clarity and instructiveness, Benjamin provides an example of what he means:

When Lucy said, "I'll never get married now that I'm crippled," what did you do? You know you felt terrible; you felt that the whole world had caved in on her. But what did you say? What did you show? Did you help her to bring it out: to say it, all of it; to hear it and examine it? You almost said: "Don't be foolish. You're young and pretty and smart, and who knows, perhaps. . . ." But you didn't. You had said similar things to patients in the hospital until you learned that it closed them off. So this time you simply looked at her and weren't afraid to feel what you both felt. Then you said, "you feel right now that your whole life has been ruined by this accident." "That's just it," she retorted, crying bitterly. After a while she continued talking. She was still crippled, but you hadn't gotten in the way of her hating it and confronting it.[10]

Again, the helping response is a mirror that reflects the counselee's words and thought, indicates that you are listening intently, and can face the words and thoughts without fear or judgment. The focus of the interview must always remain on the counselee. Resist responding to questions about yourself or how you feel about an issue. Sometimes it is difficult to frame a response or question without a judgment, but it must be done. If you are counseling an employee who is regularly having dramatic outbursts during the working day when faced with criticism or frustration, you can't say, "Don't you know that it is wrong to behave in this manner; that it disturbs your fellow workers?" Rather you might say, "How do you think your moods may be affecting the other people in the office?" or, "You seem to be having some trouble lately; is there anything I can help with?" If the response is, "Yes, I'm afraid I have been a bit disruptive lately," you once again avoid moralizing like, "Well, then, I guess we can assume that this disruptive behavior will stop." Try something like, "Can you tell me about it?" or the mirror, "So, you feel that something has been causing you to respond disruptively."

Benjamin asks some more evaluative questions:

Did you let the interviewee explore what he wanted to in his own way, or did you lead him in a direction you chose for him? Did your behavior truly indicate the absence of threat? Was he afraid to express himself, and if so, what did you do to relieve this fear? Did you really want to listen to him, or did you want him to listen to you because you already had the answer to his problem, because you were anxious to "give him a piece of your mind," or because you really didn't want to hear more as you wouldn't have known what to do with it anyway.[11]

What emerges clearly in the counseling interview is that there are several questions you should not ask and statements you should not make. While these restrictions will come naturally to the experienced counselor, it is worth listing some of them here:

1. Do not agree, condone, moralize or judge what you hear.
2. Do not lead the counselee in a direction you want to go.
3. Do not cut off a response because you feel it strays from the subject.
4. Do not fill every silence with questions or statements.
5. Do not respond defensively to resistance.
6. Do not contaminate the interview with personal examples.
7. Do not provide hollow encouragement like, "It may seem rough right now, but by tomorrow you will probably feel better about it all."
8. Do not tell the counselee what you would do in the same situation.
9. Do not say, "I know how you feel."
10. Do not try to solve the problem for the counselee.

In each of these instances, the effect is to get in the way of the counselee's ability to help him or herself; to inhibit, as Benjamin puts it, the counselee's ability " . . . to recognize, to feel, to know, to decide, to choose whether to change."

The Use of Questions As in all interview situations, the question is the basic tool for uncovering information. However, the special nature of the counseling interview requires a special sensitivity to the notion of questioning. The skilled counselor will phrase and employ questions that do not appear as questions. The normal question and answer pattern suggests to the counselee that he or she is the object of the experience rather than the subject of it. We cannot create a helping environment if we are perceived as purely an authority figure.

Perhaps the notion of questions is too limited for our discussion of counseling. We probably should expand it to include other possible responses by the counselor, like mirror statements, because these responses also call forth additional information from the counselee and, as such, function as questions in fact if not in form. Because we want to provide the greatest possible opportunity for the counselee to explore his or her own thoughts, the majority of our questions should be phrased in the open mode, as in the following:

"How did you feel after the meeting today?"
"Your sales seem to be dropping; what do you think the problem might be?"
"When you picture yourself in the school setting, what do you see?"
"You say you haven't been feeling well. Can you tell me what symptoms you are having?"

Leading questions such as, "You didn't mean to do that, did you?" should be avoided, as should forced-choice questions like, "Do you think that this job has been good for you or that you should have stayed in school?" They limit the development of the counseling relationship by underscoring the authoritarian character of the counselor's position, and they also limit the range of the counselee's responses.

Before asking a question, consider the reason you are asking it. If you are asking the question: (1) to clarify or confirm something the counselee has said; (2) to get specific information such as age or years of employment; (3) to make sure the counselee has understood something you have said; (4) to probe a specific problem area; or (5) to encourage a counselee to speak who is reluctant to do so, then the question is probably appropriate and helpful. If the question you are about to ask is self-serving, changes the direction of the interview, limits the counselee's response unnecessarily, or contains a judgment, do not ask it.

Strategy The most important thing about the application of strategy in the counseling interview is that very often there is none. Strategy refers to the conscious and purposeful arranging of questions in a sequence to achieve a predetermined end. When we take on the role of counselor, we usually do not have a predetermined end. We know or suspect that a problem exists, but the actual problem and how and when the counselee will reveal it begins as a mystery. Instead of a pattern of questioning, we try to discern a pattern of response. In a sense, the strategy of a counseling interview exists within the counselee. The counselor takes the counselee's lead and helps carry him or her as far as possible in any given direction. This phenomenon is most evident in the psychotherapeutic construct. On the counseling continuum, psychotherapy is at the extreme end. The process requires multiple interviews, sometimes over a period of years. However, examining the work of a skilled therapist is instructive for anyone who is called on to provide counseling.

I have selected two excerpts for us to examine from Carl Rogers' *On Becoming a Person.* These are transcriptions of actual therapeutic interviews, and they demonstrate effectively what I mean when I say the counselor follows the strategy that exists within the counselee. They also point out some very special differences in what the counselor says as compared to other types of interview. In the first example, Rogers shows a client in the process of accepting the notion of experience and self as being one. Note as you read the excerpt that, in this instance, Rogers never uses a question as we have come to understand the formation of questions:

> Mrs. Oak was a housewife in her late thirties, who was having difficulties in marital and family relationships when she came in for therapy. Unlike many clients, she had a keen and spontaneous interest in the processes which she felt

going on within herself, and her recorded interviews contain much material, from her own frame of reference, as to her perception of what is occurring. She thus tends to put into words what seems to be implicit, but unverbalized, in many clients. For this reason, most of the excerpts in this chapter will be taken from this one case.

From an early portion of the fifth interview comes material which describes the awareness of experience which we have been discussing.

CLIENT: It all comes pretty vague. But you know I keep, keep having the thought occur to me that this whole process is kind of like examining pieces of a jig-saw puzzle. It seems to me I, I'm in the process now of examining the individual pieces which really don't have too much meaning. Probably handling them, not even beginning to think of a pattern. That keeps coming to me. And it's interesting to me because I, I really don't like jig-saw puzzles. They've always irritated me. But that's my feeling. And I mean I pick up little pieces (*she gestures throughout this conversation to illustrate her statements*) with absolutely no meaning except I mean the, the feeling that you get from simply handling them without seeing them as a pattern, but just from the touch, I probably feel, well it is going to fit someplace here.

THERAPIST: And that at the moment that, that's the process, just getting the feel and the shape and the configuration of the different pieces with a little bit of background feeling of, yeah they'll probably fit somewhere, but most of the attention's focused right on, "What does this feel like? And what's its texture?"

C: That's right. There's almost something physical about it. A, a ...

T: You can't quite describe it without using your hands. A real, almost a sensuous sense in ...

C: That's right. Again it's, it's a feeling of being very objective and yet I've never been quite so close to myself.

T: Almost at one and the same time standing off and looking at yourself and yet somehow being closer to yourself that way than ...

C: M-hm. And yet for the first time in months I am not thinking about my problems. I'm not actually, I'm not working on them.

T: I get the impression you don't sort of sit down to work on "my problems." It isn't that feeling at all.

C: That's right. That's right. I suppose what I, I mean actually is that I'm not sitting down to put this puzzle together as, as something, I've got to see the picture. It, it may be that, it may be that I am actually enjoying this feeling process. Or I'm certainly learning something.

T: At least there's a sense of the immediate goal of getting the feel as being the thing, not that you're doing this in order to see a picture, but that it's a, a satisfaction of really getting acquainted with each piece. Is that ...

C: That's it. That's it. And it still becomes that sort of sensuousness, that touching. It's quite interesting. Sometimes not entirely pleasant, I'm sure, but ...

T: A rather different sort of experience.

C: Yes. Quite.

> This excerpt indicates very clearly the letting of material come into awareness, without any attempt to own it as part of the self, or to relate it to other material held in consciousness. It is, to put it as accurately as possible, an awareness of a wide range of experiences, with, at the moment, no thought of their relation to self.[12]

Rogers actively participates in the experience. The excerpt as transcribed seems to show Rogers actually sharing the consciousness of the client—finishing sentences and beginning others, leaving gaps for the client to reenter the verbal stream. Each response on the part of Rogers confirms his understanding of what has just been said, mirroring in many instances not just the words but enlarging on the experience being described. Although this is a therapeutic example, there is much to be generalized that is of value to any counselor. First, there is no doubt as to who is the central figure in the interview. The client is clearly the subject and not the object of the exchange. Second, there is no apparent judgment in any of Rogers' responses. Third, no questions are asked.

In the next excerpt from a later interview with the same client, Rogers does intersperse conventional questions along with the conforming statements:

> Here then is the quotation from one of the later interviews with this young woman as she has begun to realize that perhaps she is partly responsible for the deficiencies in her own education.

C: Well now, I wonder if I've been going around doing that, getting smatterings of things, and not getting hold, not really getting down to things.

T: Maybe you've been getting just spoonfuls here and there rather than really digging in somewhere rather deeply.

C: M-hm. That's why I say . . . (*slowly and very thoughtfully*) well, with that sort of a foundation, well, it's really up to *me*. I mean, it seems to be really apparent to me that I *can't depend on someone else* to give me an education. *(Very softly)* I'll really have to get it myself.

T: It really begins to come home . . . there's only one person that can educate you . . . a realization that perhaps nobody else *can give* you an education.

C: M-hm. (*Long pause—while she sits thinking*) I have all the symptoms of fright. (*Laughs softly*)

T: Fright? That this is a scary thing, is that what you mean?

C: M-hm. (*Very long pause—obviously struggling with feelings in herself*).

T: Do you want to say any more about what you mean by that? That it really does give you the symptoms of fright?

C: (*Laughs*) I, uh . . . I don't know whether I quite know. I mean . . . well it really seems like I'm cut loose (*pause*), and it seems that I'm very . . . I don't know . . . in a vulnerable position, but I, uh, I brought this up and it, uh, somehow it almost came out without my saying it. It seems to be . . . it's something I let out.

T: Hardly a part of you.

C: Well, I felt surprised.

T: As though, "Well for goodness sake, did I say that?" (*Both chuckle.*)

C: Really, I don't think I've had that feeling before. I've . . . uh, well, this really feels like I'm saying something that, uh, *is* a part of me really. (*Pause*) Or, uh, (*quite perplexed*) it feels like I sort of have, uh, I don't know. I have a feeling of *strength*, and yet, I have a feeling of . . . realizing it's so sort of fearful, of fright.

T: That is, do you mean that saying something of that sort gives you at the same time a feeling of, of strength in saying it, and yet at the same time a frightened feeling of *what* you have said, is that it?

C: M-hm. I am feeling that. For instance, I'm feeling it internally now . . . a sort of surging up, or force or outlet. As if that's something really big and strong. And yet, uh, well at first it was almost a physical feeling of just being out alone, and sort of cut off from a . . . a support I had been carrying around.

T: You feel that it's something deep and strong, and surging forth, and at the same time, you just feel as though you'd cut yourself loose from any support when you say it.

C: M-hm. Maybe that's . . . I don't know . . . it's a disturbance of a kind of pattern I've been carrying around, I think.

T: It sort of shakes a rather significant pattern, jars it loose.

C: M-hm. (*Pause, then cautiously, but with conviction*) I, I think . . . I don't know, but I have the feeling that then I am going to begin to do more things that I know I should do . . . There are so many things that I need to do. It seems in so many avenues of my living I have to work out new ways of behavior, but . . . maybe . . . I can see myself doing a little better in some things.[13]

Note how Rogers uses his questions. The first in this excerpt comes after the client has had a long pause and has described her symptoms as fright. Rogers asks a confirming question, "Fright? That this is a very scary thing, is that what you mean?" The client is then described as " . . . struggling with feelings within herself" but she is silent. Rogers uses another question to coax her into verbalization of the feeling. He phrases the question very carefully, keeping the client's interests at the center of his concern, "Do you want to say any more about what you mean by that? That it really does give you the symptoms of fright?" A bit later, Rogers uses a question to help the client put a feeling into words. The use of a question here is skillful in that it doesn't tell the client what she is feeling; rather it asks her to confirm Rogers' understanding. "That is, do you mean that saying something of that sort gives you at the same time a feeling of, of strength in saying it, and yet at the same time a frightened feeling of what you have said, is that it?"

We can see how the technique and strategy of questioning differs from other types of interview. Both the locus of the information and the vehicle for discovering it exist within the counselee. The counselor employs active listening skills with particular attention on clarifying and conforming behavior. The more the counselee believes through your responses that you are listening, understanding, and sharing the experience, the more he or she will be induced to find answers to the problems.

Breaking Contact The end-game phase of the interview takes on special significance for counseling. After all, if events have been moving ahead successfully, the counselee has become very self-disclosive. Any abrupt or otherwise ungraceful completion can leave the counselee with the feeling of being embarassed or violated in some way. Such an ending can undo all of the good work that has preceded it and close off the possibility of productive interviews in the future. The question of how to end must begin with when to end. Often, this is determined by factors other than the desires of the participants; the therapist may have another patient waiting, the supervisor must get back to the job, the student has a class, or any number of other situations that place limitations on the amount of time available for the interview. Bessel tells us that "... the recognition of limitation can be a source of strength."[14] Speaking primarily to the social worker, he underscores the need to make use of time as an active force:

> For instance, if an interview has no limitation of time, it is very difficult to prevent it wandering aimlessly, whereas if it becomes progressively more difficult to justify after about half an hour, there is pressure on both social worker and client to make the best use of the available time. It is the hallmark of the skillful social worker to use such limitations to help the client increase his understanding of the realities of his situation.[15]

Bessell uses the chess analogy to describe the closing stage:

> When considering the termination of the individual interview, it may be profitable to return to the analogy of the literature of chess in which the end-game is dealt with neither in the specific terms of the opening nor the general principles of the middle game. The end-game comes somewhere in between, with the main emphasis on situation and relative position.[16]

Benjamin is also sensitive to the counselor's feelings as well as those of the counselee. He points out that both participants may be reluctant to part. He outlines two factors that he says are basic to the closing phase:

1. Both partners in the interview should be aware of the fact that closing is taking place and accept this fact, the interviewer in particular.
2. During the closing phase no new material should be introduced or at any rate discussed, for closing concerns that which has already taken place. If there is more new material, another interview will have to be scheduled.[17]

The counselor must indicate that the time is almost up. Give the counselee some warning such as, "I really think we have covered some important issues, and I have an appointment at 3:00 that I must keep. Is there something else that we need to deal with before we wrap it up?" If the counselee introduces new material or issues at this stage, schedule an additional interview. As in any end game, you must summarize what you feel are the major points of the exchange, indicate your perception of these points, and outline what events will occur next: another interview, an action plan, a shift in responsibility, a change in class schedule, and the like. It is sometimes useful to have the counselee describe what he or she has taken from the experience. The counselor encourages this by making a statement like the following: "All right, I think we have this problem settled, but just to be sure, let me hear in your own words what your understanding of the situation is."

Closing effectively is difficult to do, but it could determine the overall success of the interview. What occurs during the last stage strongly influences the counselee's impression of the whole experience. Always leave enough time for what needs to be done: recap, summing up, making a subsequent appointment. How long you leave for the end game will vary with the situation and the type of counseling. Edinburg, Zinberg, and Kelman provide some parameters for the therapeutic interview. They suggest that ten minutes before the end of the traditional 45- or 50-minute interview the counselor begins thinking about ending the session.[18] They hold that finishing the interview on time reminds the client that there are boundaries to the session as well as the relationship.

The Counselee

Obviously, the conduct of the counselee during the interview will have a profound effect on the outcome. It is difficult to establish a helping relationship with an individual who either does not believe help is required or just refuses to accept it. If you are involved in a counseling interview as the counselee, you have arrived in this position for one of two reasons; you have sought help of some kind or you have been singled out for some reason to receive help. In order to participate fully in either of these circumstances, you must understand the cause for the counseling, and you must develop trust in the counselor.

Even if you initiate counseling, you may find it difficult to ask for help. Those of us who have been brought up with an individualistic and self-reliant outlook tend to feel as though we should be able to handle our own problems without burdening others with them. In many cases the solution to a problem is readily at hand and understood by the counselee. The real problem at this stage is that he or she will not take the necessary action to set the matter right. A good counseling relationship can help overcome this barrier. When you are considering counseling, here are some guidelines to follow:

1. Assess your problem as objectively as you can. Try establishing criteria for what you would like to accomplish with a solution to the problem, and then list some solutions that seem to satisfy these criteria.
2. If you feel that your problem requires psychotherapy because you are having unrealistic fears, problems coping with life in general, or other symptoms that lead to a sense of hopelessness and anxiety, do not put off seeking help. Ask a friend who has been involved in therapy for a

referral. If your company or school employs a mental health professional, make an appointment. Talk to your family physician about a referral or call the local hospital for names of participating psychiatrists and psychologists. Remember, you need not commit yourself to years of psychotherapy, but you owe it to yourself to participate in one or two evaluative interviews so that you can have the facts about what you are dealing with and what the recommendations of a professional are.

3. If your problem appears to be caused primarily by something outside of yourself—situations at school, at work, in the home—you need to address them with the people most directly in a position to provide you with help—your teacher, your boss, your parents. There are so many different kinds of needs, it is difficult to generalize a specific approach. One that works quite often is to prepare yourself with some of the things that you feel may relate to the solutions to your problem. This at least gives the person whose counsel you have sought something to work with, particularly if they have not had prior knowledge of the problem or adequate time to prepare for the interview.
4. Try to set realistic goals for what you hope to accomplish through the counseling. If your expectations are too high, you will be disappointed. If the outcome exceeds your expectations, consider it a plus.
5. Do not enter a counseling situation with the notion that the counselor has the answers to your problems. You have the answers to your problems; the counselor will help you find them.

When we seek counseling, it is easier to make preparations and set goals. In the other circumstance, where the counselor seeks us out, there is a different set of concerns. First of all, there is a natural reaction to be defensive, "Who says I need help?" While this is difficult to control, make an effort to be open to the suggestion. Try to accept the approach in the manner it is offered. If you are in a job situation, you may mistake an attempt at counseling for a disciplinary action. Here are some guidelines for responding to an unsolicited counseling approach:

1. Do not respond immediately. Listen to everything that is being said and ask for repetition or clarification if you are not sure of the purpose of the counseling that will take place.
2. If you have the option, allow a little time to elapse between the request for your participation in a counseling interview and the actual interview. This will give you time to think things through and gather facts and ideas that have a bearing on the counseling.
3. Consider the risks and try to focus on what may be gained from the counseling interview.

4. If you do not already have a relationship with the counselor, try to find out what he or she is like from others who have had relationships. Has their experience with the counselor been positive?
5. Express a willingness to cooperate, but do not be afraid to state your reservations and concerns about entering into counseling if you have any.

Once you enter into the counseling interview, it soon matters little whether you got there by your own suggestion or someone else's. If you have been sought out for counseling, there may be some residual tendency toward defensiveness, which should fade as the necessity for the counseling and the trust in the counselor begin to assert themselves. Here are some suggestions for the counselee's behavior during the counseling interview:

1. Listen carefully to what the counselor is saying, how it is being said, and who or what appears to be the central issue. Remember, if you are being counseled, you are at the center of the experience.
2. When you respond, note how the counselor reacts. Can you determine through words or actions that the counselor is open and nonjudgmental?
3. Does the counselor mirror your statements and allow you to take the lead or are a lot of questions being asked that tend to lead you in a particular direction?
4. Be sensitive to the counselor's limitations. You must allow the counselor to help you find solutions. Also, realize that the counselor is working with some limitations of time. Be respectful of those limits.

These factors will serve to convince you whether the counselor can be trusted with your confidence or not. An effectively handled counseling interview can be an exhilarating experience for both participants.

SUMMARY

The counseling interview differs from other types in several respects. It is an enabling act that allows the counselee to receive help in meaningful ways. The counselor should create all conditions in such a way as to make this helping relationship work. There should be no interruptions, and the setting should be conducive to interaction. In order to be effective as counselors, we must truly want to help and must have a willingness to go through this experience with the counselee regardless of where it might go, and to do so without judgment.

When we take on the counseling role, we must reexamine our use of questions. The most productive questions are open and not leading. We will find ourselves using mirror statements frequently. We also discover that the locus of the interview strategy exists within the counselee and cannot be imposed from without.

If we are the ones being counseled, we must be attentive and cooperative. We must set realistic goals and expectations. We must participate actively in the process in order to assure the best possible outcome.

Carl Rogers summarizes his view of the counseling relationship this way:

> Thus the relationship which I have found helpful is characterized by a sort of transparency on my part, in which my real feelings are evident; by an acceptance of this other person as a separate person with value in his own right; and by a deep empathic understanding which enables me to see his private world through his eyes. When these conditions are achieved, I become a companion to my client, accompanying him in the frightening search for himself, which he now feels free to undertake.[19]

Questions for Study and Discussion

1. How does the counseling interview differ from the other types we have covered?
2. The term *help* is at the center of the counseling interview. What does it mean in association with the following terms?
   a. enabling act
   b. self-disclosure
   c. mind-set
   d. trust
3. What gives a therapist power?
4. Why are mirror questions and statements so important in the counseling interview?
5. How does the counselor's wilingness to enter subjectively into the problem provide the vehicle for the counselee's objectivity?

Suggested Activities

1. Create an opening statement for the following situations:
   a. A person is sent to you for counseling who has been described as a chronic absentee and an alcoholic.
   b. A person knocks on your door and says she needs to talk to you.
   c. A friend calls and says that he has left his wife and wants a divorce.

Notes

1. Carl R. Rogers, *On Becoming a Person* (Boston: Houghton Mifflin, 1961), 31–32.
2. Alfred Benjamin, *The Helping Interview* (Boston: Houghton Mifflin, 1969) ix–x.
3. Ibid., 5.
4. Jerome D. Frank, *Persuasion and Healing* (New York: Schocken Books, 1963), 115.
5. Rogers, *On Becoming a Person*, 16.
6. Golda M. Edinburg, Norman E. Zinberg, and Wendy Kelman, *Clinical Interviewing and Counseling: Principles and Techniques* (New York: Appleton-Century-Crofts, 1975), 11.
7. Benjamin, *The Helping Interview*, 13.
8. Robert Bessell, *Interviewing and Counseling* (London: B. T. Batsford, 1971), 104.
9. Benjamin, *The Helping Interview*, 21.
10. Ibid., 22.
11. Ibid., 23.
12. Rogers, *On Becoming a Person*, 77–78.
13. Ibid., 121–122.
14. Bessell, *Interviewing and Counseling*, 111–112.
15. Ibid.
16. Ibid.
17. Benjamin, *The Helping Interview*, 30.
18. Edinburg, Zinberg, and Kelman, *Clinical Interviewing and Counseling*, 40.
19. Rogers, *On Becoming a Person*, 34.

Index